A Biography

ACCUSED

To Tara,

June 25, 2019

Best wishes — enjoyed the book club.

Steve Cockerham

BY STEVE COCKERHAM

TRITON PRESS • OXFORD, MISSISSIPPI

For information, contact the Nautilus Publishing Company, 426 South Lamar Blvd., Suite 16, Oxford, MS 38655

ISBN: 978-1-949455-00-7

The Nautilus Publishing Company
426 S Lamar Blvd., Suite 16
Oxford, MS 38655
Tel: 662-513-0159
www.nautiluspublishing.com

First Edition

Cover design by Nautilus Publishing
Interior design by Sinclair Rishel

Library of Congress Cataloging-in-Publication Data has been applied for.

1   2   3   4   5   6   7   8   9   10

Table of Contents

"Slanders which can neither be proved nor disproved are long lived and die hard."

William S. Speer referencing Jacob Thompson in
Sketches of Prominent Tennesseans published in 1888

PREFACE

It is shocking how easily history forgets. Most Mississippians have no idea that a politician named Jacob Thompson played a major role in the history of this country, and, in particular, Mississippi. He is one of the unknown giants of Mississippi history, forgotten in the fog of passing time. Today, he tends to get no more than a passing mention in Mississippi history textbooks and is often ignored altogether.

Yet Jacob Thompson is one of the most important men in state history. Seldom has any Mississippian done so much in so short a time.

He served as Secretary of the Interior under President James Buchanan. Acting as behind-the-scenes kingmaker, he launched the successful political career of his close friend L. Q. C. Lamar, who later became Secretary of the Interior and eventually Mississippi's first U. S. Supreme Court Justice.

Elected to Congress at the tender age of 29, Thompson quickly became not only a power broker in Mississippi but a major influence on the national scene as well. A friend, confidante and adviser of presidents, he was instrumental in the elections of James K. Polk, Franklin Pierce and Buchanan. A feared debater, his was an influential voice in virtually every major decision by Congress during his XII-year tenure there. He was a key player in the great debates surrounding the Mexican War, the Oregon boundary issues, the Compromise of 1850, the annexation of Texas, and the nationwide banking failures following the Panic of 1837.

In Washington, he and his wife Kate were the toast of the town. Everyone who was anyone coveted invitations to their legendary parties, where they charmed the power elite of the nation's capital with smooth southern manners. It was no accident that President Buchanan was a frequent guest, just as Jacob Thompson was a frequent guest at the White House. Unfortunately for Thompson, his meteoric rise coincided with the tense and angry buildup to the Civil War, America's bloodiest conflict.

An outspoken advocate for the South in rough-and-tumble Cabinet meetings leading up to the war, Thompson was often able to bend the president toward his way of thinking. Along with Secretary of the Treasury Howell Cobb of Georgia, he became President Buchanan's point man on the administration's most sensitive matters. When necessary, he was also Buchanan's hatchet man.

War changes everything. Like Robert E. Lee and Jefferson Davis, Thompson's life and reputation were forever sullied when he sided with the South in the great conflict that tore the young nation asunder. Thompson's fate was sealed when Confederate President Davis dispatched him on a desperate mission for which he was ill-suited—ultimately a violent espionage campaign against the North along the Canadian border.

It was that role that turned the previously charmed Thompson into arguably the most loathed person in the North with the possible exception of Davis himself. The former congressman who once held presidents in thrall wound up accused of treason and terrorism, and there may have been more than a modicum of truth in some of the charges.

Through his secret operations, including trying to set northern cities ablaze, he attempted to give the North a taste of the same pain the South had endured at the hands of the Union army. His hope was that once the North had to deal with the terror of war on its own ground, the electorate would grow weary of conflict and pressure Lincoln to sue for peace. For his trouble, the northern press turned him into a pariah. Federal troops took pains to burn his lavish home in Oxford and Union General Ulysses S. Grant personally searched for evidence to be used against him.

For a time, Thompson was even suspected of having played a role in the assassination of President Abraham Lincoln. A $25,000 bounty was offered for his capture, and he and his wife were forced to flee to Europe until the charges were finally dropped three and a half years later.

Somehow, he found time to found and nurture two universities—the University of Mississippi in 1848 and, after the war, the University of the South in Sewanee, Tennessee.

Postwar, he was able to restore some of his wealth and make a name for himself as an influential leader of the business community in Memphis, Tennessee.

It was an extraordinary life. It is an extraordinary story. But after wars, the victors write the histories, which may help account for his name being so unfamiliar to students of history today.

This preface serves as an all too brief attempt to summarize Jacob Thompson's unusual career. There is much more to the story, including the recurring claims that he maintained his lavish lifestyle in European exile with funds from the Confederate treasury. It will all unfold in the following pages.

This book contains an inordinate number of quotations I thought necessary, primarily because of the controversial nature of so many of Thompson's activities. My goal was to present both sides of the several issues in doubt with a caveat. Again, it is important to remember that the victors wrote the histories, causing some incorrect or exaggerated versions of the truth to have been repeated for over 150 years. Too, I have personally long been intrigued by the relationship of L. Q. C. Lamar and Jacob Thompson, two Oxonians who served as Secretary of the Interior; therefore, I confess to being at least a little biased in spite of efforts not to be.

I am neither an academician nor a trained historian. On retirement after a busy career as an oral and maxillofacial surgeon, my wife Mary Ann and I moved from Hattiesburg, Mississippi, to Oxford. Here I have had time to compose this book in Jacob Thompson's hometown.

RESIGNATION

At the fateful dawning of 1861, secession fever held the South in thrall, roaring through the region like wildfire fed by a wicked wind. In this intensely emotional atmosphere, there could be no sober reasoning, no last minute compromise, no negotiated settlement. The exuberant young men of Dixie were stoked with southern patriotism, their hearts pounding in anger. They fashioned their cause as a second Revolution, seeking to gain freedom from an overbearing bully.

Helpless to stop the steamrolling juggernaut of imminent war, Thompson watched events unfold from the nation's capital, fully cognizant of the perils facing his beloved southland. He had done all he could to avoid armed conflict.

Now on this morning of January 8, 1861, Jacob Thompson steeled himself for something he had long dreaded and hoped to prevent. He was to resign as the Secretary of the Interior. President James Buchanan had already been informed of his intentions. Secretary Thompson and the President had enjoyed a close, convivial relationship until recently. President Buchanan, although from Pennsylvania, loved the company of southerners including the Thompsons. Jacob and his vivacious wife Kate regularly entertained him at their home, a center of the increasingly vibrant Washington social scene. There, Buchanan found welcome respite from the pressures of the presidency. Like the rest of the nation, the cozy friendships nurtured at the Thompson home were about to be torn asunder.

Thompson no doubt reflected on his years of service to the Federal government. He had been a six term Congressman from Mississippi and was nearing completion of four years in the Cabinet. He had played a significant role in Democrat politics, helping to secure the nominations of James K. Polk, Franklin Pierce, and James Buchanan. Abraham Lincoln, the President-elect, was an acquaintance. They had a mutual respect for each other due to common frontier backgrounds. But that bipartisan friendship was soon to be forgotten, as Lincoln's election would become the catalyst that stirred the South to action, touching off a conflict whose scars continue, some 150 years later.

South Carolina had already seceded from the Union. Jacob Thompson had been apprised that Mississippi, his adopted state, was poised to follow on January ninth.

The disturbing news came as another issue greatly vexed him. After Thompson pleaded with the President not to inflame the South with any provocative actions, Buchanan, buffeted by pressures of his own, gave the go ahead to resupply the Federal forts in Charleston, South Carolina harbor. To make matters worse, the President chose not to inform his friend Thompson. Jake felt betrayed.

He and his wife, Kate, packed and vacated Washington, after dealing with a pending investigation en route to their palatial home in Oxford, Mississippi. Their only child Macon resided here as well as several of Jacob's siblings and his mother-in-law. Jacob had made his fortune in Oxford as an attorney and as a businessman. He owned considerable farmland and other assets including slaves. Certainly, slave labor had facilitated his march to prosperity. And just as certainly, he wanted to maintain the peculiar institution that maintained his wealth.

As he ruminated on all this, his decision to resign had not been a very difficult one. Many southerners at every level of government and the military were leaving the Union or contemplating such. Much like Robert E. Lee's legendary fealty for Virginia, Thompson's primary allegiance was to Mississippi, his family, and his way of life. Still, he left the Capitol with much trepidation. Jacob Thompson was a realist. He anticipated the trials, tribulations, and anguish of a civil war. What he did not know--could not know--were the accusations and vitriol that would plague him throughout the remainder of his life and far beyond!

Nicholas Thompson house, birthplace of Jacob Thompson,
Leasburg, North Carolina

NORTH CAROLINA ROOTS

Jacob Thompson was born on May 15, 1810, the third son of Lucretia and Nicholas Thompson. The Thompsons resided in Leasburg, then the pretty little county seat of Caswell County, North Carolina. Caswell County is in the northern tier of North Carolina counties, having a common border with Virginia. Danville, Virginia is nearby.

This was tobacco country, but Nicholas Thompson initially became wealthy through his tannery with farming following later. He had arrived in Leasburg as an itinerant leather tanner. Specializing in harness making, a necessity at the time, he was very successful from the outset.[1]

In 1804 Nicholas married Lucretia Van Hook from Leasburg. Her father Jacob (Jacob Thompson's namesake) had participated in the Revolutionary War and was a "man of considerable influence." The Van Hooks also had "extensive land holdings" in Caswell County, which contributed significantly to the Thompson family's rapid road to prosperity.[2]

By today's standards, Lucretia turned out to be an exceptionally fertile woman. The Thompsons soon had a growing family of seven boys and two girls. Joseph Sidney born in 1805, Young in 1808, Jacob in 1810, Ann Eliza in 1812, John in 1816, William in 1818, Sarah in 1821, Lawrence in 1827, and Nicholas in 1832. Lawrence died in childhood at age nine. Amazingly, five of these sons would ultimately graduate from the University of North Carolina.[3]

Nicholas was an authoritative and strict father, especially with timid Jacob. By contrast, his mother Lucretia was nurturing and kind, a counterpoint to her driven husband. The strictness toward Jacob had its origin partly in the conduct of his two older brothers. Troubles presented by the siblings coupled with Nicholas Thompson's iron-fisted, no compromise nature soon would drive a wedge between Jacob and his father.[4]

Joseph Sidney, the eldest, was the apple of his father's eye. Nicholas Thompson envisioned him as a highly educated planter and politician. To this end, Joseph Sidney was sent to a nearby preparatory school and subsequently graduated from the University of North Carolina at Chapel Hill. Unfortunately, the son was not nearly as driven as his father expected. He rarely exerted himself, reflected by mediocre grades. Throughout his formative years he displayed little initiative.

Young was next in age and he too managed to consistently try his father's patience. He was handsome and gregarious with a charismatic personality. Enjoying his youth to the fullest, Young loved imbibing, gambling, fox-hunting, fine horses, high fashion, and the ladies. He exhibited an air of nonchalance, which, along with his rather profligate lifestyle, aggravated his diligent father to the extreme.

In the process Young became engaged to a somewhat older lady through a misunderstanding. Realizing the error of his ways, he attempted futilely to break the engagement. She sued for "breach of promise." Ultimately, his father had to pay several thousand dollars for "heart balm" to settle the dispute. Chastened by this episode, Young meekly modified his behavior and promised his father he would study medicine. He wound up with a medical degree from the University of North Carolina, making excellent grades and pulling off a stunning reversal of character—from careless bon vivant to responsible physician.

Jacob was close in age to Young and was greatly influenced by him. His father had always hoped that one of his sons would become a minister. Studious, shy Jacob was deemed the suitable choice. After all, he had required Joseph Sidney to be a planter, and Young certainly was not suited for the ministry. Jacob was it by default. Mr. Thompson could be termed a religious fanatic. In return for his financial success, he felt obligated to provide a son for God's work. Oddly, this zealotry did not extend to attending worship services as he rarely entered a church and apparently was never a member.[5]

A letter from Nicholas Thompson to eighteen-year old Jacob written September 19, 1828, provides insight into his religious thoughts.

Sir. This day I Rec'd a few lines from you Saying that you had looked for a few lines from me to give you some Direction. You know my [views] and all the Bairing points in my advice. Humility because it is a Duty you ow to God. Obedience to your Rulors if you think it nessary for Rulers it is really Necessary that their order should be to. Industry and Economy Because it is the Strait Road to Honors & Wealth and A Contented mind Which is better than—Vice and immorality is the Strait Road to poverty and disgrace. Imploy your time well. So that you Can not 10 years after say O, if I only had my time to go over I would do so and so. How simple that is. Never look back. Imploy each hour well and if it do not turn out well you feel Cleir that you have don your Duty which is comfort.

Your situation in life is at this time a good one if improved if Not—

Knowledge is Strenth & Wealth, if a parent can give his Son Strenth & Wealth What more Need he want… we Should be Thankfull to the great Giver of all Blessings. We are all well. Thank God.[6]

After attending Bingham Academy, a military school, in neighboring Orange County, Jacob duly followed his brothers to the University of North Carolina. He was seventeen, still very shy, and preparing for the ministry as his father wished. But even at college, he could not escape their tense relationship.

Although Nicholas obviously believed in higher education and had ample money to pay for it, he sent Jacob to Chapel Hill on a "flea-bitten mule" in contrast to his high-living elder brothers. Once there, the intransigent father was miserly with Jacob, allowing him little spending money. It was almost as if he were preparing his son for the more humble lifestyle of a man of the cloth. If so, it didn't take.

Jacob penned a series of pleading letters over the need for money to purchase proper clothing, which Nicholas grudgingly gave but not before warning Jacob that he was putting it on his ledger. In one of the final letters to his son near the completion of college, Nicholas bluntly stated that he would not further advise him. He had washed his hands of Jacob for the time being, leaving him to decide for himself his course in life.

But his father had missed something. In his zeal to choose a career for his son, he had been blind to the boy's real talents. By all accounts, Jacob was a brilliant, energetic student with a strong will to succeed. He never missed a lecture except for illness. And succeed he did, graduating in 1831 with first honors in his class. Immediately upon graduation he accepted an appointment as tutor at North Carolina, rejecting his father's desires.

The decision not to pursue the ministry left his father heartbroken and angry. They had reached a breaking point in their strained relationship. The rough and tumble tanner never understood his gentle son, but since Jacob had achieved financial independence, he could now do as he wished. It was a far cry from the pulpit, but Jacob did join the Milton Presbyterian Church in Caswell County and was baptized on July 10, 1831, shortly after college graduation.

Jake enjoyed the university environment and the freedom it gave him. Teaching gave him the confidence to outgrow much of his timidity as he weighed options for his future. It didn't take long. He resigned his tutorship at North Carolina after eighteen months to study law. Jacob eagerly began his preparation under the guidance of Judge John M. Dick of Greensboro, North Carolina. After a year and a half of diligent study, he was admitted to practice in the inferior courts of North Carolina. In 1835 he was further licensed as an attorney and counselor-at-law in the superior courts.[7]

Appearance was important to Jacob Thompson, made manifest by his always appropriate and stylish dress; however, he did not possess classical handsomeness. His biographer, Dorothy Zollicoffer Oldham, kindly observed that, "he was not a man of prepossessing appearance." She attributed his success to "his ability to make friends with all classes and types of people." Jacob unfailingly exhibited "charming personal manners" to one and all. What he lacked in looks he more than made up for with his personality and powerful oratory.[8]

Armed with those formidable social weapons, he was about to show his father that he was much better suited for the law of the land than the Law of Moses.

Jacob Thompson in his Congressional career

SEEKING HIS FORTUNE

Later that year, Thompson deliberated over where to hang up his shingle. He could start a practice in one of America's emerging cities or seek a place with less competition. At that very moment, the young nation was expanding its reach across the continent and settlers were pushing farther and farther west. He thought an ambitious young lawyer could quickly succeed on the rapidly developing western frontier.

That frontier was the state of Mississippi. With the advent of the cotton gin, cotton had quickly conquered the South. Almost overnight, it revolutionized the clothing industry and became the world's most valuable commodity. With slave labor and the right combination of knowhow and luck, a man could make a fortune from the alluvial soil along the Mississippi River and its tributaries, especially in the Delta where regular overflows had deposited deep layers of rich, fertile earth.

The port city of Natchez excited his imagination. He had heard of its splendid mansions and Parisian luxuries so, being unfettered, Jacob struck out for this seeming utopia. Before leaving, he requested a letter of disunion from Milton Presbyterian Church, which was granted on June 8, 1835.[9]

After sending his possessions ahead by wagon, Jacob departed Greensboro. He traveled by horse through North Carolina, South Carolina, Georgia, and Alabama arriving at Columbus, Mississippi on the Tombigbee River just over the Alabama border. Columbus was a frontier crossroads large enough to provide accommodations. He decided to rest and regroup here after the strenuous and intense journey fraught with potential danger from robbers and Indians. Being refreshed, a few days later he resumed the trip to Natchez. Then came one of those extraordinary coincidences that change history.

Shortly after mounting his horse, his brother Young rode up. Young, now Dr. Young Thompson, informed Jacob that he had not settled down but had become intrigued by the vast fertile lands opening up an area formerly owned by the Chickasaw Indians. This land basically comprised the northern fourth of Mississippi plus a small part of Alabama.[10]

President Andrew Jackson had aggressively prodded the Chickasaw and other southeastern tribes to cede their immense homelands. In return for their tribal lands, Jackson promised the Chickasaw various concessions including money and new lands in Indian country west of the Mississippi. Under duress, the Chickasaw capitulated. The result was the Treaty of Pontotoc Creek signed on October 20, 1832, transferring 6,283,804 acres of land to the United States.[11]

Almost immediately, white settlers rushed into the area in violation of the Treaty, which clearly stipulated that the Chickasaw receive suitable lands in Indian Territory (Oklahoma) before departing Mississippi. Finally, the Chickasaw Nation sadly left en masse in 1837 on what became known as the Trail of Tears. By this time, the land rush was into its fifth year.

At Young's urging, the siblings set out from Columbus to Pontotoc where the United States Land Office had been located for the surveying and sale of Chickasaw lands. Natchez was off the table. Young had told him that much of the area formerly occupied by the Chickasaws had already been surveyed and that soon sales would commence. Pontotoc, close to the center of the cession, had become a "boom town" almost overnight.

People of every ilk flooded into Pontotoc, which was not yet incorporated in 1835 when the brothers arrived. An Indian Agency soon opened there in addition to the Land Office. Naturally, Chickasaw Indians were present in great numbers and were freely spending their newly obtained money from land sales.

Land seeking speculators poured in from across the Union, especially Georgia, the Carolinas, Virginia, and Tennessee. Every type of vice, particularly gambling, thrived. Immense crowds milled about the muddy streets of the frontier settlement while quickly erected shops could not obtain enough inventory to meet demand. This mass of humanity slept in tents, log shanties, wigwams, and covered wagons. Inns and taverns rapidly replaced these rude campsites and were always filled to capacity.

Crime inevitably followed this frantic rush. The responsible law enforcement agency for Pontotoc was situated in Monroe County some 50 miles through dense forest. This distance emboldened highwaymen, who frequented the rugged roads through the woods, eager to relieve travelers loaded with cash for land purchases. Lawlessness and debauchery thrived and criminals had little fear of being brought to justice.[12]

Into this crude rural environment rode the young attorney Jacob Thompson. He established a busy law practice literally overnight focusing on land sales as he represented both Indians and Caucasians. Jacob was amazed at the fees he generated, though they were in keeping with the general overheated economy of the area. It was a lawyer's paradise!

His brother Young soon had a thriving medical practice. In addition to the mundane, he was kept busy with trauma from the inevitable altercations in this rather wild frontier environment. Law enforcement was lacking and alcohol was plentiful—a lethal combination sure to send a continuous supply of patients to the good doctor's door.

As the money piled up, the siblings quickly concluded that Mississippi really was the place to be. Pontotoc was home. What it lacked in sophistication was offset by the vibrancy and profitability of the former Chickasaw tribal center.

TIME FOR POLITICS

In the wild, superheated boom environment of the crude north Mississippi frontier, many were on the make for more—more land, more money, more influence. For a smart, prosperous young lawyer with a talent for persuasion, it was inevitable that politics—and the power that went with it—would soon beckon. If he wanted to advance quickly, Jacob Thompson had come to the perfect place.

For two years, he had thrown himself body and soul at a busy, exhausting law practice. The rewards were great. Financially secure, Jacob could afford to devote time and energy to follow the siren's call of Mississippi politics. Then, as now, a law degree provided the introduction to a political career. Money helped too.

Thompson found his opportunity in the very partisan banking issues plaguing the state. Mississippi had chartered several banks during this period of rapid growth and speculation. These banks essentially loaned money indiscriminately with the result that the state faced potential financial ruin. Incredibly, the state sought to counter the looming bankruptcies by creating another bank to make more loans. The Union Bank was organized with the proposal that Mississippi would endorse $5,000,000 of its bonds.[13]

At a public meeting in Pontotoc for the purpose of encouraging the legislature to endorse the bonds, Jacob Thompson rose in opposition. This was the first public political speech of his career. The majority of those in attendance were in favor of the state backing the bonds. Their opinion was more banks meant more money, hence more prosperity—the same philosophy that got the state into its banking crisis to begin with.

Thompson ably and vigorously pointed out the fallacies of the "banking mania" that possessed the state. He warned that banks run by speculators had previously failed and that the Union Bank might well continue this trend. Then, he asked the audience if they were prepared to be taxed to make up the $5,000,000 if this bank also failed.[14]

The speech was favorably received and discussed throughout the state. However, greed prevailed. The legislature endorsed the bonds in a close vote, unwittingly rushing headlong into more trouble.

It was not long until the words of Jacob Thompson proved prophetic. Mississippi's house of cards was about to collapse. At this precise moment, a banking panic was rapidly sweeping the entire United States. It was particularly hard felt in Mississippi with its already fragile banking system. Issues revolving around the resultant Union Bank failure and the state's responsibility would resonate through Mississippi politics for years. Jacob Thompson would be a major player in those arguments.

Thompson came up with a potent argument designed to save the state from further financial embarrassment. He declared that the Union Bank bonds were issued in violation of the state constitution and then sold in violation of the bank's own charter. Additionally, neither the state of Mississippi nor its citizens had received funds from these bonds. Therefore, by his reasoning, the state was not liable for the bank or its bonds.[15]

In all, the state had issued $18,000,000 in bonds during the reckless 1830's to charter the Planters and Union banks. These banks primarily financed cotton planters with their bonds being bought by English investors. After the Panic of 1837, Union bank officials refused to allow their books to be audited by state commissioners, asserting that "their minds were biased."[16]

Concurrent with the mushrooming banking woes, in 1837 the legislature divided the Chickasaw cession into ten counties. At the time many of Mississippi's men of wealth and influence were Whigs. They resisted giving representation in the legislature to the newly established counties even though the state Constitution expressly required it. This was a patently political move as the new settlers tended to be Jacksonian Democrats. Governor Charles Lynch, a Whig, actually refused to issue the writs required for election of a representative from each county.

This naturally incensed the Democrats including their spokesman in Pontotoc, the rising star Jacob Thompson. A public forum in Pontotoc pitted Whig proponents against Thompson. After a lengthy debate, Thompson carried the day. He was elected to address all the Chickasaw counties over the attempted slight by the Governor and his Whig cronies. The resulting address was printed and widely distributed throughout the disregarded area.[17]

Thompson won this battle along with much acclaim for his prowess and tenacity as an orator. He became more prominent by the day as his law practice grew by leaps and bounds. Money continued to flow in primarily from land deals. He was also instrumental in establishing circuit courts in each of the ten new counties. As he traveled around north Mississippi organizing county courts, he befriended many people, enjoying great popularity with both attorneys and average citizens. Although altruistic to a point, Thompson was also laying the groundwork for a political career.

As his name spread and his popularity grew, the bar of north Mississippi urged him to run for attorney general. This brilliant newcomer had been in the state for only two years when, at the insistence of his supporters, he accepted the nomination. The timidity of his youth long forgotten, he canvassed the state making incisive speeches and with his low-key demeanor gained many converts. Alas, it was not quite enough---he lost by a small margin. In his home base of north Mississippi, Jacob Thompson received overwhelming approval.[18] Not a bad start for a political newcomer's first statewide race. But if he thought losing was tough, he was about to learn that winning could take a toll as well.

Subsequent to the suspension of banks in 1837, Democrats nationally fell into disarray. This loss of support was primarily the result of nationwide banking woes under Democrat President Martin Van Buren. As a result, Mississippi Democrats were left especially vulnerable. A generalized air of despondency followed the suspension of all banks. From this gloomy outlook, nominations were made with little expectation of winning. A. G. McNutt became the gubernatorial nominee with Albert Gallatin Brown and Jacob Thompson nominated for Congress. All Congressional candidates ran statewide at this time, as districts had not been established.

Faced with daunting odds, the Democrats began a resolute, almost desperate, canvass of the state. Their main campaign focus was the blatant mismanagement of the banks and the resultant grief and distress it created. Thompson, of course, could say that he headed off the crisis by warning state officials what would happen if they jumped behind the Union Bank. The Democrats stirred the electorate to a fever pitch. Pushing their radical approach of forcing banks to resume operations or forfeit their charters, the Democrat nominees aroused resentment from both banks and Whigs. The cry of "resume or forfeit" resounded throughout the state.[19]

Elected To Congress

With their one paramount issue and smart campaigning, the Democrats won handily. Jacob Thompson, age 29, was a member of the U. S. House of Representatives. It had been an arduous campaign, but he had no time to rest. He and fellow Congressman Brown were needed in Washington immediately as near political gridlock reigned, though neither of them knew of this.

President Martin Van Buren had written to Governor McNutt to urge the Democrat nominees to hurry to the Capitol for the opening session if they were elected. Since no telegraph system existed at this time, couriers rushed to inform the newly elected Congressmen. Jacob Thompson was briefed at one A. M. and was en route at daybreak, arriving in the House chamber barely in time for the opening gavel.

If these events were not exciting enough, Jacob Thompson took his seat and proceeded to create a tie in the House with his first vote. It was a stunning start. The vote was on a New Jersey election where the popular vote was for the Democrat members, but the certificate of election had been given to the Whig members. This issue continued to be debated with hard feelings for most of the entire session. Then as now fiercely partisan politics were the norm both in Mississippi and in Washington.[20] But they were not nearly as fierce as the debates to come, including one that would force Thompson to choose between home and country.

Although immature in political terms, Representative Thompson had already formed opinions and principles that would last a lifetime. Early on, he became an adherent of fellow North Carolina native Nathaniel Macon. The Thompsons, or in reality Jacob, named their only child Caswell Macon Thompson. Richard Caswell was a Revolutionary War general from North

Carolina who had given his name to Caswell County, the birthplace of Jacob Thompson, while Macon had also been a Revolutionary War general and hero from North Carolina.

Nathaniel Macon espoused limited government, honesty, integrity, and opposed taxes, especially protective tariffs. His positions won him a reputation as the "most prominent naysayer" in Washington. In spite of his hard-line stances, Macon was revered on both sides of the aisle. He rose to become Speaker of the House of Representatives and later President pro tempore of the Senate. As a sign of future troubles, Macon's no compromise approach extended to slavery. Indeed, he thought secession the only alternative to the northern antislavery movement.[21]

The *Mississippi Intelligencer* of June 4, 1839, reported that Jacob Thompson was "a true disciple of that great and good man (Nathaniel Macon.)"[22] They were in total harmony with their dislike of banks underwritten by the government. Their thoughts on an over-reaching federal government pertaining to slavery and taxes perfectly coincided even though Macon died at the advent of Thompson's career.

No doubt Thompson patterned his politics after Macon, but they differed in other ways. While Macon chose to live humbly, Thompson built an imposing home. Although Macon had no strong affiliation to any political party, Thompson generally promoted Democrats and their positions. Thompson supported government backed railroad expansion and other internal improvements, which would have been anathema to the hard-nosed Macon.

Thompson began his life in Washington by treading carefully, taking time to quietly learn how Congress worked. But by 1841 he had observed the perceived failings of the House of Representatives long enough to voice his frustration. He confessed to being primarily a silent voter while explaining to his colleagues in Congress, "I know well the party organization of this House—the blindness, deafness, and stubbornness it engenders. I know the impotence of argument; and the futility of reason and principle here; but my constituents do not; and they expect me, frankly and openly, to meet these various questions and maintain their interests...."

He continued, "In a Government embracing every variety of interest, agricultural, commercial, and manufacturing, like ours, inherent difficulties will always exist in fixing upon a proper and equal system of taxation. If all party distinctions could now be wiped out of the public mind as with a sponge, society would again immediately divide into tax-paying and tax-consuming parties, and interest, no doubt, would be the controlling principle…"

Then he presented a prescient conclusion on economics and the government. "That it is the duty of Government to leave capital free to seek its own investments; giving protection and security to all—advantage to none."[23] Now 175 years later similar words are still repeated in the halls of Congress by those favoring less government intrusion.

When traversing the Chickasaw cession area on business, Jacob Thompson stayed in private homes out of necessity. Hotels and boarding houses were few and far between and rudimentary at best. One of these homes in soon to be Lafayette County belonged to Peyton Jones. The Joneses had migrated to north Mississippi like so many others to purchase and farm the rich bottomlands south of the Tallahatchie River. Influential from the first, he was one of the four commissioners appointed to organize Lafayette County in 1836. These commissioners designed the layout of the nascent towns of Lafayette County, including Oxford.[24]

That same year Peyton Jones bought a section of land some eight miles from Oxford where he built a home on a rise named Woodson Ridge. It was a large one-story log building with wide verandas on all sides. The fireplaces were oversized and, along with the chimneys, were made of native stone. Here Jacob Thompson and Peyton Jones struck up a life-long friendship. Jacob became a frequent guest. They had much in common. Both were from relatively wealthy families and both were ambitious. They also shared an intense desire to keep abreast of and control local events, political and otherwise.[25]

Peyton Jones was a success from the outset as a planter in this rapidly developing area of North Mississippi. He had arrived with a few slaves and his family, traveling from South Carolina. By 1850, he owned 3200 acres of land in Lafayette County and reportedly 300 slaves.[26] Jones taught Jacob

Thompson how to make money farming. Jacob was an apt student, quickly applying the knowledge gained. And just as quickly profiting from it.

In 1837, he bought his first land in Lafayette County. The census of 1850 revealed that he owned 2400 acres in Lafayette County valued at $10,000. The farm produced 500 bushels of corn and 120 bales of cotton. A decade later, he was the biggest producer in the county with 2500 acres valued at $50,000, generating 5,000 bushels of corn and 392 bales of cotton. All the while, Jacob was a member of Congress, obviously spending much of his time in Washington, depending on underlings to keep the farm going.[27]

From that first humble law office in Pontotoc, he had expanded to offices in the planned town of Panola (near current Batesville) on the Tallahatchie River in Panola County as well as Oxford. Like his friend Jones, he rapidly increased his land holdings. His property ledger from 1854-1856 reveals just how much his empire had grown:

> Home Place 717 acres, 18 slaves
> Clear Creek including 960 acres in Panola County, 38 adult
>   slaves, 40 children
> Woodson Ridge 3360 acres, 48 adult slaves, 53 children
> Mississippi River Plantation Tunica County, 10,395 acres, 53
>   adult slaves, 23 children
> Choctaw Cession 1000 acres
> Lands belonging to Jacob Thompson and William G. Ford of
>   Louisville, 1899 acres on Tallahatchie River
> Other large tracts in several counties
> Multiple blocks and lots in Oxford
> Bonds in St. Louis Company and Mississippi
> Central Railroad[28]

The Thompsons were quite wealthy, the importance of which would become evident much later when Jacob would be accused of embezzlement. But that was a long way off.

For now, Jacob appeared to be a charmed man. His soon to be wife Kate Jones, daughter of Peyton Jones, had only one sibling and in time that seemingly arcane fact would only serve to increase Jacob's wealth. Thomas, her brother, died in 1846 on his way to the Mexican War, leaving her as the only heir of the affluent Peyton Jones and his wife Tabitha. Peyton Jones died in 1853 and Tabitha in 1873. Tabitha lived with Kate and Jacob during the latter stages of her life with Jacob managing her business.

Courtship And Marriage

During his frequent social and work visits to Woodson Ridge and Oxford, Jacob, age 26, met the charming Catherine Ann (Kate) Jones, the fourteen year- old daughter of Peyton and Tabitha Jones. It was love at first sight. Kate was reportedly beautiful and personable with the added attraction of being an heiress to the large estate of her parents. Kate's parents approved of this match, and the romance blossomed until Jacob had to go to Washington. Jacob proposed to the fun-loving, adventurous Kate, and she readily accepted. He was apparently afraid to wait longer as eligible suitors were literally at her doorstep. The wedding took place in Lafayette County on December 18, 1838.

The seventeen year-old bride had received a very basic education on the newly settled frontier. Jacob, now 29, thought it inadvisable to take Kate to Washington with him at her age and level of sophistication. He instead accompanied Kate to a finishing school in France. Jacob quickly returned home to his busy schedule, leaving his newlywed wife. In Paris she completed her training, gaining in literary skills along with a distinctive French flair. The now twenty-year-old cultivated young lady traveled to the capital city to be with her husband. There they lived together as a married couple for the first time. She would soon be acclaimed as a very popular hostess in Washington society. Her invitation became one of the hottest tickets in town.

They had one child, Caswell Macon Thompson, born on November 11, 1839, eleven months after their wedding. Whether Macon was born in Paris or Lafayette County is unclear. He never was strong physically and a large defect over his left lower jaw can clearly be seen in adult photographs. This disfigurement occurred at age nine after an illness and was the result of surgery.[29] The most logical explanation for his defect was from the aftermath of an abcessed tooth requiring drainage. Macon probably developed osteomyelitis of the jaw from the abcess with the resultant loss of bone and probable pathologic fracture.

Macon had a playmate in his formative years. Jacob's much younger orphaned first cousin Samuel Maverick Thompson came to live with the Thompsons at age eight, residing with them in Oxford and Washington. Samuel was very close in age to Macon, providing him with ready companionship. Kate and Jacob Thompson remained Samuel's foster parents through college.

After graduating from the University of Mississippi, Macon took an extended trip to observe Indians in the lands west of Kansas. He would return to serve as quartermaster for a unit established by his father at the advent of the Civil War. Seeking active duty, Macon received a staff position from General James Longstreet with the aid of Jacob. He would serve on this staff through the early Virginia campaigns. However, Macon's physical disabilities soon dictated an end to his military career.

Although Jacob maintained a rather standoffish relationship with his father, he corresponded frequently with his siblings in North Carolina. While he had no intention of returning to Leasburg, he encouraged them to come to Mississippi. His reports of happiness and prosperity worked.

He learned that his close friend Abner Lewis from Chapel Hill days had married his sister Sarah. After marriage, they soon began their trek to Lafayette County, traveling in a caravan of covered wagons, a trip of three months. With Jacob's help, the Lewises bought a plantation ten miles from Oxford on the Tallahatchie River. They later moved from the bottomlands to the hills of Oxford since it had a healthier environment.

Later Eliza Ann Thompson visited sister Sarah Lewis on the Tallahatchie River farm and decided to stay. She subsequently married North Carolina native Yancy Wiley. John and William Thompson joined the influx to Oxford. John was a physician like his brother Young, while William had become an attorney, associating with Jacob in his law practice.[30] While Young settled in nearby Monroe County, five of the siblings were now proud inhabitants of Lafayette County.

POLITICAL CONTROVERSIES

J acob came home from Washington in the summer of 1840 to help
President Martin Van Buren, who was running for re-election. It was a bruis-
ing race. Despite Jacob's best efforts, the unpopular Van Buren lost in a land-
slide both in the state and nationally to the Whig candidate William Henry
Harrison. Voters bitterly blamed Van Buren, labeled "Martin Van Ruin," for
the financial panic that saw hundreds of banks fail and thousands of people
lose their land in what was the nation's worst financial crisis at that point.
The very same banking mess Thompson had tried to head off in Mississippi
had complicated his and fellow Democrats' political fortunes in Washington.

Though still learning his way, the new congressman showed he was a
man of action by his impatience with the slow pace of the House. He was
ever ready to vote, often calling for the question. Too, Thompson demon-
strated a ready willingness to defend a colleague, in this case fellow Mississippi congressman, Albert Gallatin Brown. Whig Representative Daniel
Jenifer of Maryland had verbally attacked Brown on the floor of the House,
while knowing the recipient of his barbs was not present. In Brown's absence, Thompson quickly rose to defend him, vigorously chastising the attacker for going after a colleague who was unable to defend himself.[31]

Meanwhile, the Democrats were once again in disarray. Following the
latest Van Buren debacle in 1841, Jacob had had enough. He decided to
retire from politics to tend to his business and domestic interests. However,
the state Democratic convention unanimously re-nominated him, and he
reluctantly agreed to run again.[32]

Whenever he had a chance to get away from the campaign trail, Jacob
supervised the construction of his elegant mansion on Taylor Road in Oxford. He chose the setting on a slight rise amid beautiful hardwood trees.

The best available lumber was imported by wagon from Memphis. Slaves on site manufactured the bricks used in the foundation and exterior. A large wrought iron fence surrounded the entire property. Outbuildings included an office, carriage house, gate- keepers lodge, gardener's house, smokehouse, and kitchen. Cedars were planted lining the curving drive. He laid out beautiful gardens that would be visible from the spacious verandas of the house.

Fine European artwork obtained during the Thompsons' extensive travels hung in twenty rooms. Stained glass windows added sparkle to the drawing room. A dining room spacious enough to seat a hundred guests was lined with gilded French mirrors. The vastness of this room lends credence to the Thompson's alleged purchase of two hundred soup bowls on one of their Continental visits as well as silver and other china. Jacob named the elaborate home and surroundings Home Place for its pastoral, peaceful setting. It was truly a splendid southern antebellum home.[33] The mansion reeked of opulence, power, and taste, a metaphor of the southern planter class.

The compelling issue in the summer of 1841 was once again the Union Bank. By now the bank was totally bankrupt—it had failed just as Jacob Thompson had predicted. Governor Alexander McNutt refused to redeem the bonds insisting that the state was not legally or morally bound to do so even though the state had backed the bonds with its credit and taxing power. So hotly was this debated that the congressional candidates obviously had to take a position on this looming disaster. Jacob Thompson wrote a forceful letter to a Mr. Webster of Vicksburg maintaining in a clear and concise fashion his agreement with the Governor in denying the state's obligation. This letter was later wholly incorporated into the legislature's response.[34]

As might be expected, after taking his seat in the House of Representatives in November, Jacob Thompson had to defend the state against allegations of wrongdoing in this sordid affair. The primary attack on Mississippi's position came from the outspoken, grumpy former president, now congressman, John Quincy Adams.

Other nationally known Mississippi politicians including Jefferson Davis agreed with Thompson that Mississippi should not honor the bonds.

As Thompson had warned, the whole affair was a disaster for the state.

Every bank in Mississippi shut down and stayed closed for several years afterwards, which made it harder to borrow money, even at exorbitant rates. Mississippi's national reputation was blackened, but every candidate who endorsed the state's refusal to redeem the bonds won in the elections of 1843. Such is politics.

During debate on the repudiation and its ramifications, John Quincy Adams thundered that Mississippi's failure to pay its debts could precipitate war with Great Britain since it held many of the Union Bank bonds. Adams followed through by introducing a resolution stating that if the United States had to go to war because a state refused to pay its debts, then that state would be removed from the Union.

The repudiation issue was not unique to Mississippi. Other states were in debt also. This prompted the Ways and Means Committee to propose the Federal government borrow the necessary money to assume all their debts. Amid this debate in the House Jacob Thompson rose to defend Mississippi by claiming the Mississippi Union Bank had been unconstitutionally chartered; hence, Mississippi did not have to honor the $21,000,000 debt.

As for the proposal of the Ways and Means Committee, he declared, "this happy and glorious Union will soon be forever severed in twain, because no state would ever submit to pay the debts of another." Ultimately Mississippi did indeed default along with Arkansas and Florida. Other states defaulted on interest payments as well.[35]

The next session of Congress was consumed with the annexation of Texas. There were many angles to this thorny issue including the expansion of slavery and charges of blatant imperialism hurled by opponents. At such opportunistic crossroads can political careers be built. Thus it was that the rather emaciated, energetic, and cunning Senator Robert J. Walker of Mississippi realized that support of annexation was his possible road to the White House.

Walker had been born into a family of prominence and wealth in Pennsylvania. Following his relocation to Mississippi, he succeeded as a lawyer, planter, and land speculator. Walker's career path was similar to Jacob

Thompson's in many ways. The glaring exception was that Jacob was typically forthright in contrast to the sly and conniving Walker.

The fateful letter, widely distributed, written by Senator Walker promoting the immediate annexation of Texas was purportedly co-written by his then ally Jacob Thompson. Certainly, the issue of Texas had been of supreme importance to Robert Walker, and Thompson fervently assisted him in his efforts. The letter did achieve the result of blocking Van Buren's bid for the Democratic nomination for president.

Senator Walker knew that his constituency supported annexing Texas as did the South in general. Walker also was aware of the outspoken opposition to annexation of Martin Van Buren, the overwhelming favorite for the Democrat nomination. Jacob Thompson and the Mississippi delegation had already been instructed by the state legislature to vote for Van Buren.

When Van Buren frankly stated his anti-annexation position, the Mississippi delegation at the Baltimore convention, including Jake Thompson, violated their instructions, voting for the pro-annexation candidate, a little known Tennessee protégé of Andrew Jackson, James K. Polk. Jacob Thompson was on intimate and friendly terms with both Polk and the New Yorker Van Buren. Although not without political risk, he lent his considerable support to Polk as he felt certain the annexation issue would wind up defeating Van Buren.[36]

Immediately after Polk's nomination, Thompson wrote him a congratulatory letter that included: "We have in our ranks four to 8 aspirants to the Presidency whose souls are bent upon the over loved object… I know nothing on your part which will have so great a tendency to cause harmonious co-operation, with them all, as an intimation in your acceptance of the nomination that your course will be to serve but a single term."[37] Polk evidently agreed with this suggestion since he announced that he would serve only one term and then kept his word.

Senator Walker had cleverly helped engineer the nomination of Polk. Since Polk had avowed not to stand for reelection, Walker asked to be Secretary of the Treasury, realizing this office was the typical springboard to the presidency. Polk apparently agreed but, after winning the election, rued the day he had made the promise. He was afraid of the politically astute but manipulative Walker. Instead of treasury, Polk offered him the less prestigious cabinet position of attorney general.

Thompson, who had done so much to elect Polk, was asked by Walker to intercede with the president-elect on his behalf. At this point, Walker had become resigned to his fate and was ready to accept the appointment of attorney general to avoid being completely left out of the cabinet. True to form, Thompson approached, even perhaps cajoled, Polk over the perceived slight to his friend and fellow Mississippian. At the insistence of Thompson, Polk acquiesced and promised to offer Walker the treasury post he so desired. A seemingly grateful Walker thanked Thompson profusely and accepted the position.[38]

While this was transpiring, Governor Albert Gallatin Brown of Mississippi wrote Jacob Thompson inquiring if Walker would ultimately get a cabinet seat. He replied in the affirmative. To make sure the state was fully represented at the upcoming March session, the governor prepared to appoint Jacob Thompson senator in Walker's place. The commission was duly forwarded to Walker, appointing Thompson senator with the date left blank because Walker had not yet been officially named to the cabinet.

Walker actually had the commission when Thompson met with Polk on his behalf but said nothing about it. They remained friends until March 1845 when Thompson returned to Oxford after being unanimously re-nominated for Congress. Soon thereafter, Governor Brown requested to meet him in Grenada to discuss politics.

During the conversation, Brown revealed that he had issued the commission and given it to Walker to be executed. He further stated that Dr. William Gwin, a close friend and confidante of Walker, almost begged him to be appointed senator and that he had Walker's support.

Governor Brown then offered the still open appointment to Jacob Thompson, but he declined since he had already accepted the nomination of his party for Congress. He thanked Brown, adding that he would have been honored and pleased to be appointed senator had he known before agreeing to run for Congress.[39] After Thompson's refusal, Brown appointed

Robt. J. Walker.

Robert J. Walker, who deprived Thompson of a Senate seat,
starting an ongoing antagonism

Judge Joseph W. Chalmers of Holly Springs to fill the senate seat vacated by Walker.

William Gwin, the son of a well-known Tennessee Methodist preacher and close friend of Andrew Jackson, studied law initially and later received a medical degree from Transylvania University.

He began his medical practice with his brother Samuel in Clinton. Using Jackson's influence, both brothers soon obtained lucrative federal appointments.

William Gwin became a mover and shaker in state Democratic politics, utilizing his energy and political skills to elect Robert J. Walker to the United States Senate in 1835. Gwin himself was elected to Congress in 1841 on the Democratic ticket along with Jacob Thompson. Gwin was an entrepreneur and a risk taker, making and losing fortunes in the process.

In the meantime, Walker continued to cause trouble for Jacob Thompson. It was as if he had suddenly decided to devote his life to plaguing the man who once helped him accelerate his political career.

Dr. Gwin was incensed that Jacob Thompson had helped defeat a bill in which Gwin had a great deal of interest. Ever the speculator, Gwin hoped to achieve financial gain from its passage. Never mind the ethics of the matter. The bill was supposed to be for the relief of the Chickasaw Indians while the reality was far different. Thompson aggressively fought against the "Chickasaw bill" to protect the very Indians it was supposed to favor.

Gwin was so mad that he challenged Thompson to a duel. Jacob chose Jefferson Davis and John A. Quitman as his representatives. These two were premier leaders of Mississippi and arguably of the South. They both soon were to distinguish themselves in the Mexican War. With these men of prominence intervening, cooler heads prevailed and bloodshed was avoided.

Walker and Gwin both left Mississippi after the Chickasaw bill controversy. Robert Walker never returned to Mississippi, ultimately moving to Kansas where he became the territorial governor. A consummate opportunist, Walker went overnight from an ardent proponent of the South and slavery to an anti-slavery nationalist. He traveled to Europe during the Civil

War, undermining and successfully removing sources of Confederate credit in England and France.

William Gwin intrepidly moved to the new state of California in 1849. There he was elected U. S. senator, California's first along with John C. Fremont, serving during the 1850s. Putting past conflict behind them, a warm friendship developed between the Thompsons and the Gwins while both couples lived in Washington.

The words of Jacob Thompson in a letter to J. F. H. Claiborne best express his feelings: "But while I became reconciled entirely to Gwin, I never could tolerate Walker. He was a man devoid of opinions of his own, controlled by any man who had will and decision; he had a fertile genius as readily employed on one side of the question as the other. He was true to a friend only so far as that friend could serve him in his designs."[40]

By 1843 the 33 year-old Jacob Thompson was a seasoned heavyweight in the House of Representatives. He had become comfortable in this environment, exhibiting none of his former shyness. As his influence grew, he delivered several key, succinct addresses on the current issues of the day; i.e., Texas annexation and the northern boundary of Oregon. On both of these important topics, Representative Thompson vigorously supported the Polk administration's positions.

The increasing price of public lands was an issue dear to Thompson's heart. The millions of acres of lands ceded by the Chickasaws and Choctaws had to be disposed of by the federal government. Thompson earnestly fought for the yeoman farmer to be able to acquire a small portion of this land cheaply. In so doing he reflected the views of Thomas Jefferson who had promoted yeoman farmers as the backbone of a strong America.

The large purchasers would have to pay more per acre similar to our present graduated tax system. The more you buy, the more you pay per acre. This naturally encouraged migration and settlement into the vast area of the cessions. Cynically, most of these small farmers would tend to vote Democrat, of which Thompson was well aware.[41]

Generally speaking, Congressman Thompson had the personality to separate the message from the messenger, thus keeping him from personally attacking colleagues. This ability to be unfailingly polite in trying circumstances created respect and friendship even as the political situation in the country steadily deteriorated. He was always ready to defend Mississippi, the South, and the continuation of slavery, though he was not one of the firebrands. Of course, he had some political enemies and was capable of being implacable when pushed to the extreme.

His nearly contemporary fellow Mississippian, one term congressman, historian, and author J. F. H. Claiborne described him as, "Cautious and deliberate in taking positions on all new issues, yet firm and resolute in maintaining them, he was ever consistent, and became a leader on whom the most explicit reliance could be placed. Always prudent, yet firm and determined, sure of his position and well able to defend it, no constituency was ever served with more fidelity, honesty, and efficiency, and none ever trusted a representative with more constancy and confidence. He was never known to dodge an issue, or fail to maintain the course he advocated, or prove untrue to a colleague or political friend."[42] High praise indeed!

The Thompsons' homes in both Oxford and Washington became centers of hospitality, primarily for Democrat politicians. Kate, his wife, still in her twenties, energetic and outgoing, loved to entertain. And entertain she did. As a result Jacob quickly developed warm and intimate friendships with many Democrat leaders on both a state and national level. He utilized these close personal friendships to intervene with President Polk on behalf of different people, including the aforementioned Walker.

Another indication of Jacob's standing with Polk came when he was approached by General John A. Quitman at the end of the Mexican War. Quitman, a hero of that war, was determined to maintain his rank of major general. He had been promoted to brevet major general during the conflict and after the war reverted to the rank of brigadier general. Polk was disinclined to ask Congress to restore his rank as the war had ended and volunteers were returning home. Too, the President thought Quitman was unduly pressuring him through every means possible, which he resented.

Thompson intervened, soothing Polk with assertions that Quitman had not threatened him. Ultimately, Polk acquiesced and Quitman kept his rank. Jacob Thompson brokered a deal to make both parties happy, showing that he had developed into a trusted statesman, wielding wide influence as a man wise enough to solve thorny problems.[43]

Two years later in 1850, Quitman was governor of Mississippi and sought the counsel of Thompson in another sticky matter. The Governor had been indicted by a Federal Grand Jury in New Orleans for violating the Neutrality Act of 1817. Quitman had with others been involved in trying to annex Cuba, apparently believing this was part of America's "manifest destiny." Quitman contended that the indictment was an attempt to bully him for advocating secession.

Thompson told the governor that "arresting him would annihilate state sovereignty. The governor was the sole representative of the sovereignty of Mississippi, and the very idea of sovereignty carried with it the sequence of impunity in action and conduct." Thompson did not believe a warrant for his arrest would be issued; however, if it happened "you owe it to yourself to refuse the mandate... The times are out of joint... The first effort to degrade the State will be made in your person, and, by all power above, I would resist it."[44]

Thompson was wrong about the arrest. A warrant was indeed issued and this early fight over states' rights was on. After resigning as governor to fight the charges, Quitman endured three hung juries before the case was ultimately dismissed. Although both were Mississippi Democrats, it is strange that Quitman would seek the opinion of Thompson on this issue. Quitman was a radical proponent of secession, a southern fire-eater. Also, he was a general and a governor. Thompson by contrast was much more pragmatic and moderate. Both did staunchly believe in states' rights, holding that state sovereignty was paramount.[45] Perhaps, Quitman simply appreciated the growing influence of Jacob Thompson in the Capitol.

Two difficult international issues confronted the country during the Polk presidency. One was the Mexican War, including what to do with the territory gained as a result of the war. Naturally, this became part of the increasingly heated debates over slavery and its extension. The second issue involved the persistent dispute with Great Britain over ownership of the Oregon territory.

Oregon presented a special problem since the powerful British Empire was the adversary. Also, the American South was very dependent on the British to buy its primary product—cotton. Thompson succinctly reviewed the history of the territory in a Congressional address, admitting that the claims to the area between the 49th and 54th parallel were vague. However, he was not prepared to concede all that contiguous territory to the British. His reasons, it seemed, were strongly patriotic ones.

He concluded his remarks in a speech before Congress on February 2nd, 1846: "Gentlemen should remember that there may be differences of opinion between individuals from different sections of the Union; but as regards the South as a whole, they have never actuated by any narrow or contracted considerations when national interests or national honor were involved. In every national dispute, the South has always been with the country … I am ready to go to the utmost verge sanctioned by honor and a just policy to make these emigrants (to Oregon) feel that they are American citizens, and that they will receive the protection and defense of the Government of the United States."

"To do nothing is wrong," he exclaimed in regard to abandonment of claims. "Enamored of quiet and afraid to act, you do nothing, and thereby abandon the country and secure your peace. Are gentlemen willing to purchase peace at such a price? The hour has not yet arrived when we will shrink back from the assertion of right or the vindication of truth."[46]

His voice among others carried the day and a negotiated settlement was reached without resorting to war. Certainly, Thompson did not want war on multiple levels, but he realized that all would be lost unless the United States stood its ground. Interestingly, Thompson's fervent patriotism had a limit. That would become clear later on.

On January 9, 1847, almost a year later, Jacob Thompson made an impassioned, fairly lengthy address in the House of Representatives during the often bitter debates over the Mexican War. This speech still in print further revealed his position regarding patriotism as well as the damage done by those opposed to the administration and its prosecution of the war.

"This debate, Mr. Chairman, presents the American Congress in a strange light before the country and before the world…. This same Congress… declared with a most remarkable and astonishing unanimity, that 'by the act of the republic of Mexico, a state of war existed between that Government and the United States,' and authorized the raising of fifty thousand volunteers for the prosecution of the war."

He warned that with the enemy strong and defiant, "we are gravely debating the causes of the war, endeavoring to make it appear that our own Government is wrong, and that the enemy is right, indulging in criminations and recriminations, abusing the President in the coarsest and most vulgar terms, asserting in the most positive and decisive manner what shall and what shall not be done with the spoils of victory. This picture is so revolting that it will cause the cheek of the patriot to mantle with shame as he beholds it…."

Warming to the subject, Thompson continued, "A sentiment of familiar quotations in these days is one expressed long since by a gallant officer of our navy, (Commander Stephen Decatur,) and well became the man who uttered it: 'Our country, may she always be right; but, right or wrong, our country…' Let us direct our attention to the present existing condition of things in this country. Our nation is in war; we have drawn the sword…. And it is a vain and base shrinking from duty to waste our time in idle debate. Action, prompt and decisive action, is demanded. We all desire peace…."

His extemporaneous remarks (Thompson had forgotten his prepared speech) included the support for raising ten additional regiments of volunteers to be attached to the regular army in the field, the selection of a commander-in-chief to oversee and direct the three armies in Mexico, a necessary tax increase to finance the war, and a plea to not divide the country at this critical time over the slavery issue as it had already been debated.

He concluded, "As one man let us put forth the power of this nation, and first secure our country's honor and rights; and then I have an abiding confidence that the patriotism of our people will triumph, and save every portion of this country from dishonor and injustice."[47]

These comments and proposals were in basic support of the desires of President Polk. The bill authorizing the tax increases and war loans Thompson promoted passed overwhelmingly but only after a prolonged contentious attack on Polk and his allies, especially Jacob Thompson.

It started when Tennessee's John Crozier, "a haughty young Whig," offered an amendment "for the sole purpose of opening up the measure for a long and spirited disquisition on the War's lack of legitimacy." Quoting from Thompson's speech, he excoriated him repeatedly in a mocking and insulting manner. Much of Crozier's venom revolved around Thompson's implications that General Zachary Taylor and General Winfield Scott were not prosecuting the war in a timely fashion; thus, the need for an overarching commander. Thompson held his own, patiently, calmly, and frankly responding to each question and accusation.

Ultimately, Crozier confronted Thompson over the trivial issue of mentioning Mississippians before Tennesseans in his comments regarding the volunteers' charge at Monterey. According to Crozier, the Tennessee volunteers preceded those from Mississippi, thus mandating that he name them first. The whole issue had become ridiculous, but, throughout it all, Jacob Thompson had kept his cool.[48]

The *Congressional Globe*, analogous to today's *Congressional Record*, frequently contained motions, amendments, clarifications, and probing questions from Jacob Thompson. He would quickly, forcefully, but graciously rise to offer defenses of his positions when challenged. Prepared speeches were less commonly delivered, thereby giving them more import. Jacob was particularly fixated on points of order and was a stickler for following proper parliamentary procedures, much like the powerful southerners who would build up seniority and control the senate through sheer clout and shrewd parliamentary maneuvers a century later.

In 1850, Thomas Prentice Kettell published a resume of Thompson's political career to that point in *The Democratic National Review*. Kettell wrote that Jacob's initial ventures into politics meant four months of visiting most counties in the state with speaking engagements for six days out of seven. To accomplish this he often had to ride horseback for thirty miles between speeches.[49]

Kettell then recounted an anecdotal story that was supposed to have occurred when Jake first ran for Congress at age 28. "An old man remarked, "Young man, I fear you won't do—you are too young for Congress," Thompson promptly replied, "Hear me before you make up your mind; and as to age, I will get older as fast as I can." After listening to Thompson, the old man rose and laughingly declared, "enough, enough, I'm satisfied—you are old enough for me."[50]

The brief review of specially highlighted Democrat politicians by Kettell continued with a rehash of the Union bond default. Was the state liable for bonds issued "in violation of the constitution and sold in violation of the charter of the bank and no funds had been received by the people of the state?" Thompson was lauded for "defending Mississippi through knowledge of the facts and eloquence… As this was the most trying, it is certainly the most praiseworthy achievement of his public life" to 1850.[51]

Kellett finished, "He has been emphatically a working member of Congress, ever in his seat, ready to meet any responsibility which may be thrown upon him, regular in his habits, indefatigable in his attentions to the private interests of his constituents, and diligent in the discharge of every duty devolved upon him in the Hall, the committee-room, or before the departments. Though yet a young man, Mr. Thompson is, in the duration of service among the oldest members of the House…"[52]

To be fair that was a Democrat publication touting Thompson as a party leader. This exalted opinion of him clearly was not universal. Many Whigs in Mississippi detested Thompson for his aggressive campaign methods that would be considered tame by today's standards. Millington Walker, a struggling medical student from north Mississippi, noted in his diary entry of June 5, 1849, "They announced the nomination of Jacob Thompson, the damndest nomination that could have been made." In 1851 Walker recorded that "Jacob Thompson and friends resort to low, undermining subterfuges for the purpose of arousing the sympathies of the people and thus gain their votes."[53]

ESTABLISHING
A UNIVERSITY

Concurrently, back in his adopted state of Mississippi, exciting events were happening. The population had exploded from 136,000 in 1830 to 376,000 in 1840 primarily because so many were so eager to settle on prior Chickasaw and Choctaw lands. This was an amazing increase of 175 per cent overall with "persons of color" now constituting some 55 per cent of the population. These were indeed the flush times of Mississippi, notwithstanding the banking panic of 1837.[54]

Political leaders pushed for a state supported university to serve the needs of the rapidly growing population. After much deliberation and delay, Oxford, a town of 400, was chosen as the site of the fledgling University of Mississippi. Its selection over Mississippi City on the Gulf coast by a vote of 57 to 56 reflected a shift in political power from south to north Mississippi. The 26 counties created in north Mississippi from the Indian cessions resulted in this dramatic swing with Oxford the beneficiary.[55]

The charter of the University, adopted in 1844, established a powerful board of trustees consisting of thirteen members selected statewide. Jacob Thompson was appointed by the legislature to this original board. He continued to serve until 1857 when he resigned to become secretary of the interior. At his resignation from the Buchanan cabinet in early 1861, he was reelected to the board.[56]

When the University officially opened on November 6, 1848, Jacob Thompson gave the inaugural address on behalf of the Board of Trustees.

At the end of the first session, the University still had no library. Ever education oriented and civic- minded, Jacob donated books from his library in addition to funds for the purchase of much needed reference works.

His main focus while serving on the board was the establishment of a school of law. Addressing the Mississippi legislature in 1854, he said, "that for a thousand years the Bar has been the road to the titles and the power. Our ambitious youth go to the East for instruction in this department for it is to be found there alone." He stated his desire that the University of Mississippi should have "a professorship of law [but] not of law alone." Thompson continued, "in the science of government we think of high importance to the Southern youth."

He reiterated that "we live in a confederacy of states" and that the "political relationships of the states to each other are looked at in somewhat different light according to the geographic points of view." Appealing to the legislature via the states' rights approach secured its approval along with funding for the first publically supported law school in the deep South.[57] This was shrewd as Mississippi and affiliated states would need brilliant home-educated lawyer defenders.

Thompson's role in the establishment and early development of the University as "the most eminent Trustee" was significant. He put his heart and soul into its success until his appointment as Secretary of the Interior by President-elect Buchanan. During his cabinet tenure, while continuing to closely follow happenings at the University, two events occurred which reveal elements of his character.

The first began with a letter from Secretary Thompson in the spring of 1860 to board member James Howry. Thompson lamented that he had heard of the impending bankruptcy of Lafayette County businessman William F. Avent. The clear implication was to help his friend in time of need if possible. Voila! Message received. The board quickly voted to secure "suitable rooms for a year or term of years" in Oxford "for a lecture room, law library room and a room for the law professor's study." Avent and Lyles bank building on the Oxford square was soon selected to provide the necessary space. It was a case study of how a politician—in this case Thompson—could subtly, unobtrusively wield considerable influence and power for a friend. All it took was a mention of sympathy at just the right moment. Before he knew it, Thompson had quietly accomplished his goal without ruffling feathers.[58]

The second is more complex, involving a concerted effort to remove Chancellor Barnard in part because because he hailed from the North. A Yale graduate and accomplished academic, Frederick Augustus Porter Barnard joined the University faculty in 1854. He became chancellor upon the forced resignation of Chancellor Augustus B. Longstreet in 1856. Barnard's vision for and direction of the University was unparalleled. Under his guidance the University flourished, moving into the top tier of American academic institutions.

Nonetheless, he had his incessant detractors. The detractors, most notably Dr. Henry Branham, were upset over his perceived role in the ouster of his predecessor. The animosity and dissent culminated in an event known as the Branham Affair. Branham, a local physician and rabid pro-slavery advocate, had been waiting for an opportunity to undermine and get rid of Chancellor Barnard for one of the oldest motives known to man. As the son-in-law of former chancellor Longstreet, Branham wanted revenge. He would soon have just the contentious issue he had been looking for.[59]

While the Barnards were attending a meeting in Vicksburg in May 1859, two students clandestinely entered their residence, viciously attacking and raping their maid Jane, a slave. A professor heard the assault, saw the boys leave, and days later learned their identity from other students. Jane identified her attacker (the second was a non-participant) to Mrs. Barnard who in turn relayed this incriminating information to her husband.

Barnard flew into a rage. At a called meeting, the faculty reviewed evidence, ultimately finding the accused "morally convicted" but took no action. The problem: Under Mississippi law slaves could not testify against a white person. Barnard then asked the attacker's parents to remove their son from school. They complied. However, the culprit applied for readmission the next semester. Barnard promptly denied this request.[60]

This gave Branham and his cohorts their opening. They tried to destroy Barnard through a "smear campaign." They alleged that he used "negro testimony" and was "unsound on the slavery question." The campaign eventually divided the faculty and students. As the controversy swirled out of control, Barnard received death threats. He was disillusioned and upset, almost beside himself. Finally, he asked the governor to investigate the allegations against him. A board of inquiry unanimously found in his favor, absolving him completely.

Still, the backstabbing and threats continued unabated. Barnard, at his wits' end, decided to resign as chancellor and return to his native Massachusetts. Before he could act, Jacob Thompson wrote Barnard a letter stating, "I am convinced that you have no cause to fear either personal insult or personal violence from anyone in Oxford...I wish you would go on as you have always done, believing that you have friends who will stand by you." The message was unmistakable. A powerful Cabinet member and trustee was putting his clout and reputation solidly behind the chancellor. And solidly in the path of anyone who might attack him. It worked. Barnard agreed to stay.[61]

Once more, Thompson had separated himself from the rash tactics of southern fire-eating fanatics. Chancellor Barnard was a friend and a superb scholar. For that, Thompson, who also did not want the University's respected academic credentials sullied, would back him to the hilt against Branham and his fellow accusers. If Thompson needed another reason to stand with the embattled chancellor, he needed look no further than St. Peters Church in Oxford, where Barnard happened to be an ordained Episcopal minister, often conducting services as Thompson and his family sat in a pew as communicants. Thompson had grown up in a Presbyterian household but became an Episcopalian at marriage, choosing to join the denomination of his wife.

At the outbreak of the Civil War, Barnard would leave Oxford to become head of Columbia University in New York City. The University would not be the same for a long time to come.

Thompson's growing clout came from more than the fact that he was a former congressman and current Cabinet secretary. He had built an impressive network of powerful friends and political allies. He made it a point to

LQC Lamar, Thompson's longtime friend and ally

support his Democrat friends, both North and South. His tireless work on behalf of Martin Van Buren of New York, James Buchanan of Pennsylvania, and Franklin Pierce of New Hampshire helped each achieve the presidency, a fact they never forgot.

The University was not Thompson's only foray into education. He also promoted female and Indian education. He served on the Board of Oxford Female Academy, donating "extensive" books and public documents to that institution. Likewise, he used his position on the Committee for Indian Affairs to obtain an academy for the struggling Choctaw Indians in Mississippi.[62]

Thompson gave the Choctaws further assistance through a bill he introduced in 1841. Through the negligence of the local Indian agent, Choctaw land had been inadvertently sold by the government. The bill corrected the error, giving relief to the destitute Indians. Thompson wrote of this issue, "I introduced a bill which will mete out ample justice to the miserable Indians who are in a state of want and wretchedness." Resulting from his extensive dealings with the closely related Chickasaws in north Mississippi, Thompson stated that he learned to speak their language, making it easier to understand their needs.[63]

In 1849 soon after the University opened its doors Jacob Thompson first met L. Q. C. Lamar as the brilliant young mathematics professor (and attorney) joined the faculty. They quickly struck up a lifelong friendship in spite of a fifteen-year age difference. Lamar had followed his father-in-law Augustus Baldwin Longstreet from Georgia to Mississippi. Longstreet had headed Emory College prior to accepting the chancellorship of the University of Mississippi. Lamar truly loved his father-in-law, which seemingly would create tensions in his relationship with Thompson since Thompson had supported removing Longstreet as chancellor in favor of Barnard. However, this was not the case.

Addressing this unlikely relationship, Lamar's biographer Edward Mayes wrote that Lamar "entertained always the highest regard" for Thompson. He said the congressman's "kindness to (Lamar) and encouraging attentions he ever held in grateful remembrance."[64] Jacob Thompson in short order was offering advice to his new friend Lamar on matters political and financial.

Lamar's national political career began in one of the many Democrat strategy sessions held at Home Place, the Thompson's spacious home. Jacob Thompson was without doubt the political boss of the Democrat party in Lafayette County and much of north Mississippi, using his dining room as a base to develop a plan of action in these troubling times. Jefferson Davis and Governor John Pettus frequented these work sessions. In June 1857, the topic was the need to select a viable candidate for Congress from north Mississippi. The incumbent Democrat congressman, Daniel Boone Wright, had chosen not to run for re-election in favor of resuming his law practice in Ashland.

The debate over whom to recommend and promote as the Democrat candidate for Thompson's old House seat continued well into the night. Finally, Jacob Thompson rose and stated that the candidate should be highly intelligent, cultured, eloquent, and above moral reproach. When asked where this person could be found, Thompson enthusiastically replied over a wine toast, "Gentlemen, I present to you our next congressman, Lucius Quintus Cincinnatus Lamar."[65]

That endorsement began the impressive political career of Lamar, the Congressman, Secretary of the Interior, and Supreme Court Justice. Lamar is credited with using his political skills to end Reconstruction in the South and became one of eight leaders included in John F. Kennedy's *Profiles in Courage.*

Jacob Thompson advised Lamar on many things, but when it came to financial advice, he was a spectacularly unsuccessful mentor. It was not for lack of trying, however. Thompson seemingly made money at every endeavor-- from law practice to cotton farming to investments-- while Lamar struggled at each. Thompson obviously had the inclination and knack in matters financial as opposed to his dreamy, academically motivated protégé.

Jacob gave the land for a cemetery to St. Peters Episcopal Church in the growing town of Oxford. This filled a need and also provided revenue for the church through the sale of plots. At this time, he half-jokingly told Lamar that he had deeded a plot to him since he was afraid Lamar would not be able to bury himself otherwise.[66]

Thompson had followed his wife Kate in becoming an active member of St. Peters. It probably did not take too much persuasion on her part for him to leave his puritanical Presbyterian background, especially as interpreted by his oppressive father. Besides his gift of the cemetery and direct monetary support, his slaves made the brick for the beautiful sanctuary built in 1859-1860. While in Europe after the war, he asked Macon to purchase six additional acres for the cemetery. Macon bought the land and it was donated shortly after Jacob's return home.[67]

Despite house construction, escorting his wife home from Paris, helping establish a university, and attending to his plantations and law practice, Thompson somehow always found time for politics. Fortunately, his very capable brother William handled much of the day-to-day management of their busy legal office. Congressman Thompson was undoubtedly both intrigued and frustrated by national politics. Being in Congress with the necessity to run every two years was time consuming and wearying. Making running even harder, until 1847 he had to campaign statewide as an at-large candidate.

Yet, Thompson had made himself a Washington power broker, a man courted by presidents, governors, and congressmen alike. He consistently had the ear of Democrats in the Oval Office. And why not? They found him usually to be a loyal supporter of their agendas. At the same time, he was able to maintain good relations with many on the other side of the aisle. Things were different back then. The Democrat party to which he remained devoted was not a proponent of a powerful central government, as are today's Democrats. It was instead the party of small central government (hence states' rights) along with a strict interpretation of the Constitution.

THE SLAVERY ISSUE

But the times were changing. Attitudes on both sides of the aisle in Congress were hardening. Compromise was harder to achieve. Thompson realized that the South was being increasingly marginalized, largely over the slavery issue. The enslavement of human beings, though legal, could not be defended morally. As more free states entered the Union, the slaveholding states were losing their power and control. Jacob Thompson could see no way out of this evolving situation except to oppose altering the ratio of free states to slave states.

Bad as the situation was, it was about to get worse.

As a result of the Mexican War, the United States picked up more territory out west. Northern congressmen rushed to block any expansion of slavery into the new territory. Their opening salvo in an attempt to prevent expansion of slavery into territory acquired as a result of the Mexican War was a measure introduced by Democrat Congressman David Wilmot of Pennsylvania in 1846. The proviso was a rider on an appropriations bill and it passed the House but was defeated in the Senate. Later, it was reintroduced and again failed in the Senate. Ultimately, the proviso met failure when attached to the Treaty of Guadalupe Hidalgo, which had ended the Mexican War.

The proviso was dead, but Thompson knew this was no time for celebration. He appreciated the Wilmot Proviso for what it was—a direct attack on slavery. The combination of all northern Whigs and the majority of northern Democrats would be unstoppable. He realized that his beloved Democrat party would never be the same. He doggedly continued to work for party and national unity, but he could see the political handwriting on the wall. This, he knew, was a pivotal moment from which there would be no turning back. While fixated on the slavery issue, Thompson surmised that power motivated northern politicians more than morality.

A frustrated and saddened Thompson warned as much when he wrote the *Oxford Organizer* on June 19, 1849: "I am not unconscious of the fact that my experiences in legislation has given me great advantages, but that very experience teaches me the importance and difficulty of the present crisis. A majority of the people of the United States give unmistakable evidence of their fixed determination to overthrow our domestic institutions.... A total abolition of slavery is the avowed object, yet cautiously do they approach this end in their legislative action."[68]

John C. Calhoun, the great orator and defender of southern rights, had a large influence on Jacob Thompson, beginning early in Thompson's political career. This is hardly a surprise as their views regarding slavery and state's rights were similar though Thompson was more realistic. Jefferson Davis, perhaps the best-known Mississippian at the time, was also under the sway of Calhoun.

In "An Address of the Southern Delegates in Congress to their Constituents" drafted by Calhoun and adopted on January 22, 1849, he concluded that the abolitionist movement was intent on nothing less than the immediate overthrow of southern white supremacy. The lengthy address was calculated to warn and unite the South in opposition to this movement. It argued that the abolitionists' goal was unconstitutional and a violation of current law. In the end, less than half of the southern delegation signed the address. There was no disagreement in Mississippi however. Every member of the Mississippi delegation including Jacob Thompson and Jefferson Davis were signatories.[69]

The Compromise of 1850, growing out of the Wilmot Proviso, became the latest attempt to find some middle ground that all parties could accept. It was fostered and promoted by Henry Clay and Stephen Douglas. The Compromise passed in five separate bills after failing to get enough votes in one omnibus bill. As adopted, Texas surrendered claim to New Mexico plus claims north of the Missouri Compromise line while transferring its public debt to the federal government; California was admitted as a free state; the Wilmot Proviso that the South found so onerous was rejected. Thus, the new territories of New Mexico and Utah would decide on their own whether slavery would be allowed. (In reality, both were unsuited to plantation agriculture.) Finally, slave trade was banned in Washington, D. C. (but not slavery.)

Predictively, Thompson voted against the Compromise of 1850 and was outspoken in his opposition. Addressing Mississippians from Washington on February 13, 1851 he said, "Thus divided upon what we can not do, I despair. All hope of resistance to the late measure which passed Congress, to any satisfactory end, is gone. I believe there is patriotism, justice, and love of the Union still existing in the free States to an extent sufficient to enable the South to obtain whatever, with a united voice, she might demand as necessary for her security and protection for the future. But if the South is divided in her requests or demands, nothing of course, will be obtained. It is vain and futile to expect it… I regard secession for Mississippi alone, hemmed in and compassed about as she is, as impracticable. And to make the attempt will injure the cause which we seek to maintain."

Later, he dissected the bills point by point, giving his reasons for rejecting each part, in an address printed in the *Oxford Constitution* of March 22, 1851.[70] After his vote on the Compromise along with his very vocal dissent, Jacob knew he was in political trouble at home. A strong Unionist movement had swept through the state. He had gone against the popular tide to vote his convictions. The rest of the Mississippi delegation, including Senator Jefferson Davis, also opposed the Compromise except for the mercurial Senator Henry Foote, who strongly supported the bills.

Amid the growing tension, Congressman Thompson decided once again that he could think of nothing better than to get out of the Washington rat race and return home to a calmer and simpler life. He announced to his friends his intention to retire. A letter to his Aunt Rebecca dated March 16, 1849, gave reasons beyond his disillusionment with national politics. In the letter he wrote of his chronic bronchitis and "a perfectly torpid liver." He explained, "I want to get away, I want exercise in the open air. These winters here will kill me if I continue to come to Washington; necessity will force me to stay at home."[71]

It was not to be. When the state Democratic convention in 1851 could not agree on a suitable candidate for his district, he was persuaded to run yet again. He agreed after the convention "unanimously resolved that the party needed the use of his name and services in that canvass."[72] In the end, he and most of the Democratic ticket were defeated. The Unionist platform and its candidates were that strong in Mississippi. The Congressional career of Jacob Thompson had come to a bittersweet end. The man who preferred to stay home got ordered by voters to do just that.

Mississippi had recently split into Union and States' Rights parties. The head of the state Democratic Party, Governor John A. Quitman, was a radical states' rights advocate who scared many Mississippians. The populace was not yet ready for disunion. The Union party consisted of Whigs and disaffected Democrats but was not as pro-Union as the name implies. Their platform, adopted from Georgia's, stated that any assault on slavery and its expansion or changing the Fugitive Slave Laws should be resisted by all means including secession.

The States' Rights Party had been formed by Democrats to counter the Union movement with the local organizational meeting held in Oxford in March 1851. At that meeting L. Q. C. Lamar, Thompson, and four others were selected as representatives to the state convention in Jackson. Jacob Thompson, Jefferson Davis, and other Democrats vigorously canvassed the state to promote the Democrat or States' Rights candidates of 1851. It was to no avail.

The strong secessionist sentiments advocated by Governor John A. Quitman were too much to overcome even though the Democrat candidates sincerely protested that they too were against secession. Cleo Hearon in "Mississippi and the Compromise of 1850" wrote that "Jefferson Davis, A. G. Brown, and Jacob Thompson would have supported secession only if by several states and actually believed that the threat of secession would be sufficient."[73]

In the election of 1851, Thompson ran against the Whig or Unionist candidate, B. D. Nabors, a clergyman. During this campaign, Thompson delivered one of his "characteristic humorous speeches:" He wittily addressed the audience: "Gentlemen, I have now been your Representative in Congress for twelve years and understand all the routine of business there, and have sustained all the impressions which the life in Washington City is capable of making upon a man's character and morals. Now, if you send Mr. Nabors there, you will spoil a good preacher and make a very poor Congressman, and I confidently predict that if you do send him there he will never preach again. I know the influence that society at the capitol has upon new men." Nabors was elected and Thompson's prediction came true. Nabors never preached another sermon.[74]

POLITICAL DEALINGS

During his influential years in the U. S. House of Representatives, Jacob Thompson had served as Chairman of the House Committee on Indian Affairs and Chairman of the Committee on Public Lands. He had become increasingly active both on the floor of the House and behind the scenes in promoting Democrat agendas. All the while, he kept a wary eye on those who sought to undermine southern positions on slavery and tariffs. Like many a southern congressman in the seniority-driven years after World War Two, he became a master of arcane political and parliamentary maneuvering, adept at accomplishing his goals through tact, gentle persuasion, or, if deemed absolutely necessary, frank coercion.

Knowledge and experience garnered from his committee chairmanships translated into power. That power aided greatly in promoting Mississippi's interests. For example, in 1850 Washington made the nation's first significant grant of public lands to railroads. It consisted of land grants to Illinois, Mississippi, and Alabama. With Thompson's strong backing, large grants to the Illinois Central Railroad and the Mobile and Ohio Railroad were approved. The Mobile and Ohio, so vital during the Civil War, ran almost the entire length of Mississippi.[75]

A second issue of local importance in which Thompson wielded considerable influence was the "Chickasaw bill" previously chronicled. The bill would have permitted Indians to file claims in United States courts instead of through executive departments of government. Opponents, including Thompson, argued that legal fees would consume any compensation to Indians. He thought it was a bald-faced scheme for lawyers to improve their livelihood at the expense of the Indians. It was his role in defeating this bill that brought the antipathy of Walker and Gwin to a boil.

While Jacob Thompson genuinely tired of the House of Representatives, he always deeply desired to be a senator. After refusing to accept Governor Brown's appointment to the Senate out of party loyalty and anger over the deviousness of Walker, Jacob made attempts to be elected by the legislature as was the method at the time.

His problem was that he could not beat his contemporary and fellow Democrat, Jefferson Davis. The power base of Mississippi politics was in the southwestern part of the state, the home territory of Davis. Too, Davis was a better public speaker and more handsome. Also, their political views were similar on most issues. All this presented an uphill struggle for Thompson, but one he met head on. He was absolutely not lacking in ambition.

Davis and Thompson crossed paths many, many times in their political careers. Davis had visited Thompson at his home on several occasions for strategy sessions. The two campaigned together across Mississippi in support of Democrat candidates and Democrat positions. They even lived and shared a "mess" at the same boardinghouse, Mrs. Potters, on Pennsylvania Avenue along with their wives during Jefferson Davis' one term in the House of Representatives.[76] But were they friends?

The answer is probably yes at times and no at other times. Politics can cause strained friendships or worse. According to Mrs. Davis, she and Jefferson had an amiable relationship with the Thompsons. Over time, they both proved their respect for each other. Jefferson Davis as president of the Confederacy tapped Jacob Thompson in 1864 to head his secret service with wide latitude to act and spend the Confederacy's dwindling resources. Thompson in his turn showed deep, heart-felt concern for Davis after his capture at war's end.

Later, after the two were reunited in Memphis, Jefferson Davis was often a guest of the Thompsons. Jacob also generously helped Davis financially during his postwar difficulties. James T. McIntosh, the early editor of *The Papers of Jefferson Davis* summarizes their relationship: "The differences between them were probably only political, reflecting the sharply divisive politics of the 1850s…"[77]

In the Senate race of 1849, many north Mississippi Democrats promoted the idea of electing a senator from that newly settled and rapidly growing region. Jacob Thompson heartedly agreed that it was north Mississippi's turn (meaning *his* turn) and that Davis should wait. Jefferson Davis, however, was the incumbent senator, having been appointed by Governor Brown in 1847 on the death of the sitting senator. Shortly thereafter, he was elected by the legislature to complete the term. As such, Davis had the power of the incumbency as well as being a hero of the recent Mexican War. He was in no mood to wait for anybody.

Undaunted, Thompson ran against him on the premise that "Davis to say the very least stood in a negative position" with Democrat voters due to his supposed support of Zachary Taylor, a Whig, in the latest presidential election.[78] This charge was perhaps true but in poor taste as Zachary Taylor had been Davis's father-in-law for a brief time several years before. Sarah Knox Taylor, his daughter, had died of malaria after three months of marriage to Jefferson Davis.

Davis revealed his distaste for Thompson's campaign tactics in a letter to Dabney Lipscomb, President of the Mississippi Senate, "The conduct of Mr. Thompson is in keeping with his character, except that in writing to Mr. Cannon he committed himself to an open, honorable, man, one in whom he could not expect sordid motives to have an influence." Thompson's tactics infuriated Davis' much older brother and mentor Joseph, which served to harden Jefferson's feelings.[79]

A repetition of sorts occurred in the 1855 Senate race when Thompson again ran against Davis. Thompson boasted of the support from the formidable former governor and current senator, Albert Gallatin Brown, the same man who tried to appoint Thompson to the Senate only to be thwarted by the devious Robert Walker.

Brown had been in Congress with Thompson, and they had worked closely together in the establishment of the University of Mississippi. Too, Senator Brown was from Copiah County in south Mississippi, which theoretically would help Thompson in Davis' southwest Mississippi power base. Albert Gallatin Brown was a popular politician a friend, and a strong ally.

At one point in the campaign, Thompson was accused of subterfuge. A Democrat newspaper editor from Vicksburg reported that in order to get his support, Thompson surreptitiously attempted to bribe him with "pecuniary favors to any reasonable amount."[80] When the votes were counted in the Democratic caucus, Davis had won by 2 votes. Jacob Thompson simply could not beat Jefferson Davis, even with the support of Senator Brown.

Jefferson Davis biographer William Edward Dodd depicted Jacob Thompson as a major rival of Davis. He wrote, "When the Democratic caucus met to nominate their candidate, the preference of the party was much in doubt. The first ballots resulted in a tie…. While Thompson undoubtedly represented similar lines of political action, he was supported by many who opposed much of what Davis laid down as the ultimatum of the South. Thompson was said to 'know no North, no South.' (Dowd picked up this phrase from an editorial in the *Washington Union* of January 26, 1856.) He represented at the time the more timid, the politicians especially, of his party."[81]

Out of office but still active, Jacob Thompson became a delegate to the 1852 Democratic convention in Baltimore where he threw himself into helping Franklin Pierce win the presidential nomination. Thompson was one of three men elected to inform the president and vice-president of their nominations and also to seat them.

Before that occurred, on the thirty-fifth ballot, Thompson rose to respond when the state of Mississippi was called: "Mississippi came here with an anxious desire to harmonize the democracy of the whole country. She came here with an anxious desire to take some distinguished northern statesman and make him the Chief Magistrate of this Union.

"We now desire on this occasion and our whole course has been dictated but by that one object—to get some acceptable man who can bear our standard in triumph through the coming election. In this spirit we have gone for James Buchanan of Pennsylvania; but our northern friends have not come to us. We do not expect to give a barren vote. We expect to bear the man we vote for into the White House at Washington…." Then he announced, "Mississippi casts her seven votes for William L. Marcy of New York."[82]

Jacob Thompson was informing the convention that he and Mississippi extended an olive branch but expected to be met halfway. While personally supporting the ultimate winner Pierce, Thompson, as spokesman for Mississippi, announced the consensus of Mississippi for Marcy. He was comfortable with certain moderate northern Democrats as nominees while not accepting others. Thompson desperately wanted party unity and above all to win. No less than the fate of Mississippi, the South, and the United States was held in the balance. Time was running out and he knew it.

When Franklin Pierce became president, he offered Jacob Thompson the consulate of Cuba, a prized post at the time. Thompson declined. He apparently desired to remain in Oxford where he was better able to keep his finger on the pulse of the state and nation as well as keep a tight rein on his businesses.

In 1856, Thompson again represented Mississippi as a delegate to the Democratic National Convention held in Cincinnati. He actively campaigned for the nomination of James Buchanan who eventually triumphed. These were contentious times with North and South becoming even more polarized.

Buchanan, though a northerner and personally against slavery, was a constitutionalist and southern sympathizer, thus making him acceptable to the South. Buchanan won the general election to become the fifteenth president; however, he did not receive a majority of the votes cast or even win in a majority of northern states.

At this convention Jacob Thompson forcefully introduced resolutions against squatter sovereignty in any shape, form, or fashion. Squatter sovereignty, championed by Lewis Cass, soon to be Buchanan's secretary of state, was a theory that Congress had no constitutional power over slavery in territories. It held that the territories had the right to govern themselves on this matter. Not exactly what the South had in mind.

Buchanan's Cabinet: Jacob Thompson at far left. Others, left to right, are Lewis Cass, John B. Floyd, Buchanan, Howell Cobb, Isaac Toucey, Joseph Holt, and Jeremiah Black.

Secretary Of The Interior

President-elect James Buchanan wanted Jacob Thompson to serve as Secretary of the Interior and Thompson eagerly accepted. Having chaired committees on public lands and on Indian affairs, both of which fell under the purview of the Interior Department, Thompson felt the job was right up his alley. After years of contention in Congress, the challenge and excitement of governing without the hassle of running for office mightily appealed to him.

In view of the long friendship between Buchanan and Thompson, the appointment should have surprised no one. An article in the *Memphis Appeal* of March 8, 1857, addressed their relationship: "The two (Buchanan and Thompson) have been much together in Washington and were even, for a long-time, habitually seated around the same table."[83] They ate many meals at the same boarding house, giving them an opportunity to discuss the events of the day.

John Slidell of Louisiana and other southerners had recommended Thompson for the job. Their motive: the protection of slavery, the sin the South felt it could not do without. They were afraid that wild speculation would result in rapid development of newly acquired western lands, allowing these territories to rapidly develop into free states. They knew that Thompson, with his no nonsense businesslike approach and polite but exacting demeanor, was not about to permit this to happen.[84]

When the new administration took over in March 1857, Thompson ambitiously set out to reorganize the unwieldy Interior Department. The

Department, then a catchall agency, was only eight years old but was already derisively called, "The Department of Everything Else." Robert Walker, Secretary of the Treasury in the Polk administration, yes, the same controversial Walker, was the driving force behind its creation.

Lumped together in this single Department were the bureaus of Public Lands, Indian Affairs, Patents, Pensions, the Census and Statistics, the Commissioners of Public Buildings and Grounds, and other smaller offices. Through these various agencies, the Interior Department was responsible for western exploration, regulation of territorial governments, Indian issues, public lands, patents and pensions, and even Washington's water system.

Each of the bureaus ran independently of each other, sometimes at cross-purposes, and their various heads were accustomed to reporting to the President and Congress directly. It had the effect of turning the secretary into a figurehead. After seeking the approval of the President, Thompson set about cleaning up this mess by consolidating his power and unifying the department under his control.

The various commissioners were apprised of his reorganizational plans. The goal was bluntly stated—efficiency. Going forward, there would be one final arbiter—the Secretary. All old cases were to be cleared, after which the new policies were to be in effect. When any request or report to Congress was contemplated, the issues would be thoroughly discussed with the appropriate bureau, but the final decision would rest with the Secretary. Once a decision had been made, employees had to support it or resign. Hiring and firing would be at the discretion of the Secretary.

It was a frontal assault on a swamp of personal fiefdoms. Naturally, this caused some disgruntlement and pushback. Two of the best administrators felt compelled to quit. But Thompson stood firm. With his innate sense of fairness and personal work ethic, the new Secretary soon had an organized, efficiently run, and respected Department of the Interior. Recommendations to Congress were well prepared, well received, and quickly adopted. Even his detractors had to concede that he managed Interior competently.[85]

Along the way, the new Cabinet member and his wife were dissected at length in the Washington press.

The very opinionated northern journalist Mary J. Windle provided an early glimpse. She described Secretary Thompson as "a mild, pleasing-looking man of some forty years, who made a polite and satisfactory apology touching the length of time we had been kept waiting." She and her companion had been kept waiting for some thirty minutes in Thompson's office before the interview.[86]

Later, in February 1858, Kate wowed the same snooty journalist at a soiree at the Thompson's residence. "The political as well as the fashionable world seemed for a time to have laid aside its scheming, to pay their respects to the charming hostess, who had a smile and a word of graciousness for every newcomer, and a still sweeter glance of intelligence for those endeared to her by the tenderness of private friendship. The piquant animation of her manners has made this lady conspicuous in society from the first appearance."[87] Kate had made a very favorable impression on the snooty journalist.

Although Kate's southern charm and social graces were great assets to Jacob's political career, she still retained some of the old frontier vernacular. French schooling greatly boosted her skills as a hostess but did not completely eliminate the tendency to use the everyday language of her youth. Mary Chesnut in her famous diaries quoted Lizzie Browne, wife of William Montague Browne, editor of the *Washington Constitution*: "I shall never forget her making me shudder when I first went to Washington, saying, 'My son can't get shut of the chills,' and she, then and there, covered with diamonds."

Mrs. Browne was being spiteful after being shunned by President Buchanan, which she blamed on the Thompsons; however, Mary Chesnut thought it important and credible enough to enter that gossipy tidbit in her diaries. The well-spoken Mrs. Chesnut was acquainted with the Thompsons and would have known her speech well enough to judge the accuracy of Mrs. Browne's catty remark. Also, Kate Thompson's letters seem to validate a lack of total command of English, though perhaps not enough to make anyone "shudder."[88]

In addition to Jacob Thompson at Interior and Lewis Cass of Michigan at State, Buchanan's initial cabinet consisted of Howell Cobb of Georgia at

Treasury; Jeremiah S. Black of Pennsylvania, the Attorney General; John B. Floyd of Virginia, Secretary of War; Postmaster General Aaron V. Brown of Tennessee; and Isaac Toucey of Connecticut, the Navy Secretary. The Vice President was 36 year-old John C. Breckinridge of Kentucky, though he did not participate in regular cabinet meetings. This cabinet, dominated by southerners, exerted a big influence over the President. None would exercise more influence than Jacob Thompson.

Not to be deterred by the gloom of America's deteriorating political system, the new cabinet promptly began to prepare for the social season. President Buchanan, a life-long bachelor, loved parties, loved to entertain, and had his comely niece, Harriet Lane, to fulfill hostess duties. The Thompsons eagerly participated in the ongoing, elaborate rounds of social events. Catherine Thompson had the energy, style, grace, and manners to be either hostess or a valued guest.

She also had the assistance of their teenage niece Sallie Wiley, who lived with the Thompsons. Wiley's mother, Jacob's sister Eliza, had died so the Thompsons brought her to Washington with them to provide structure in her life while furthering her education, both formal and informal. This social whirlwind could obviously be a learning experience for Miss Wiley with the Thompsons continuing a pattern of rearing relations in need.[89]

In October 1860, the Prince of Wales, the future Edward VII of Great Britain, reached Washington on his grand North American tour. A reception was held at the White House and the Thompsons attended. The nineteen- year old Prince was introduced to the Thompsons and the effervescent Kate made a big impression on him. He asked her to lead the ball with him, which thrilled her immensely. Later, when the Thompsons travelled in England, Edward introduced them to his mother, Queen Victoria, who presented Kate with a diamond-encrusted thimble.[90]

On their arrival in Washington, the Thompsons rented an elaborate house on G and 18th Streets from Edward Everett, a Massachusetts Unionist. The prior occupants, recently departed, were ironically Jefferson and Varina Davis. This house served the new occupants well through many hospitable social functions. Here the Thompsons entertained frequently and lavishly with President Buchanan often a guest.

When the Thompsons decided to leave Washington in January 1861, Jacob asked Mr. Everett about breaking the lease early. The old New England Whig agreed forthwith, writing that the Thompsons were "very desirable tenants." In a letter to Mr. A. Hyde, his Washington business agent, Everett said, I "had rather give up every thing than that Mr. Thompson shd think he was hardly dealt by. I am quite willing to settle on any basis agreeable to Mr. Thompson. I have been entirely satisfied with him as a tenant, & he shant go away dissatisfied. Rather than have had him and his state secede, I would have let him live in my house rent free to the end of my days, though I had to go to the poor house for a shelter myself."[91] Quite an endorsement from a political opposite.

WALKER ONCE AGAIN

Early in the Buchanan administration, as the clock ticked closer to the inevitable breakup, the boiling Kansas issue had to be dealt with. The Kansas territory had already degenerated into near civil war over the slavery issue. As Kansas was applying for statehood, it was necessary to adopt a constitution. A first attempt at a constitution, written by anti-slavery zealots, failed to be adopted. The second, the Lecompton Constitution, was put forth by the constitutional convention containing a majority of pro-slavery delegates; hence, a pro-slavery document resulted.

This convoluted draft contained a provision that amounted to an up or down vote on slavery, but only pertaining to future slavery, since slave ownership was currently protected in Kansas according to the U. S. Constitution. Though controversial, a yes or pro-slavery, vote resulted and was incorporated into the proposed Kansas constitution. Then the constitution was submitted to Congress for approval.

As luck would have it, Robert J. Walker had been appointed territorial governor of Kansas. He had quickly managed to inflame pro-slavery advocates by throwing out prior election returns that were in favor of slavery, though in truth the results were very questionable. Thompson, certainly no friend of Walker at this point, along with Howell Cobb decided to take action. They felt that Walker was creating an embarrassment for the administration and set out to at least further evaluate the situation.

Colonel Henry L. Martin of Mississippi, a clerk in the Department of the Interior, was sent to Kansas to investigate land records since charges had been brought by the Interior Department against land officers there. Supposedly, he then surreptitiously advised the convention meeting in progress on the main floor at Lecompton while he was there to examine records in the basement. The allegation was that he delivered a message from the administration that a constitution must be forthcoming, and that he assisted in the effort.

Walker believed that Thompson was behind his miseries. He knew that Thompson was a constant, close adviser to the President and believed that he was out to destroy him. Upon returning to Washington at Buchanan's behest, Walker told the President that he wanted to start over again with yet another constitution. That the President would not contemplate. Walker, admittedly in a difficult predicament trying to keep the peace in bloody Kansas, had nevertheless put the administration in a bad light and done much to divide Democrats in the process. After the meetings in Washington, Walker resigned, apparently under duress.

The controversial Lecompton Constitution was approved in Kansas and submitted to the U. S. House of Representatives where it was promptly rejected after having passed in the Senate. Kansas was ultimately admitted to the Union as a free state in 1861. Did Jacob Thompson undermine Walker and promote the adoption of the Lecompton Constitution? And how? This letter and subsequent answers provide some insight.

Sir: My father has received information from a source which he is not at liberty to divulge, that a schedule proposed for adoption by the Lecompton Convention was prepared* under the eye of Mr. Secretary Thompson, and was forwarded to the Convention in Kansas, through this confidential clerk, Mr. Henry L. Martin; also that this fact# has been made known to some, ultra men of the Southern delegation in Congress, who have boasted of it, as an instance of concession forced from the Administration. The Govr. (Walker) is somewhat disturbed by these statements, which have reached him under a plausible appearance, and earnestly requests that you will furnish him with some reliable information concerning the matter.

With very high respect
Yours truly, A. Jennings Wise

*This is utterly false
His Excy
James Buchanan
President of the United States
This is equally false.
J. Thompson[92]

The President and the Secretary categorically denied the letter's accusations in spite of circumstantial evidence that Thompson, with the knowledge of the President, had sent an agent to Kansas to intercede on behalf of the administration. Whether or not Buchanan had been informed of Thompson's and Howell's plan, he certainly took pains to deny it forcefully. Precisely what Colonel Martin's role was, or if he were strictly following orders, will never be known. Walker had proven himself unreliable, and Thompson was a man of action, the President's operative. And as a result of their past difficulties, Thompson in all likelihood would not have missed an opportunity to sabotage Walker.

Soon after Thompson became Secretary of the Interior, Congress passed the Pacific Wagon Road Act. Thompson was charged with implementing the act. It was designed to find a way to improve and shorten the overland route through the Rocky Mountains via the Fort Kearney, South Pass, and Honey Lake Wagon Road. Thompson directed chief engineer Frederick W. Lander to expeditiously search for a shorter travel route, which eventually shortened the arduous trip by 85 miles.[93]

The upgraded road met with Thompson's full approval even though he knew that as settlers flooded westward, new states without slavery would ultimately result, further altering the balance of power. Here, his patriotism collided with his southern interests. He opined that the "hardy pioneers… with their stout hearts and brawny arms" were now moving across mountains that were once a formidable barrier.[94] As a southerner, Thompson was an undying defender of slave labor in the cotton field. As an American, he believed in Manifest Destiny with its unstoppable push across the Continent.

Aaron Brown, the congenial Postmaster General, died in March 1859 leaving a vacancy that needed to be quickly filled. This was an important position at the time due largely to patronage. On the recommendation of Jacob Thompson and Senator David Yulee of Florida, Joseph Holt, a native Kentuckian was promoted to the position. Holt had been serving as the Commissioner of Patents in the Department of the Interior.

As a result of the re-organization of the Interior Department by Secretary Thompson, Holt had to report to him, not to Congress directly. This loss of power rankled the difficult and stern Holt. Though he had practiced law in his native Kentucky as well as Vicksburg, Port Gibson, and Natchez, all in Mississippi, Holt considered himself an outsider. He developed a decided dislike for Thompson, which transcended Thompson's endorsement. For his part, Secretary Thompson was prepared to reciprocate.

Holt had been an efficient Commissioner of Patents with a reputation for being hard-hearted. By contrast, General Brown had a problem saying no to friends and office seekers, resulting in large financial deficits in the office. In the cabinet meeting when Holt was selected, Thompson later wrote that Buchanan "wanted a man for the Post Office Department who has no heart." Thompson responded that he was prompted to propose Holt, "causing laughter all around."[95] This was a precursor of the coming rancor between these two.

Joseph Holt, a former employee at the Interior Department,
who became Thompson's longtime nemesis

PRELUDE TO WAR

With no solution in sight to the growing national crisis, the 1860 Democratic National Convention convened on April 23 at, of all places, the South Carolina Institute Hall in Charleston, S. C. The choice of location was controversial since Charleston was likely the most pro-slavery city in the country. Rabid pro-slavery spectators packed the hall. In this setting, the tiniest of sparks could be expected to trigger conflagration. Sure enough, in no time at all, the convention wound up escalating the regional tensions that would lead to the breakup of the Union.

On April 30, the convention voted 165 to 138 to adopt a platform that rejected southern delegates' demands that slavery be protected in the territories. This was no spark; it was a full-fledged forest fire. Fifty southern delegates, including the entire Mississippi delegation, bolted in protest.

The convention failed to nominate a presidential candidate and was forced to recess, later reconvening that year to finish the job.

Meanwhile, the southerners held caucuses and meetings to decide their next course of action. At a meeting in Memphis, Jacob Thompson's May 5 letter from Washington was read to the gathering.

In the letter Thompson offered his support to the delegates who had walked out of the Convention and regretted that all delegates from the South did not leave together. Dramatically, he declared that "as soon as the Democratic party ceases to be the party of the Constitution and the Union it should be dissolved."

Thompson stated his devotion to the Constitution and the Democratic party, then described the crux of the controversy: "Have you the right, under the aegis of the Constitution, to remove to a Territory with your slaves, and there enjoy your unmolested, unimpaired right of property? The

Republicans deny this right. They assert that Slavery exists only by virtue of local law; and that, as soon as you pass the boundary of the local municipal jurisdiction, and enter a common Territory with your slave, he becomes free, because, as they contend, the Constitution of the United States does not recognize property in slaves.

"The Democracy, on the other hand, deny the power in Congress to establish or prohibit Slavery in the Territories. It was agreed, on all hands, that when the people of a Territory met in Convention to form a Constitution, preparatory to admission into the Union, they had the indefeasible right to adopt or reject Slavery, and to claim admission under their Constitution, as framed. But a difference existed whether the Constitution proprio vigore (by its own force), recognized and protected the right of property in slaves in the Territory. This question was left to be settled by the Supreme Court (in the Dred Scott case,) to whose decision all Democrats agreed, in good faith, to submit…"

After quoting the famous Supreme Court decision that ruled a slave was not free just because he lived for a time in free territory, Thompson concluded that the Democrat party must accept this sentiment. The refusal to adopt a plank similar to this letter had precipitated the departure of the southern delegates. His frank letter ends with a warning. "The agitation of this question of Slavery will never cease till this end is attained; and I am firmly persuaded that the Democratic Party of the North will be stronger with the people with this sound, conservative, manly avowal, than they would be by shrinking and skulking from the issue."[96] Thompson left no doubt where he stood on this inflammatory topic.

The Democratic convention reconvened at Baltimore, away from the pro-slavery fanaticism that reigned in Charleston. Tensions were still high at this gathering, but delegates finally nominated Senator Stephen Douglas of Illinois, "the little giant," for president. Douglas had espoused popular sovereignty on the slavery question, but his position was not nearly pro-slavery enough to satisfy the southern fire-eaters, who were increasingly dominating southern politics. And in one final, fatal blow to the hopes of the South, delegates again refused to insert into the platform the pro-slavery position pushed by Thompson and the southern coalition.

Representing the administration, Cobb and Thompson attended, as they "were the active political minds of the administration and had each an eye out for possible lightning bolts." They were supposed to encourage harmony among the many combative cliques with the hope of including the slavery plank, which they saw as the salvation of the Democrat party. It was an impossible job.[97]

They did manage a pyrrhic victory in the end as the southern delegates along with those of California and Oregon, 11 from Pennsylvania, 2 from New York, and 1 from Minnesota hastily met and adopted the majority report that had been defeated at Charleston. The report affirmed "it is the duty of the Federal Government in all its departments to protect, when necessary, the rights of persons and property in the Territories, and wherever else its constitutional authority extends."[98]

John C. Breckinridge, Buchanan's vice-president, was the presidential nominee of a separate, primarily southern, "rump" convention with the virtually impossible task of attempting to re-unite the party. Alas, the party was hopelessly split, setting the stage for the election of the Republican candidate Abraham Lincoln. That was a result that none of the warring Democrats wanted. It was devastating to Thompson and Cobb.

Acutely aware of the potential consequences of a Republican victory, Howell Cobb and Jacob Thompson, accompanied by his wife Kate, travelled to New York in the fall of 1860. Their mission was to persuade New Yorkers of the seriousness of the situation should Lincoln be elected. Cobb and Thompson continued to be the front men for the Buchanan administration as they attempted to convince Gotham financiers that a Republican victory could result in a repudiation of debts owed by the South.

New York Mayor Fernando Wood and other Democrats had already issued dire warnings over the financial repercussions of a Lincoln victory, and it was understood that New York was essential to Republican success—they could not win without it. President Buchanan's representatives were making a last ditch effort to prevent New York from assuring Lincoln's election.

New York staged a three and a half hour torchlight parade in favor of an anti-Lincoln fusion ticket, which was observed by Thompson and Cobb. Cobb wrote that the two of them had "been mingling with our friends and fellow citizens here pretty freely and I hope with some success. There is certainly a far more favorable feeling for the defeat of Lincoln than I had expected to find and it is certainly improving. I cannot say that I feel confident but I can say that I am hopeful. The commercial interest begins to realize the danger and that is a great point gained." Thompson and Cobb were continuing to try to save the Union through stopping Lincoln. The alternative was grim. If Lincoln won, they were sure secession would follow.[99]

Their public reason to be in New York was to raise money for a U. S. government loan, which turned out to be successful. This gave further credence to the argument that the North did not appreciate the gravity of a Lincoln presidency. They obviously believed the South was bluffing once again. In spite of Thompson and Cobb's efforts, New York voted Republican. Lincoln had won nationally while receiving less than forty per cent of the votes cast.

After the election of Lincoln, Thompson wrote to his friend, former president Franklin Pierce, seeking his help in calming the rapidly worsening South Carolina situation. Pierce, still popular in the South, replied on November 26th. The former president proposed "federal recognition of coequal rights with the states." Pierce concluded "if (the federal government) could gain a little time, there would seem to be grounds of hope that these causes of distrust and dissatisfaction might be removed. Thompson tried, but once again nothing positive resulted.[100] The drumbeat for secession grew louder.

SCANDAL

Until late in the Buchanan administration, Jacob Thompson had experienced a charmed life. From a backwoods attorney to a cabinet secretary, with few setbacks he had risen like a comet through the political system. He had a delightful, loyal wife, powerful friends, and had become wealthy. In 1860 Thompson possessed $500,000 in real estate and $400,000 in personal property, a vast sum at the time.[101] It equates to approximately $26,000,000 in today's money. It had been a charmed life. But it was about to dramatically and forevermore change.

In December 1860, nearing the end of his tenure as Secretary of the Interior, Jacob Thompson became aware of a serious transgression in his Department involving the Indian Trust Fund. The fund contained some $3,000,000, primarily in bonds held in trust for various Indian tribes. Goddard Bailey, a talented clerk from Alabama, administered the fund. Bailey had been hired on the recommendation of Secretary of War John B. Floyd, a distant relative.

A large transportation company, Russell, Majors, and Waddell, had government contracts to deliver supplies to frontier army posts. Somehow this company experienced financial difficulties in spite of their multi-million dollar contracts with the War Department. In desperation, Mr. Russell of Vermont asked Secretary of War Floyd to help extricate the company from its predicament. Together they hatched a scheme to keep Russell, Majors, and Waddell out of bankruptcy.

As a solution, the War Department started anticipating earnings of Russell, Majors, and Waddell by accepting drafts for future work. These negotiable drafts, signed by Russell and Floyd, were then used as security to borrow money. Of course, this was not remotely proper or legal, and, to top if off, Russell did not even use the money to pay off existing debts, which was apparently Floyd's intent.

Now more desperate, Russell was introduced to Goddard Bailey, the custodian of the Indian Trust Fund. He persuaded Bailey to secretly transfer to him $150,000 of bonds supposedly secured by bills of corresponding amounts from Russell, Majors, and Waddell. This occurred in July. Later, in October another $387,000 was taken from the trust fund. On this occasion Bailey clipped off the January coupons in an attempt to avoid detection. In December 333 bonds were obtained. Again, Bailey kept the coupons. All together $870,000 in Indian Trust Fund bonds had been given to Russell in lieu of bills of equal amounts that Bailey called "collateral security for the return of the bonds."[102]

Goddard Bailey became increasingly suspicious and fearful, requiring Russell to produce the acceptances of the War Department for the bonds delivered. Russell promptly complied with Secretary Floyd's knowledge and endorsement. A routine audit during this time did not reveal any discrepancies as the coupons were produced, and the accounting by Bailey showed all securities were intact. How easy it seemed to steal from the federal government.

Shortly afterwards, Bailey learned of Secretary Thompson's imminent resignation and realized the jig was up. He anticipated an examination of the safe by the chief clerk, which led him to confess to Thompson on December 22nd. Secretary Thompson, appreciating the gravity of the situation, immediately informed the Secretary of State and the Attorney General. The safe was opened in their presence along with the oversight of three clerks. In the safe Floyd's drafts were found in place of the missing bonds. Thompson notified President Buchanan of the sordid affair and had Bailey arrested.

The very next day Thompson, briefed the House of Representatives and requested an investigation. At his instigation, the House appointed a five-member committee to thoroughly analyze the abuse of the Indian Trust Fund. Only one member was a States' Rights Democrat, the rest politically opposed to Thompson. The committee delivered its report on February 12, 1861, after Mississippi's secession and Thompson's resignation.

This was a time of great regional and personal hostility, both North and South. With Thompson's exit southward, some northerners were already accusing him of being a traitor. The committee report nonetheless stated, "They deem it but justice to add that they have discovered nothing to involve the late Secretary, Honorable Jacob Thompson, in the slightest degree in the fraud, and nothing to indicate that he had any knowledge of it until the time of the disclosure of Goddard Bailey."[103]

In 1881, long after Jacob Thompson had been thoroughly and repeatedly defamed in the North, former U. S. Attorney General Jeremiah Black was quoted in the *Philadelphia Press*: "Having mentioned the name of Mr. Thompson, I ought to say the most infamous slander ever uttered against any public man in this country was the charge against him of abstracting bonds belonging to the Indian Trust Fund. He was and is a man of unspotted integrity; a committee of his enemies declared that in this transaction he was entirely faultless, and yet the accusation is continually repeated for the gratification of mere political malice."[104]

President Buchanan asked for Secretary Floyd's resignation over the fraud. Russell had been arrested along with Bailey, but Floyd and Bailey testified before Congress, thus escaping liability for criminal prosecution. Before appearing in Congress, Bailey had been indicted, not tried. The government quietly replaced the missing funds in 1862. So the scandal was over, but Jacob Thompson would be plagued by vicious accusations related to this same issue for the remainder of his life. Actually, the accusations continue 150 years later with not a scintilla of new evidence having emerged.

President James Buchanan

Commissioner To
North Carolina

Events were moving fast now. They were soon to move so fast that reason would be a rare thing indeed. The election of Lincoln had galvanized the lower South. The governor and legislature of Mississippi appointed Jacob Thompson as Commissioner from Mississippi to North Carolina for the explicit purpose of encouraging the Tarheel State to act in concert with the other Southern states; i. e., to be prepared to secede in unison. Being a native of North Carolina, Thompson's selection was fitting, but he was still a member of Buchanan's cabinet.

When the request came on December thirteenth, Thompson saw the conflict immediately. How could he miss it? He quickly met with the President to seek his approval. Buchanan was naturally skeptical of this request by one of his cabinet members to promote secessionist activity.

Thompson made the case that the only chance of a compromise was for the South to present a united front, thus getting the attention of the North as well as buying time in the South. Then, he shrewdly told the President that the proposed time for any southern action would be after March fourth when Buchanan would be out of office. With the understanding that this constituted a stalling action, the President gave his consent.[105] Those who wanted to view Thompson as a traitor were to be given new fodder.

Some North Carolinians probably recalled that Thompson had addressed the people of the state at Raleigh in 1859. His speech strongly criticized radicals on both sides of the increasing sectional strife, attacking first the radical Republicans for trumpeting the "irrepressible conflict." Then he denounced the southern fire-eaters who advocated a resumption of the African slave trade. If the southern radicals had their way, Thompson averred that he would "rally under the national banner."[106]

Now in December 1860, here he was again in Raleigh, this time bluntly advocating secession. After a cordial meeting with Governor John W. Ellis on his arrival, Thompson wrote a letter to the Governor later that night warning that the "irrepressible conflict" proponents were now coming into power. He said he feared when Lincoln took office on March 4th, the South would be faced with "a majority trained from infancy to hate our people and their institutions."[107]

The ensuing open letter from Thompson to Governor John W. Ellis and read before the North Carolina legislature was printed in the December 22nd issue of the *Raleigh State Journal*, giving insight into his frame of mind: "Common dangers threaten the peace, honor, and safety of both (North Carolina and Mississippi;) and it is certain that an unresisting submission to the aggressive and hostile policy of the Northern States will inevitably involve both in a common humiliation and ruin." In time, his prophecy would turn out to be at least half right. But he was just warming up.

"The crisis demands action. It is unbecoming a free people to close their eyes to the issue forced upon them, and to cry peace, peace, peace, when there is no peace. The antagonism of opinion, upon the questions growing out of the recognition by the Constitution of the right of property in slaves, so long and angrily discussed, has at last culminated, in the adoption, by a majority of the Northern people of the doctrine of the Irrepressible Conflict. The leading idea of this creed is that the Union of these States cannot endure, half of them slave-holding and the other half non-slave-holding...."

"It is admitted that each State must decide for herself, both the mode and measure of redress for present and prospective grievances. One destiny, however, awaits all the slave-holding States of this Union, and fate has indissolubly linked their fortunes together; Therefore, it is meet and wise, and proper and expedient, that they should consult and advise together, for their common defence and general welfare...."

"The Constitution of the United States already affords guarantees which are ample for our security. But they are found on parchment only. The people of the Northern States have not kept faith with us. Not only have a majority of the non-slaveholding States rendered all legislation for our protection nugatory and inoperative by State enactments, but on the 6th of November last, a majority of the people of all the free States endorsed a platform of principles in direct conflict with the Constitution and the decisions of the Supreme Court and thus the will of a numerical majority—a majority trained from infancy to hate our people and institutions, are to be substituted in their stead.

"The Executive and Judicial departments of the government, and the Senate of the United States have always held that property in slaves was recognized by the Constitution, and therefore, under a common flag was entitled to protection. The dominant party denying this proposition, and thus, by their construction, the Constitution will be changed. This common Government will be revolutionized, and instead of throwing its broad shield over all the citizens of all the States, protecting each and all equally in the possession and enjoyment of their rights of property, it will be perverted into an engine for the destruction of our domestic institutions, and the subjugation of our people...."[108]

Thompson took his role as commissioner to North Carolina seriously. He and others with like opinions were known as "co-operationalists" because they attempted to get the South to act as one. Thompson had long espoused the need for coordination and cooperation as essential to preventing conflict by demonstrating to the North that the South was together and deadly serious. Too, if war resulted, he realized that the entire South would have to organize into a functional unit in order to possibly prevail. Even at this late date, Thompson had hope, though waning, that war could be avoided by a show of strength and unity.

As might be expected, Thompson's mission soon created an uproar in the North that would continue long after the conclusion of the Civil War. Both Buchanan for approving the commission and Thompson for carrying it out were chastised to the extreme. The northern press led by Horace

Greeley, coming on the heels of the Indian Trust Fund scandal, felt it had further reason to label Thompson as a traitor. The *New York Times* opined, "Secretary Thompson has entered openly into the secession service, while professing still to serve the Federal authority."[109] Buchanan was not treated much better.

Always keen to defend his actions, and in this instance Buchanan too, Thompson replied to these charges post war. In a letter published in the *Lancaster Intelligencer* of September 29, 1877, he recounted his remembrances of the mission, particularly as it related to President Buchanan. An abridged copy of this letter had appeared in the *New York Times* on the day prior. He stated that Buchanan relied on the Constitution in his treatment of southern issues. The President, per Thompson, believed that a state did not have the right to secede and that the government likewise had no right to use force against the state if it did. Status quo would prevail during the remainder of the Buchanan administration.[110]

Thompson then took pains to review the North Carolina mission as has already been described. While this was occurring, Thompson wrote, Buchanan had delivered his message to Congress in which he "denounced secession as heresy, unconstitutional, and unauthorized. I differed from the message in this: That while I admitted the Constitution did not provide the remedy for the States, yet each had retained this right, from which they had never parted, to withdraw for cause the powers they had conferred upon the general government and resume the full exercise of them. But as I held, no man could justify secession which was not sufficient to justify revolution, and as there was not and could not be during the administration of Mr. Buchanan any justifying cause of secession, and as our difference was a mere abstract one I could with propriety hold my place in the cabinet."

He concluded the rather long and defensive missive with typically effusive Thompson praise, "I cannot close this letter without bearing testimony to the greatness, goodness, and worth of our departed chieftain. It was his fortune to live amid dissolving empires. But a purer man, a more sincere friend, a more devoted patriot, an honester citizen, and truer guardian of the public interests never lived or wielded power."[111]

Buchanan's message to Congress, referenced by Thompson in his letter, went through several drafts with active input from the Cabinet. Thompson objected to the acceptance of the Lincoln election and what it entailed, including hostility to secession. Attorney General Black had advised the President that it was constitutional to use force against a state and furthermore that a state had no right to leave the Union under any circumstances. Cobb, Floyd, and Thompson strongly disagreed with this interpretation.[112]

After the meeting, Thompson "went to the President quietly and asked him if he would go with me over the Constitution and the Convention that framed it. I said to him that there was certainly no expressed power in the instrument itself that gave him the right to use force against a State...." After a review of the pertinent parts of the Constitution, Thompson left.

At a subsequent Cabinet meeting "he (President Buchanan) said: 'Thompson you are right on one important point; it is clear to my mind that there is no reserved or expressed power granted by the Constitution to use force against a State for any purpose. It is also apparent that the framers of the instrument intended to deny both to the President and to Congress any such power. I am also convinced that a State has no right to secede from the Union.'" Thompson was obviously pleased, and the Congressional message was altered to the consternation of Attorney General Black.[113] Once more, Thompson had done his best work behind the scenes.

Constitutional powers weren't the only subject of discussion at this session. Together, they passionately discussed the deteriorating state of affairs in South Carolina, again allowing input from each Cabinet member. President Buchanan proposed a convention of the states in hopes of reaching a compromise over the disputes between the regions. Thompson quickly endorsed such a peace convention. Ominously, he also warned against coercion, which he said would cause Mississippi to respond with "direct action."[114] Before long, some of the men in that room would have more direct action than they cared for.

THE WAR BEGINS

The equivocal message to Congress that ultimately resulted from the deliberations did not please activists in either North or South. These were very contentious times with much distrust and misunderstanding between the regions. South Carolina soon took its often-threatened step to secede. Fatefully, now the administration would have to decide what to do about the federal forts smack in the middle of Charleston harbor. Were the garrisons safe? Did they need reinforcing? And how would the most pro-slavery city in the most pro-slavery state respond to that?

Years later, Thompson wrote that initially he had little participation in decisions regarding the forts since they did not directly involve his department. Critics may be excused for finding this a little disingenuous since he was a close friend and confidant of President Buchanan and not at all tentative in offering his opinions, especially when closeted with the President. Thompson did warn that reinforcing the forts would lead to conflict, which he deemed "disastrous."[115] You didn't have to be a prophet to figure out what might happen next.

It was at that point that Major Anderson, commanding United States forces in Charleston harbor, exercised the discretionary orders given him to move from Fort Moultrie to the much more defensible Fort Sumter, which lay in the middle of Charleston harbor. It was a prudent and sensible move under the circumstances, but these were not normal times.

This troop movement, clearly visible from shore, enraged the trigger itchy South Carolinians who thought they had assurances from the President that no movement or reinforcement would take place. South Carolina demanded that Sumter be evacuated with the troops returning to Moultrie.

All this served to unnerve the President. He summoned the Cabinet for an emergency session.

Edwin Stanton, the outspoken anti-secession Ohio attorney, was now a member of the lame-duck Cabinet, having been appointed attorney general after the resignation of Cass. He consistently nudged the President into taking a hard line approach to South Carolina in contrast to Thompson, who echoed the demand of South Carolina for Anderson to leave Sumter.

Stanton recalled, "Thompson was a plausible talker—and, as a last resort, having been driven from every other argument, advocated the evacuation (of Sumter) on the plea of generosity. South Carolina, he said, was but a small State with a sparse white population—we were a great and powerful people, and a strong, vigorous government. We could afford to say to South Carolina, 'See we will withdraw our garrison as an evidence that we mean you no harm.'"[116]

To rebut Thompson's argument, Stanton reminded the President of the loss of public confidence in the administration. He then reminded him, "Only the other day it was announced that a million dollars had been stolen from Mr. Thompson's department.... Now it is proposed to give up Sumter. All I have to say is, that no administration, much less this one, can afford to lose a million of money and a fort in the same week." His pointed barbs were also aimed at the embattled Floyd, who resigned the next day.[117]

Since Thompson's friend and ally Howell Cobb had already resigned, Floyd's departure meant that Thompson was the Cabinet spokesman for the South. He did have some assistance from Phillip Francis Thomas of Maryland, the new Secretary of the Treasury. Thomas had been Commissioner of Patents in the Department of the Interior before being promoted. He would serve only a scant month, following Thompson in resigning from the Cabinet in January.

Arrayed against Thompson in addition to the formidable Stanton was the testy Holt, secretary of war and sworn enemy of Thompson. Jeremiah Black was the new secretary of state after serving as attorney general. He respected Thompson and his views, and while remaining on friendly terms, urged the President to reinforce Sumter. Black had used his influence to convince Buchanan that Stanton should fill his old job of attorney general, revealing clearly his strongly held anti-secession sentiments.

Thompson persevered in this hostile climate. He continued to have the ear of the President, although Stanton, Holt, and General Winfield Scott, the septuagenarian, vain, corpulent commander in chief of the United States Army, exercised ever more influence. These three convinced Buchanan to adopt Black's recommendations that all federal property would be maintained, including the garrison at Fort Sumter.

After New Year's celebrations, the never-ending Cabinet meetings resumed. Thompson with new ally Thomas was not happy with the determination to immediately reinforce Sumter. They pleaded with the President to alter his decision based on reports from Anderson that Sumter was unassailable. Thompson and Thomas suggested sending a messenger to assess the situation. Buchanan agreed. Precisely at this point, a scathing letter from the South Carolina commissioners arrived at the White House. It basically called the President a liar.

From here things get a little clouded. The letter no doubt angered Buchanan. He was supposedly heard to say that reinforcements should be sent forthwith; however, Thompson, Thomas, and Black did not realize that such a decision had been made. Perhaps, it was done that way intentionally to keep Thompson and Thomas in the dark.

Taking advantage of the opportunity, Holt and Scott hastily ordered the Star of the West, a merchant vessel, to sail with reinforcements and military supplies to Charleston. While the Star of the West was at sea, a report was received from Major Anderson at Sumter confirming his confidence in being able to hold the fort without additional troops. The President countermanded the order for reinforcement but he was too late. Alas, there was no available mode of rapid communication. Wireless telegraph awaited discovery by Guglielmo Marco in the early twentieth century.

A sickened and disappointed Jacob Thompson wrote to Howell Cobb, now back home in Georgia, about these events. "The President and Holt played the meanest trick on me in the world in sending the Star of the West to Charleston. I told him (Buchanan) the assignment of Holt to the War

Department was considered by me the adoption of his line of policy… The President replied—not—at all, and no order should be issued without being first considered and decided in Cabinet. With this promise I could not resign…

"The movement of Star of the West was a strategical movement of Gen'l Scott. He convinced Holt he could steal into Fort Sumter without discovery or collision. To do this it was necessary to keep the movement a secret, and as they all knew I would resign for such an order and thus blow the order, it was necessary to keep me in ignorance of it… Old Buck, at heart, is right and with us but after Stanton came in, I have seen him gradually giving way…" Thompson concluded the letter, "The President still adheres to his position that he has no power of coercion but he has a most curious idea that enforcing the laws at the point of a bayonet is not coercion."[118]

LEAVING WASHINGTON

The curtain was rapidly falling on Jacob Thompson's tenure as a member of the Buchanan Cabinet. So many things had occurred in such a short time. December 1860 and January 1861 would prove to be fateful times for Thompson and the country. On January 8th Thompson received the information that Mississippi would secede on the 9th.

The 9th would also turn out to be the same day that the Star of the West appeared off Charleston harbor, eliciting cannon fire from South Carolinians manning the batteries. The ship speedily withdrew without sustaining significant damage or injury to personnel; however, this whole affair did serve to exacerbate the crisis on both sides. After all, southerners had proved that not only would they try to leave the Union but that they were also audacious enough to attack the U. S. government.

Jacob Thompson marched into the President's office to hand in his resignation on January 8th after hearing of Mississippi's plans and learning that the Star of the West was nearing Charleston. Though Buchanan believed his old friend and confidante was making a mistake, he grudgingly accepted the resignation.

Thompson was exasperated that he had not been notified in advance of the attempt to reinforce Sumter, but his determination to follow his beloved Mississippi out of the Union was foreordained. Way back in 1850, while in Congress, Thompson had written, "When the President of the United States commands me to do one act, and the Executive of Mississippi commands me to do another thing inconsistent with the first order, I obey the Governor of my State."[119]

In retirement Thompson would reflect upon his mindset on the day he quit the Cabinet:

My own position was made plain to the President very early in the action. I told him if it were possible I would like to remain with him until the close of his administration, but if Mississippi seceded I must go out too. I went to Mississippi when a young man, and anything I am she made me. There I had a handsome property. My family, my relatives, and my friends were in Mississippi. If I remained in the Union I would be denounced as a traitor to my state. If I resigned when my state seceded I would be called a traitor to my country. All this I laid before the President and asked which horn of the dilemma I should take. His reply was: 'When your state secedes, I will not insist upon your remaining.'[120]

Unquestionably, loyalty to one's state had more import at that time than it currently does. Many southerners chose their state over the Union. The prime example is Robert E. Lee, a dedicated soldier and the son of a Revolutionary War hero, who was offered command of the Union armies. After agonizing over the decision, he chose his revered native state of Virginia. The list goes on and on of the public servants, from senators to army privates, who were loyal to their state. There were notable exceptions, but the vast majority of southerners reflected the opinion and action of Jacob Thompson.

Within days, Secretary Thomas followed Thompson out of the Cabinet, leaving the ultra-Unionists in ascendancy. Thompson had spent twelve years in Congress, nearly four years in the Buchanan administration, and untold time campaigning for national Democrat candidates. What an ignominious end—certainly very frustrating as he left Washington for Oxford, Mississippi, and home. He was not a rabid secessionist, even hoped still for a peaceful solution, but he had observed first-hand the acrimony among former friends and current colleagues, which led him to conclude that war was almost inevitable.

Kate Thompson provided a plaintive view of Washington as the split between regions and cultures intensified. She was a keen observer of events from a social viewpoint while her husband was fully engaged in politics. She was also well acquainted with most of the Democrat principals and their wives due to her standing in Washington society.

Her status can be clearly seen in a report by the editor of the Washington *Constitution*, William Montague Browne, writing about a trip the President took in the summer of 1859. On this two-week trip, he had invited a party of ladies to the Pennsylvania resort of Bedford Springs. Browne wrote, "It need scarcely be added that Miss Lane (niece of and White House hostess for Buchanan) and Mrs. Thompson, by their admirable social tact and the mingled grace and affability of their address, impart a charm to the presidential circle that leaves nothing to be desired."[121]

Mary Ann Howell, wife of Secretary of the Treasury Howell Cobb, and Kate Thompson had become close friends. The two were dissimilar in that Mrs. Cobb had a large family that she doted on while the Thompsons had only one child, now a young adult. Mary Ann, though held in high social standing, was reserved in contrast to the effervescent Kate, who entertained frequently and grandly. In spite of their differences, they established a regular correspondence in Washington that continued until the hardships of war dictated otherwise. Kate's letters reveal the tensions and fears of the time.

In a letter to Mary Ann Howell on December 15, 1860, Kate wrote:

I have heard of your arrival at Macon (Georgia)—and think by this time you are rested… After parting with you at the boat—I felt like—'the last link was broken that bound me' to Washington. Mr Thompson stoped (sic) at Browns hotel—and I took your husband to the Constitution (Washington newspaper and voice of the Buchanan administration) office—and then had a slow ride home—and spent the evening all alone—and had time to think and cry over all my little troubles and anxieties and felt better…

I did not see Gov Cobb after you left… His resignation created great excitement here… The same gloom and depression is still over this city—No parties, no dinners—every body looks sad—but I think we Southern people ought to be looking up—for all seems to be going well with us… I think if you could have heard some of the Black Republican speeches that have been made here—even your devotion to this Union would have given away… Miss Lane and I continue our silence on political questions—I go to see her and the President as often as I can—because I know they feel their old friends are many of them deserting them—I will do all I can to stand by them until the 4 of March—and hope that day may come quickly...

Mr Thompson has received an appointment from the Gov of Miss to go as Commissioner to N. Carolina—and leaves here on Monday the 17. And I am going with him—he will be absent a week or ten days—and I can't stay here by myself. The President approves of his going... By way of preparation I have had my new dress made to go to N. Carolina—and I felt I must try to do my best...

I have been up (to Congress) twice—the galleries crowded—I have made no Senatorial call except upon friends—I shall not call upon or leave cards upon a single B. republican or Douglas. 'Straws tell which way the winds blow' and to be prepared for any emergency. I had 12 doz pack of cards for Mr Thompson struck off—and left off the Sec of the Interior as I have no idea of his cards ever being left any where as Mr Ex Sec... So my head is nearly crazy and my heart goes pit a pat at any sound I hear. What are we coming too? Where is the end of all this trouble—I trust there is a kind Providence—whose hand is directing this great revolution—and will—all go down—to his glory and our happiness... [122]

In her letter of January 13, 1861, Kate Thompson recounts the whirlwind of events from her perspective since her last communication with Mrs. Howell:

My last letter was written to you just as I was leaving home (for North Carolina)—I had a very pleasant visit and returned home—to enter a Sea of trouble—The same night that we reached home—Mr Thompson was informed of Mr Baileys (Goddard Bailey) defalcation—by his own confession—all of which I take it for granted you have read the papers—This was overpowering, but I stood up manfully—and Mr Thompson has done every thing in the world he could do to try to have the Bonds restored—and the guilty persons punished—he never slept for three days and nights—until he had Russell (William Russell) safe in jail—then the agony was somewhat over...

The most unpleasant part was that Gov Floyd was somewhat impli-cated, as Bailey had received his Acceptances on the War Department, for the amount of Bonds he had stolen—This worried the President and they had some unpleasant feeling about it—and on Tuesday after this happened Saturday night—the President asked the Vice Pres. to inform Gov Floyd his resignation would be acceptable—he refused—saying he could not under these circumstances—he must vindicate himself first—On Friday the dif-ficulty about the troops moving from Fort M. to Fort S. came up and Gov Floyd resigned Saturday morning…

The President behaved as mean as he could about this matter—saying one day he would send—and the next day—he would not send troops—so things went on—until Holt and Scott got things fairly under their own way—and started the Star of the West off—without Mr Thompson or Gov Thomas knowing one word about it, and Mr T (Thompson) thinks the President did not know it—till after she was out at sea—for if he did—he told stories enough about it.—So Tuesday morning (January 8th) T. sent his resignation to the President—and his answer accepting it—I think the most infamous letter ever written by any man—After all Mr T. had done in trying to sustain him—to receive such treatment. I was boiling hot—but Mr T. resented it in a very decided, but mild answer—which drew a very affectionate answer from the President—but this did not satisfy me—I hate the old man worse than ever—but I don't abuse him much.

This long, sometimes sad, sometimes bitter letter continues:

I wish I had gone from here before all this happened, such a change— the Floyds gone—I am as mad with Judge Black as I am with Holt—and I don't speak to Holt… I learn Stanton is the author of those articles in the Herald of 5th Jan—a mean low life—Pen—scamp… The last week that Mr T. was in the cabinet—Judge B (Black), Holt, and Stanton—give him unmistakable evidences of their desire for him to leave—but Mr T. still insisted the President's heart was with us and he would never send the troops—Now you can guess what I think of the President's heart, as black as the man of war—Brooklyn—Gov Thomas remained two days after they made it too hot for him…

My dear Mrs Cobb—the President has not a friend in the world… Miss Lane called to see me—twice while I was sick (before Thompson's resignation)—I have not seen her since—I am going once to say goodbye—oh how I hate it. I had a very pleasant visit from Mrs Floyd—she spoke so kindly of the President and Miss Lane—Went twice to see them—you know how good she always was—but this seemed like overdoing the thing—indeed I cant feel so kind to-wards them—and I can't help it—I was not able to finish this letter last evening—because I was so interrupted with company—all to say goodbye. Everybody is going away—The city looks deserted.

There are three company of troops somewhere in the city—none in sight of us as yet—The Departments are all filled this morning with guns and pistols—stacked ready for use—Was there ever such Tom-foolery. When nobody here is thinking about making an attack on any thing or any body—You can form some idea—how grand and happy old Scott is—just in his glory… I feel as light and happy as a bird I am out. Yes out of the union too.

"Let come what may, I can never be more unhappy than I have been ever since you left here—or these troublesome times commenced… I have nearly all my furniture—glass china wine and trunks packed—will be ready when ever Mr t. says the word—We would be off—now, but not entirely through with the Bailey robbery investigation.[123]

The final letter in this series was written on February 3rd from Brown's Hotel in Washington:

…You will see I am now at Browns—made the first move toward home—We have been here for ten days and leave tomorrow morning at 6 o'clock for Miss. I am anxious to start –my patience all gone—

I must give you a full account of my last visit to the White house—Last Wednesday evening—Mr T. and myself went up to say Goodbye—but saw only the President and Miss Hetty (Esther Parker, Buchanan's housekeeper and intimate friend) … The President received us very cordially and he and

Mr T. talked—and Miss Hetty and I—He then insisted on our coming to dine with him socially before we left for home—I accepted—slightly thinking that would be the end of the invitation but Thursday morning we received a very sweet note from Miss Lane—saying the 'President and herself'—would expect us on Friday at 5 o'clock—We went—I went in with the old chief. Mr T. with Miss Lane—and Genl Dix (who was staying there) with Mrs Ellis—and Mr Glosbrenner (Adam Glossbrenner, Buchanan's private secretary)—composed the dinner party—There was nothing disagreeable said or done—but I felt very much embarrassed—[124]

These three lengthy letters provide great insight into the thoughts and actions of both Kate and Jacob Thompson. Their frustrations and even anger is apparent, but they managed to keep their composure and civility through the ordeal of watching the nation being torn asunder. The close relationship they maintained with the President and his niece Harriet Lane to the end is quite evident. Too, it is commendable that they delayed leaving while Jacob dealt with the Indian Trust Fund scandal. The easy way out would have been to leave post haste since he certainly knew he would be labeled a traitor and a thief no matter what.

From the time of the Indian Trust Fund debacle nearly to the end of his life, Jacob Thompson had no real public forum in which to properly review and defend his actions. The pro-Union fervor of a sanctimonious northern press has shaped impressions of him almost entirely, whether accurately or not. Fortunately, personal letters and a few anecdotes and remembrances are available to give balance to the war years.

One corroborating view of happenings in the Cabinet leading up to Thompson's resignation warrants special attention. In the last issue of the *Washington Constitution*, January 30, 1861, William Browne, the Anglo-Irish editor of this once powerful newspaper, offered some observations. He had also become *persona non grata* in Washington for his defense of the South. Browne wrote in his final editorial, "…I have been visited with the most vindictive animosity by certain members of the President's Cabinet, who never held an office of popular trust, and know nothing of the popular heart, because I did not permit their irresponsible and unwarranted conduct, exposing the country to war, and implicating the honor of their chief, to pass unrebuked.

"Having deceived the President—informing him of orders issued when it was too late for him to recall them, and knowing that those orders were opposed to the President's policy and in violation of his assurances to others (Jacob Thompson for one)—those men, elevated by chance, and to the country's misfortune, to the high offices they now hold, are the fit originators and executors of the petty vengeance…they have wreaked upon me." He continued with his diatribe, specifically against Holt and Scott, ending with "he (Buchanan) must know that the world and posterity will hold him responsible for their proceedings."[125] This editorial is consistent with the version Thompson gave to Cobb in his letter of January 16th.

Predictably, Jacob Thompson's activities and resignation created an uproar in the North. "Undertaking to overthrow the Government of which you are a sworn minister may be in accordance with the ideas of cotton-growing chivalry, but to common men cannot be made to seem credible."[126] These are the words of Horace Greeley in the New York *Daily Tribune* upon Thompson's resignation. That editorial comment would prove to be one of the subdued variety. Jacob Thompson was a marked man, his life under constant scrutiny.

After leaving his rented Washington home for temporary quarters in Brown's Hotel, Thompson continued to hope and pray for some sort of compromise, some peaceful solution. He never fully bought into secession except as a very last resort for the simple fact that he had a premonition of the disaster that war would bring to Mississippi as well as to him personally. Thompson loathed the events and people who had led to this day while still desiring a last minute reprieve. That was not to be. A February peace conference, chaired by former president John Tyler, proved nonproductive as Lincoln refused to actively participate.

This led an exasperated Thompson to communicate with former president Buchanan a few months later, "The propitious moment has arrived when Lincoln could call off his bloodhounds and make with us the most favorable terms, but he is under the influence of the mob feelings of New England." He continued, "Though the course of events has made us citizens of two different governments, my feelings of kindness and personal regard have undergone no change."[127]

Upon their return from Washington, a large, enthusiastic crowd greeted the Thompsons in Oxford. The crowd had been whipped up by speeches from local officials and inspirational music from a band. When the Thompsons debarked, thunderous applause drowned out the music. Jacob was deeply affected. The crowd called for a speech, which went unfulfilled as he responded that, for once, he was rendered speechless.[128]

In February soon after arriving in Oxford, Thompson gave a speech in which he reviewed the Star of the West issue. He related he learned of the mission to Fort Sumter while writing his resignation. Then, he revealed, he telegraphed his old acquaintance from the University of Mississippi, Augustus B. Longstreet, then president of South Carolina College, to inform him of the looming arrival of the ship. Even though Longstreet was neither a military man nor a politician, he apparently spread the word, putting the shore batteries on alert. Fort Sumter was almost assuredly already under constant observation and the militia prepared to defend against reinforcement.

These comments nevertheless created a firestorm in northern newspapers. There probably was more to the story than reported as Thompson had previously informed Longstreet that no federal reinforcements were being sent to Charleston. The follow-up message, at least according to Jacob, was to let him know he had been wrong. To do less could be construed as deceiving his old friend and the father-in-law of Lucius Lamar.[129]

Thompson stated that he was pleased the Star of the West was not destroyed and that the "concealed trick, first conceived by General Scott and adopted by Secretary Holt, but countermanded by the President when too late," had not succeeded. This speech served to rekindle the animosity between Thompson and Holt as the latter took public exception to Thompson's remarks, referring to his "arrogance" in making them. Thompson in return assailed the prickly Holt.[130] This would not be the end of the encounters between these two proud and contentious men.

Doing His Part

J. F. H. Claiborne, Thompson's early biographer, relying in large part on information from Thompson himself, concluded that Jacob Thompson took absolutely no part in the establishment of the Confederate government.[131] Certainly, he had no governmental position resulting from the convention in Montgomery. To bypass the convention with his penchant to be where the action was bears testament to how seriously he viewed the impending struggle. Two of the favorites for president were friends of his. Howell Cobb and wife Mary Ann were close friends of the Thompsons throughout their Washington years together while Jefferson Davis was considered a good friend in spite of their prior differences. When Davis was elected president, Thompson proclaimed his delight.

Instead of being caught up in the excitement surrounding the formation of a new government, Thompson prepared for the costly ordeal he expected and feared. There were so many things to do. He talked to his overseer, his slaves, and secured that part of his wealth that he could.

Then he turned his attention to outfitting various units from Lafayette County, spending large sums in the process. Thompson's Cavalry, Company B, 1st Mississippi Cavalry Regiment and Thompson's Company, Company A, 2nd Battalion Cavalry Reserve Corps, both from Lafayette County, reflect his family sponsorship. Jacob donated $2,000 to the former on their departure for Pensacola while his brother and law partner William outfitted the latter.

The 19th Mississippi Infantry had a company known as the Jake Thompson Guards. Serving in this regiment were Thompson's son Macon as quartermaster and his special friend L. Q. C. Lamar as colonel. Jacob also gave this company $2,000.00 for badly needed equipment, the gifts being reported in the *Memphis Daily Appeal* of February 9, 1861 and the *Oxford Intelligencer* of April 3, 1861.[132]

It is interesting to note that Thompson's Cavalry, Company B and the rest of the 1st Mississippi Cavalry were equipped with Maynard breech-loading carbines. This was unusual as only 3,000 of these advanced weapons were in southern armies. The procurement of these carbines almost certainly resulted from Thompson's connection with Dr. Edward Maynard, a dentist and prolific inventor. Dr. Maynard, on the faculty of the Baltimore College of Dental Surgery, had a lengthy meeting with Thompson at the Thompson home in Washington on December 15, 1860, for the purpose of selling him 3,000 Maynard rifles.[133]

The rush to war was on. There could be no turning back now. In Oxford the hurriedly formed units were mobilized as soon as possible. Enthusiasm was high—patriotism was the order of the day. Parties and ceremonies were held to see the various units on their way, and Jacob Thompson actively participated in the festivities in spite of his anxieties.

The War began in earnest in July 1861 at the battle of Manassas Junction or Bull Run in northern Virginia. Thompson soon thereafter expressed his apprehensions regarding Confederate strategy to President Jefferson Davis in a personally delivered letter. Jacob was representing the Committee of Safety from Memphis of which he was a member. He opined that "the fear [here] is that [the] eye of the Administration is so exclusively fixed upon [Virginia] that we may be neglected and stripped of the means of defence." That fear had validity, but Davis was getting similar reports from across much of the Confederacy.[134]

Thompson expressed grave concern over "the disjointed condition of the army in the valley of the Mississippi & the absolute necessity of appointing some well approved General to take charge of all the military operations in this great valley."[135] This frank assessment had its effect. Albert Sidney Johnston would soon be named that overall commander.

The problem for Davis and the Confederacy was a lack of, well, everything. There was not nearly enough manpower, equipment, and supplies to defend the entire vast perimeter of the seceded states. Unfortunately, Albert

Sidney Johnston tried to do just that, only to watch his army lose bloody battles and large swaths of territory. It was in this climate that the temperamental, vain P. G. T. Beauregard was sent to the west as a wing commander under Johnston.

After further collapse and retreat, Beauregard set up headquarters in Jackson, Tennessee, approximately 110 miles north of Oxford. Thompson paid a close eye to the worsening situation as the hostilities moved ever closer to north Mississippi. Finally, at age 51, and lacking even rudimentary military skills, Thompson volunteered to serve in Beauregard's command, the Army of the West.

Before becoming aide-de-camp to Beauregard, in the fall of 1861 Thompson's name had been placed on the ballot for governor of Mississippi. The outcome of this election was a foregone conclusion as the incumbent governor, John J. Pettus, was in the process of large- scale mobilization of troops. The populace passionately backed Pettus in his war preparations. Apparently, Thompson mounted no real campaign as he realized that it would be to no avail. Pettus won with almost 90 per cent of the vote.[136]

Johnston ordered Beauregard to move his army to Corinth, Mississippi, where units from various parts of the western Confederacy were rapidly being massed. After sustaining devastating defeats in Kentucky and Tennessee, Johnston had decided to gamble on a daring, surprise attack on Grant's army camped near the Tennessee River approximately twenty miles from Corinth.

After achieving the goal of a surprise attack on the Union army at Pittsburg Landing, the Confederates pushed the shaken Union forces back toward the Tennessee River in a vicious, bloody battle on April 6, 1862. During the assault, General Johnston was wounded in the leg and subsequently bled to death. His death and the arrival of significant federal reinforcements that evening via steamboats marked the turning point of the battle known as Shiloh.

General Beauregard acceded to command after the wounding of Johnston and soon called off the attack for the day to allow for regrouping and resupply. The Confederate attack resumed on the seventh, but the reinforced, much stronger Union army launched a fierce counter-attack. Realizing his peril, Beauregard ordered the Confederates to retreat to Corinth.

Jacob Thompson actively served as aide-de-camp in this battle that saw the most casualties on both sides yet seen in the Civil War. Thompson witnessed the full horror of mangled corpses and pitiful cries of the wounded as he carried orders and messages over the battlefield. Though an aide-de-camp, he was referred to as "Colonel Thompson" in Beauregard's report of the battle.

Thompson's report of his actions and recollections of Shiloh written to General Beauregard from Corinth on April 9th gave a good overview of the battle along with a personal accounting. On April 6th "At 6:30 o'clock I brought an order from you to General Breckinridge…that he must hurry up his troops." Then "about 7:30 o'clock I rode forward with Colonel Jordan to the front, to ascertain how the battle was going." Around 10:00 A. M., "I was charged with the duty of hurrying forward the ammunition wagons to a safe point immediately in the rear of our lines…"

The excerpts continue: "Under your order I advanced in the direction of the firing, rallying the stragglers, which were marched in double file…." He remembered that he "spent the remainder of the evening in aiding to collect stragglers…."[137] This detailed report provides evidence of Thompson's dedication and willingness to take orders.

During the wild Confederate onslaught of April 6th on the reeling Union army, General Benjamin Prentiss bravely maintained his position at what became known as the Hornet's Nest. This valiant effort perhaps saved Grant's army as it had time to regroup at positions protected by fire from the gunboats on the Tennessee River. Eventually, Prentiss was forced to surrender along with what was left of his division, some 2200 men.

That evening Prentiss was taken to Beauregard's headquarters as a prisoner. While incarcerated there, he and Jacob Thompson engaged in a good-humored conversation notwithstanding the savage events they had viewed earlier in the day. These two had been friends before the War and were reacquainting themselves.[138]

Later, Colonel Jordan, Beauregard's adjutant-general, arrived at the camp and was surprised to see Prentiss there. Jordan joined them in discussing the battle along with more trivial banter. Ultimately, the three all bedded down together on a contrived bed made of tents and captured blankets. Prentiss, the prisoner, was sandwiched between Thompson and Jordan.

"Tired as we were with the day's work, " Jordan remembered, "sleep soon overtook and held us all until early dawn, when the firing first of musketry and then of field-artillery roused us ...."[139] Even a war could not force these men to abandon certain courtesies, no matter what uniform they wore. Thompson's ability to be civil in this most trying of circumstances emphasizes that he was not the mean scoundrel as often depicted.

His role in the confused, savage combat was significant. Albert Sidney Johnston dispatched Thompson to Beauregard with instructions to move a division to a new position. Later, Thompson was confident enough to countermand the positioning of two brigades. He was back and forth accurately delivering verbal messages and personally helping align units. Evidenced by his actions, Thompson had the trust of both Confederate commanders and the obedience of their subordinates as well as a large dose of self- confidence.[140]

About 2 P. M. on the second day of the battle with the southern attack waning, soldiers began straggling to the rear, refusing to advance. The recollections of "Colonel" Thompson," capture the moment. Thompson wrote, Beauregard "seized the banners of two different regiments and led them forward to the assault in the face of the fire of the enemy. I became convinced that our troops were too much exhausted to make a vigorous resistance."

Realizing the situation, Thompson beseeched the General, "you should expose yourself no further... but to retire from Shiloh Church in good order." This was sound advice but bold coming from an aide-de-camp to the now commanding general. Beauregard heeded the counsel, ordering a withdrawal back to Corinth.[141]

Beauregard sent his lengthy account of the battle along with the "flags, standards, and colors captured from the enemy" to the Richmond authorities in the care of Thompson.[142] So it was off to the Confederate capital again, this time with the report and trophies from Shiloh, which events would show failed to impress Jefferson Davis. He was desperate for a victory to halt the Union push from splitting the Confederacy.

After completing his mission to Richmond, Thompson rejoined the army in Corinth. A massive Union army under General Halleck was slowly approaching the Confederates encamped in Corinth. The Confederate army had received reinforcements since the devastating losses at Shiloh, but much of the army was sick or wounded while remaining scattered throughout north Mississippi.

Outnumbered over two-to-one, Beauregard made the decision to retreat fifty miles south to Tupelo. The retreat was meticulously planned to be a secret maneuver. Jacob Thompson was sent in advance to select the camp positions for the army. He chose much healthier locations on higher ground than the prior campgrounds. The army achieved the stealthy withdrawal almost flawlessly, escaping a near certain siege.

After overseeing the retreat, Beauregard was replaced by Braxton Bragg. Beauregard and President Jefferson Davis had a strained relationship by this time, stemming from Beauregard's egotistical nature and Davis' iron will. Jake Thompson somehow remained on friendly terms with both but could no longer be Beauregard's aide-de-camp as he had no command, so he returned home to Oxford. This sojourn did not last long. General Ulysses Grant along with General William Tecumseh Sherman was building a large force in west Tennessee. Their goal was to move south following the Mississippi Central Railroad.

Brigadier General John Bordenave Villepigue of South Carolina, in charge of the meager Confederate forces defending the Mississippi Central Railroad, offered Thompson the position of lieutenant colonel in Ballentine's Regiment.[143] The choice was expedient as Thompson knew the terrain and the people now exposed to attack. His key role in organizing the counties formed from the Chickasaw cession and his regional and statewide political campaigns had prepared him for this role.

Grant and Sherman advanced inexorably down the railroad toward Oxford. The undermanned Confederates abandoned their position on the Tallahatchie River, leaving Oxford precariously uncovered. Thompson anxiously watched as the events unfolded. He saw first-hand the panic, the refugees filling the roads carrying all the treasured belongings they could, and then the arrival of the Yankees into his pleasant town.[144]

On the approach of the Union army, Thompson sped through the countryside akin to Paul Revere informing the landowners he knew of the dire situation. Fearing the pillaging that seemed imminent, he advised them to bring their silver and other portable valuables to his house for safekeeping.

Thompson had the collected valuables labeled and placed in the back room of his home office. Ingeniously, he stationed an old black lady along with several small, distraught black children in the front room. Above the front door Thompson placed a stark warning sign reading "Smallpox in Here."[145]

After hopefully securing the treasure, Thompson rode his horse through the square to William Turner's house to observe the inevitable. The Confederate force, probably less than 2000 men shielding Oxford from the north, resisted the Yankees as they neared town but were soon forced to retreat. Thompson, perched on the roof of Turner's house, watched the action until he unintentionally became involved in it.

Upon passing his location at the corner of North Street (now North Lamar) and Jefferson Avenue, the Yankees met with unexpected stiff resistance from a newly formed Confederate line. Several casualties resulted with the Yankees beating a hasty, though temporary, retreat. In the ensuing confusion, Thompson felt a round pass close to his head. Looking down, he saw a mounted horseman taking aim at him. As he scurried to the trap door on the roof, a second shot shattered the railing where he had just been.

The war had become real personal. Jacob, naturally unnerved, bolted down the stairs, out the back entrance, and into the street, revolver in hand. Retrieving his horse, he made good his escape, following the backroads he knew so well.[146]

This was only the beginning of his miseries. Thompson had learned of the burning of the home of his friend and political ally, former Congressman L. Q. C. Lamar. Lamar's home "Solitude" was anything but solitude as it was in the path of the Union advance. The unwarranted destruction of private property struck fear in Jacob's heart for his own home plus those of family and friends.

His fears were justified. The Seventh Kansas Jayhawkers rampaged through Oxford and the University with total impunity, looting and destroying as they went. They plundered the Thompson home, taking everything they wanted in addition to confiscating 190 bales of valuable cotton stored there. Fortunately, Kate and other members of the household had fled.

Upon completion of their ransacking, the ruffians moved on, but General Grant soon arrived at the home to personally peruse and confiscate any correspondence deemed potentially "treasonable." Grant had been instructed to do this by Secretary of War Edwin Stanton. Stanton was obsessed with those "secessionists" who had in his opinion caused the war.

On Stanton's personal list of traitors was Jacob Thompson. Stanton and Thompson had briefly served together as cabinet members in the latter stages of the Buchanan administration. They had opposing viewpoints and neither was afraid to speak his mind, although Thompson was more diplomatic. Stanton now was almost desperate to prove that a conspiracy existed before the war to destroy the government. He needed proof, so Grant at his behest collected all the personal letters and documents of Jacob Thompson and sent them to Washington.[147]

Several of these letters were later published in northern newspapers to show Thompson's disloyalty as well as to embarrass him, including one to Buchanan in which he called Lincoln a "blunderer." Further correspondence declaring his positions on secession and other matters were printed. The documents released to the newspapers were intended to sway public opinion in the North as well as being part of a vendetta against Thompson and his ilk.

Meanwhile, the Confederate army continued its retreat south of Oxford. At Water Valley, some eighteen miles from Oxford, a sharp engagement took place involving Ballentine's Regiment and its Lieutenant Colonel Thompson. During this clash, Jake Thompson had his horse shot out from under him, but he was unscathed. Coffeeville, a few miles further south on the Mississippi Central Railroad, was the next scene in the ongoing contest as the Confederate cavalry counterattacked. Thompson also took part in this hotly contested skirmish as Grant's army pursued the retiring Confederates.

This was a far sight more serious than his battles against political back-stabbers in Washington. Like many officers in the Confederacy, Thompson had no military training. He simply showed up with his sharp mind and willing spirit and became an officer. And now he was directly engaging in combat that could easily get a man killed. It also aptly illustrates the passion—some would say lack of reason—of southerners desperately determined to protect what they saw as their "way of life," a phrase that remains part of the southern lexicon 150 years later. The roots of that phrase—used in the 1960s by Mississippians trying to explain why they fought so stridently against civil rights for black people—can be traced right back to Jacob Thompson and his friends.

VICKSBURG

The Rebel army under Lieutenant General John C. Pemberton won the race to Grenada on the Yalobusha River, establishing a strong line and temporarily blocking the Union advance. At Grenada, Pemberton made Thompson chief inspector of the Department of Mississippi and East Louisiana, the forces given the difficult task of defending the approaches to Vicksburg. It was a critical job. Losing Vicksburg and Port Hudson to the south would give the North control of the Mississippi River, thus cutting off the vital trans-Mississippi section of the Confederacy and dealing a major blow to the southern cause.

Soon after accepting the staff position from Pemberton, Thompson suggested attacking the rear of Grant's army at Holly Springs where supplies were massed along the railroad.[148] General Earl Van Dorn was tapped to lead this surprise attack, involving a circuitous approach to Holly Springs, thirty-five miles north of Oxford on the Mississippi Central rail line. The raid was tremendously successful as the vast quantity of supplies built up there for the Vicksburg campaign were seized or burned, and the railroad left inoperable by Confederate saboteurs.

This stunning victory along with an accompanying raid by General Nathan Bedford Forrest caused Grant to leave his headquarters at Oxford for a more stable position in Memphis where his supply line became the Mississippi River instead of the railroad. Grant's focus shifted to approaching and attacking Vicksburg down the river instead of overland. This change of plan, naturally, caused Pemberton to counter by moving his army nearer to the river. And so, the Vicksburg campaigns began in earnest.

As the Union thrusts came ever closer to Vicksburg in the spring of 1863, Jacob Thompson tried to ascertain the strength of the Federal fleet anchored in the Yazoo River. The ships were essentially hidden from land view by thick underbrush on the banks of the River, so Thompson took a skiff from Vicksburg and proceeded upriver towards the mouth of the Yazoo.[149]

Union river guards soon spotted this daring and foolhardy attempt at espionage. A small white flag flew from the stern of the little boat, apparently a flag of truce to be of benefit if discovered. Jacob Thompson and his crew were unsurprisingly apprehended before completion of their mission. Subsequently, they were taken to General Grant for questioning. In his *Memoirs*, Grant recalled, "After a pleasant conversation of half an hour or more I allowed the boat and crew, passengers and all, to return to Vicksburg without creating a suspicion that there was a doubt in my mind as to the good faith of Mr. Thompson and his flag."[150]

Eventually, after much maneuvering and several encounters, Grant established a siege of Vicksburg. The beleaguered Confederates, 33,000 in number, finally surrendered on July 4, 1863, an enormous blow to the Confederacy. Jacob Thompson was in the besieged city, probably starving with the rest of the army. Before the capitulation General Pemberton had dispatched Thompson to communicate directly with General Joe Johnston in Canton. Jake was able to slip through the tightening Union lines to deliver the message requesting immediate help. He likely returned to Vicksburg and was captured along with the whole army, signing a parole document to remain a noncombatant until exchanged; however, his name does not appear on the roll of the parolees from Vicksburg.

He had been involved in the bloody assaults by General Sherman attempting to capture Vicksburg from the north at Chickasaw Bayou. These assaults were repulsed with heavy casualties, ending the attempts to take Vicksburg by frontal attack. Thompson also participated in the battle of Baker's Creek or Champion's Hill, a confused struggle that resulted in Union victory. This important encounter had cleared the way for the siege of Vicksburg.

The savage battle of Champion Hill as it is now generally known resulted in a war of words on the Confederate side with generals pointing fingers at each other. There is no doubt that this action was mishandled.

Pemberton, commander at Vicksburg, certainly had his critics then and now. Creating suspicion, he hailed from Philadelphia, Pennsylvania, but had married a southerner from Virginia.

Pemberton graduated from West Point and had participated in the Mexican War and the Seminole Wars in Florida, choosing the Confederacy at the advent of the Civil War after agonizing over the decision for several weeks. Jefferson Davis eventually passed over other generals to promote Pemberton to lieutenant general, thrusting him into a very difficult situation in Mississippi. Though not his fault, Pemberton had sworn enemies from jealous Confederate officers he outranked.

It is a time-honored tradition of sorts to find a scapegoat to blame for the loss of a battle as big as the siege of Vicksburg. Just as Stanton wanted to blame Jacob Thompson for secession, southerners pointed the finger of blame at the hapless Pemberton. It didn't help that he was a Yankee by birth or that General Joe Johnston blamed him for not obeying orders. Johnston was his superior and did order him to Clinton in order to combine forces, but President Davis had told Pemberton to defend Vicksburg itself to the last extremity. Upon receiving conflicting orders, Pemberton apparently did not know what to do and dithered.

Inspector General Jacob Thompson in his report of July 21st curiously came to the defense of the maligned Pemberton by writing frankly that "You gave into the views of the officers with reluctance, and expressed yourself as doing so against your convictions. But being present and hearing everything said, I did not see how you could have done otherwise, with any expectation of retaining your hold upon the army…"[151] Obviously, there had been resistance to Pemberton among certain officers leading to command breakdown and near mutiny.

Later in the report Thompson noted the difficulty in getting General William Wing Loring to follow Pemberton's orders at Champion Hill. Loring was bitter at being passed over by Davis when Pemberton was promoted to lieutenant general and clearly had antipathy to his superior. Thompson recalled, "You directed me to carry the renewal of the order, which I did, at the speed of my horse. Loring replied 'if General Pemberton knew that the enemy was in great force in his front.' I replied I did not know whether General Pemberton knew the fact or not, but I knew I repeated the order correctly; and if he did not comply with it, the responsibility was his, not mine." The report ended with "Being near your person throughout these several days of trial, I was struck with admiration at the prompt manner in which you discharged every duty devolved upon you, in your responsible position."[152]

A contemporaneous recollection by a Lieutenant Drennan gave credence to Thompson's report. "There is quite a feud existing between Loring and Pemberton—so far as Loring is concerned I heard several expressions of disrespect…. In fact it amounted to that degree of hatred on the part of Loring that Captain Barksdale and myself agreed that Loring would be willing for Pemberton to lose a battle provided that he (Pemberton) would be displaced."[153] Loring got his wish. The battle was lost and Pemberton was recalled.

Thompson's support of and loyalty to the despised Pemberton was similar to his dedication to Buchanan. He could have taken the easy path in condemning either superior, but he did not. Both were unpopular and vulnerable; however, Thompson went against the grain in defending them. He did the same with the difficult Beauregard. A word to Davis from Thompson deriding Beauregard, who had a very strained relationship with the President, would likely have totally derailed his career.

In his report to Richmond concerning the Vicksburg campaign, Pemberton praised his inspector general. "Major Jacob Thompson, inspector general of the department, also accompanied me on the field, and on that occasion, as on all others, whether in the office or in the active performance of the duties of his department, has ever shown himself zealous and competent."[154] Thompson again proved himself reliable and trustworthy, particularly in accurately relaying messages of the utmost importance.

After the surrender Thompson retreated eastward with the remainder of Johnston's army. Waiting to be exchanged, he returned to Oxford and was elected to the Mississippi legislature from Lafayette County in the fall of 1863. During his short stay in the legislature, at the session from November 3 to December 9 held in Columbus, Thompson was appointed chairman of the Ways and Means Committee. Later at a called meeting in Macon, he pleaded for more measures to be instituted for the defense of Mississippi.[155]

Thompson had seen firsthand the plight of the destitute people in north Mississippi. He had witnessed Confederate soldiers burning their cotton to keep it out of enemy hands. For many, selling cotton was the only way to earn the revenue they needed to buy even the bare necessities of life. He had watched Confederates confiscating their wagons and teams for war purposes. Likewise, the Union soldiers had ravaged the land, pillaging, burning, and destroying their crops, livestock, and homes. They were desperately trying to survive.

Thompson didn't just watch these tragedies. He tried to stop them. He wrote the local Confederate commander, Brigadier General James R. Chalmers to ascertain who authorized the policy of burning cotton and the ban on trade with the enemy with its deleterious effects on the local populace.

Chalmers responded on December 15, 1863, in eloquent fashion that he was following the orders of General Joseph Johnston. He basically agreed that the present policy, though once appropriate, was now oppressive in the current situation. He wrote, "You ask me 'to make any suggestion as to the proper remedy.' I believe that a trade should be opened, with proper restrictions, with men in the Federal lines." Chalmers further advised that he had prepared an order allowing some trade, but that Johnston overruled it.[156]

Upon receiving the answers of Chalmers, Thompson, then in Oxford, penned a letter to President Davis. He disagreed with Chalmers regarding the necessity of an order to allow trade and also with any trade by a military officer. Thompson thought Chalmers should look the other way in allowing some cotton to be sold to the enemy. Trade should be permitted "in these counties which are cut off from intercourse with the interior of the country…" he opined.

Thompson continued, "To trade with the enemy either directly or indirectly is an admitted evil: But a seeming attempt to starve a people is a greater and a more disastrous evil—To admit the people to buy in the way of barter and exchange what is absolutely necessary, will enliven our people

& greatly aid our army…"[157] Thompson forcefully tried to come to the aid of the suffering citizens of the counties he had once helped establish. Soon it would become a moot issue. In mid-May, the new Union commander at Memphis issued an order explicitly banning all trade with the enemy. And that was that.

FATEFUL TELEGRAM

By 1864 the Confederacy was on its last legs. Some victories cheered the South, but it was a downhill struggle. The desperately needed help from Britain and France had not materialized. Almost everything including manpower was in short supply. In this climate, on April 7, 1864, Jefferson Davis sent a telegram to Jacob Thompson that would radically change his life yet again, plunging him into not just physical peril, but the sort of situation that can forever change how a man is remembered.

The vagueness and simplicity of that fateful telegram belied its import. "If your engagements will permit you to accept service abroad for the next six months, please come here immediately," Davis wrote.[158] The message went to Macon, Mississippi, then the temporary seat of Mississippi government, in care of Governor Charles Clark, who forwarded it to Thompson in Oxford. After considering the pros and cons with Kate, Jacob agreed to hastily travel to Richmond to discuss the position in person.[159]

Before leaving Oxford, he took several steps that showed the seriousness of the matter. He transferred his land and other holdings to his son Macon. The prudent attorney here attempted to save his estate should tragedy befall him on what he perceived to be a perilous mission of some sort. His will, recorded in Lafayette County, provides an accounting of his extensive landholdings in 1864. The properties transferred to Macon were described thusly:

"The Oxford tract and the lots in the said town of Oxford known as the home place, containing some five hundred and fifty acres…, the Clear Creek plantation lying and being in the County of Lafayette, and containing some twenty-seven hundred & twenty acres…, also, the Mississippi plantation lying on the bank of the Mississippi River… in the County of Coahoma containing seventeen hundred & eighty-three acres… all the uncultivated land of every description whatever…in the Counties of Panola, Tunica, Coahoma, Tallahatchie, Sunflower & Bolivar."

The transfer then dealt with his slaves, "all negroes owned by me whether they be found in State of Mississippi, or Texas, or any where else." By this time Thompson had sent some of his slaves to the Huntsville, Texas area for safekeeping. The document continued to list assets as "all of my stock of horses, mules, cattle, hogs & sheep, wherever the same may be." He conceivably also had sent livestock to Texas with the slaves to protect the animals from seizure by the Federals.

While Macon received the property "To have & to hold the whole in his own right," Jacob made provision for Kate. "This conveyance however is made subject to this condition that one-third interest of the property hereby conveyed and assigned to the said C. Macon Thompson is to be held in Trust, for the use and benefit of his mother Catherine A. Thompson…." After the war, Macon transferred back most of the properties to his father, excluding, of course, the slaves.[160]

Thompson arrived in Richmond as fast as the poor Confederate transportation system allowed. He met with President Davis who informed him that many thousands of people in Ohio, Illinois, and Indiana did not support the war and desired peace. Their leaders had approached the Confederate government for assistance with further organization as well as obtaining arms. They boasted of their ability to end the war through coercion or even secession themselves.

After being told that the Confederate Congress had approved a secret mission to Canada with a large appropriation, Thompson was further advised that he would have wide discretion, including no accountability for the expenditures made. The lack of oversight immediately caused him to consider the downside of leading this mission. He envisioned the liability of being responsible for dispersing money—potentially, a lot of money—with no record required to show where it went. He instinctively recognized the danger. So he hesitated. But the rapidly deteriorating circumstances of the Confederacy coupled with his sense of loyalty and gung ho southern patriotism persuaded him to accept. Before consenting, Thompson said he needed assurances of Davis' "unlimited confidence & friendship."[161] This he evidently received.

Thus, Jacob Thompson became a spy. It was to change his life in many ways, not the least of which was a cloud over his reputation in both North and South after the gunfire had long faded. Political foes and combatants are usually recognized as such. But the enemy almost always considers spies traitors, less than honorable, their offense punishable by execution. Just ask Nathan Hale or more recently Julius and Ethel Rosenberg. And then there was the matter of all that missing money. Jacob Thompson would hear about *that* for the rest of his days.

He had not been the first to be offered this unenviable position. Alexander H. Stuart, who had been Secretary of the Interior from 1850 to 1853, was invited to Richmond to discuss heading a mission out of Canada. Jefferson Davis told him the mission "was to foster and give aid to the peace sentiment then active among the border states," as Stuart later remembered. Stuart declined. He thought the ultimate goal revolved around a "remarkable delusion" over the support to be obtained from the peace movement in the North.[162]

Jacob Thompson was a realist too. He understood this mission had long odds of success. He recognized that he possessed few of the attributes of a secret agent; however, he did have numerous friends and contacts in the North from his years in Congress. Jake wrote Kate that he was "willing to run any hazard," and then added "great good could be affected for our cause by a true man in Canada," which is exactly what Jefferson Davis had told him.[163]

There followed on April 27, 1864, a formal communication from the President to Thompson: "Confiding special trust in your zeal, discretion, and patriotism, I hereby direct you to proceed at once to Canada, there to carry out such instructions as you have received from me verbally, in such manner as shall seem most to conduce to the furtherance of the interests of the Confederate States of America, which have been entrusted to you…"[164]

Assistant Secretary of State Littleton Quinton Washington, who served

Clement Clay, Confederate commissioner to
Canada along with Thompson

under Judah P. Benjamin, then secretary of state, stated postwar, "I was present at the time when Mr. Thompson received his instructions from Mr. Benjamin. They were oral and largely suggestive and informal. Much was left to his discretion and wisely; for he was an experienced and conservative man."[165]

Davis and Benjamin apparently trusted Jacob Thompson to do his work with little input from Richmond. This was long before spy radios, and telegraph messages were unavailable as the Union was interposed between the Confederacy and Canada. So it was correspondence by messenger. Communication through enemy lines via messenger was difficult at best. Typically, it took two or three weeks to get a reply. What's more, the situation had often changed in the interim, leaving Thompson and others to decide how to proceed. They were essentially out there behind enemy lines, acting on their own with occasional, often outdated guidance from their bosses.

Former U. S. Senator Clement Clay of Alabama received a similar commission to Thompson along with James Holcombe, a University of Virginia law professor. Thompson was appointed chief of the mission to establish a second front of sorts in Canada. Holcombe left first and was already in Montreal when Clay and Thompson departed on May 3rd. William W. Cleary of Kentucky, appointed secretary of the mission, joined them for what proved to be a harrowing journey to Canada.

Like Thompson, Clay was appointed for his loyalty to Davis and the Confederacy. In all probability Davis also thought that Clay could moderate Thompson, the sometimes impetuous man of action. That was not to happen as the two differed in temperament to the degree that they barely tolerated each other and were often at cross-purposes. Clay confided, "It is a very difficult and delicate duty, for which I am not suited by my talents, tastes, or habits. I cannot enjoy secret service. I have accepted it with extreme reluctance."[166] In hindsight this was a recipe for failure from the outset.

The three commission members left Richmond for Wilmington, North Carolina, boarding the blockade-runner Thistle headed for Bermuda. After waiting for darkness on May 6th, the speedy Thistle attempted to run the blockade of thirteen Union ships. She was greatly aided in her escape by the ironclad CSS Raleigh, which acted as a decoy, later boldly engaging six of the blockaders. At daylight they were spotted and the chase was on. The captain of the Thistle announced that a Union cruiser was gaining on his vessel.

Duly alarmed, the party of three secret agents "made arrangements to burn our mail and papers, and to distribute the money." Then they resorted to fortifying themselves with whiskey from the Captain's stores. The Yankee ship seemingly closed the gap rapidly, then fell off the pace. Perhaps, they were saved by engine failure.

The rest of the trip to Bermuda was uneventful. But their journey was not over. They boarded the British mail ship Alpha bound for Halifax, Nova Scotia.[167] It had been an exciting start to their mission as well as a sobering one as the superior might of the Union was again manifested, this time through naval power.

Soon after arrival in Halifax, James Holcombe met the team. He had been sent to Canada three months prior to represent Confederate legal interests over ownership of a merchant steamer captured by Confederate sympathizers off Cape Cod and to assist in the return to the South of escaped Confederate prisoners. Holcombe enlightened the agents of his attempts to gather both escapees and blockade-runners necessary to transport them. A network of agents had been organized to get the men to Halifax and then by sea back to the Confederacy. While he reported few takers, a functional organization had been established.[168]

The Confederacy had carried out secret operations in Canada since early in the war. Confederate prisoners of war and other southerners received sanctuary there, and Canada provided a great intermediary point for communications with Great Britain. Many prominent Canadians were sympathetic toward the South. Though most Canadians favored abolition of slavery, they generally liked the genial southerners, while exhibiting a visceral dislike for Yankees, whom they perceived as overbearing.[169]

Canada was populated with former Tories who had fled the United States after the Revolutionary War and still harbored resentment and fear of their fast-growing, ambitious neighbor to the south. D'arcy McGee, Canadian cabinet minister expressed the feelings of many in February, 1865,

"They coveted Florida and seized it; they coveted Louisiana and purchased it… they picked a quarrel with Mexico, which ended by their getting California…. The acquisition of Canada was the first ambition of [America]…. Is it likely to be stopped now, when she counts her guns afloat by the thousands and her troops by the hundreds of thousands?"[170]

Two days after arriving in Halifax, Thompson and the ever- present Cleary left for Montreal. They arrived toward the end of May after an arduous land and water journey of eight days. Commissioner Thompson went to work immediately and problems arose almost as fast. Clement Clay was a near invalid by the time he reached Canada and longed for wife and home, making him cross and ineffective. He delayed making the long journey from Halifax for several days for health reasons. This was the beginning of a worrisome trend of independent action by the commissioners.

Thompson and Cleary established headquarters at St. Lawrence Hall, a large and openly pro-Confederate hotel that boasted the only bar to serve mint juleps for the hundreds of Confederates who resided in the immediate vicinity. Unfortunately, the Union was far from oblivious to what was happening in Canada. Union spies were already evident in and around the hotel, creating a hostile environment for the young mission.[171]

Realizing the impossibility of organizing a covert operation with Federal agents at every corner, Thompson moved onward to Toronto. Clay, citing health concerns, refused to leave and requested money to begin operations on his own. Thompson obligingly opened an account at Montreal's Bank of Ontario, depositing $93,000. Before leaving, Thompson met with informed friends and acquaintances from the so- called peace party of the northeastern United States. He concluded that they were too involved with profiting from the war to support ending it.[172]

Queens Hotel in 1867
Jacob Thompson used this Toronto hotel as his headquarters
while also residing here.

Clement Valladingham, Copperhead leader
courted by Jacob Thompson

COURTING COPPERHEADS

In Toronto, Thompson elected to stay at the Queen's Hotel, the city's finest, noted for being the center of Confederate activities. If he had expected to escape from enemy agents in Toronto, he was soon to be disappointed. It did not take long to spot some of the many Union agents present in Toronto as in Montreal. They were pervasive. Even with his knowledge of the espionage all around him, Thompson was too trusting, repeatedly divulging information to enemy informers, the worst habit imaginable for a spy.

He soon established contact with Clement L. Vallandingham, a former Congressman from Ohio and Grand Commander of the Sons of Liberty, one of three midwestern organizations collectively known as the Copperheads, all attempting to end the war. Vallandingham, a long-time friend of Jacob Thompson, had fled to Canada in 1863 under duress for his Confederate sympathies.

Under President Davis' orders, if he deemed the chances of an uprising in the northwest to be reasonable, Thompson was charged with supporting the movement in every way, including financially. On leaving Richmond, Thompson had been supplied with a large sum of money, probably around $600,000.

The Copperheads, per Vallandingham, proposed that Illinois, Indiana, and Ohio secede from the Union and establish a northwestern confederacy with the intent of adding the border states of Kentucky and Missouri. They thought that this further division of the Union would cause Lincoln to sue for peace.

Captain Thomas Henry Hines, a seasoned veteran and spy already in Canada, had been appointed by Richmond as head of military operations. Although still in his twenties, Hines knew how to operate across the border

Thomas Henry Hines, operational head of
Confederate Canadian operations

John Breckinridge Castleman, second in command of Canadian operations.
Postwar, he was Thompson's travel companion in Europe.

with near impunity and was the primary contact with the Copperheads. Thompson and Hines quickly established a trust in each other and bonded in their pursuit of common objectives.

The Copperheads were full of talk and bluster but short on action. They claimed hundreds of thousands of members ready to stop the war by armed intervention if necessary. Their articles of association insisted that every state in the Union was sovereign, making the Union invasion of the South unconstitutional. What the Copperheads desired was a political settlement to end the war, while the Confederates wanted out of the Union. The bottom line was that the Copperheads were not mentally prepared to go to war against the Union—they were at heart a loosely formed political organization.

"It appears that Captain Hines, in his youthful optimism, often misread the rhetoric as a guarantee of action—action that never came to fruition."[173] The greenhorn spy Thompson likewise became enamored of Vallandingham and his Copperheads. He initially gave the Copperheads $25,000, the beginning of a troubling trend. There can never be a complete accounting of the money spent on the Northwest Conspiracy, but suffice it to say that a tremendous amount was basically squandered.[174]

Thompson and the Confederacy invested considerable time and effort as well as expenditures on arms, attempting to cajole the Copperheads into action. To show his sincerity, Thompson became a member of Vallandingham's Sons of Liberty. Despite Thompson's prodding, friendships, and formidable political and organizational skills, it became apparent that the Copperhead movement had been grossly overestimated. Not only had their numerical strength been embellished, the anti-war movement also suffered from a lack of proper leadership. They could not be counted on.[175]

The plan early on seemed doable if only the Copperheads would act. The Confederacy supplied them with weapons bought in New York City and smuggled into Canada. Ultimately, the arms and ammunition were hauled by wagon, finally crossing the border into Ohio and Indiana. This time consuming and expensive effort would prove futile.[176]

Chicago was targeted for a joint mission of Confederate operatives and Copperheads. Logically, this site was selected since the Democratic National Convention was soon to be held here and a large number of Confederate prisoners were held in the area. Escaped Confederate prisoners already in Canada were organized to help liberate prisoners of war held at Camp Douglas and Rock Island, ready to act in conjunction with the planned Chicago expedition. Both of these Illinois prisons held thousands of Confederates in deplorable conditions. This expedition was one of several attempted, requiring Copperhead support to release Confederate captives and create chaos.

The former prisoners were primed to move into action when the signal was given. Dates for the operation were repeatedly set and at the last moment postposed by the Copperhead leaders. Once this occurred four times in a day as the former Confederate prisoners were on station and ready to fulfill their part of the mission. On each of the many agreed upon times, the Copperheads failed to show.[177]

It didn't help that Union spies and paid informers had thoroughly infiltrated the hapless Copperheads. While Confederates had enjoyed an early advantage in spy networks, by this time Union capabilities for espionage and counter-espionage far surpassed the South. Copperhead leaders were identified and arrested after the Chicago failure, causing the movement basically to dissolve after the fall of Atlanta.

Hines, along with Castleman, the capable second in command of military operations, had infiltrated their ninety men into Chicago prepared to wreak havoc on the city and to release the captives held in nearby Union prisons. If successful, the daring scheme would divide the former United States into three parts, in all probability allowing the Confederacy to endure. Lincoln would be defeated in the upcoming election and peace would reign.[178]

One last meeting with the Copperheads, however, convinced the two Confederate captains that the uprising could not succeed. They once again had failed to materialize in adequate numbers. Hines told the carefully selected brave men accompanying him from Toronto to Chicago that the mission was aborted and that they should scatter. Thus, for all practical purposes ended the so-called Northwest Conspiracy.

Thompson was furious when he heard the news. Hines later observed, "Mr. Thompson became thoroughly convinced that the movement could be induced, and that it would be successful. But there was always the doubt whether men bound together merely by political affiliations and oaths, behind which there was no real legal authority, could be handled like an army."[179] In fairness, the Sons of Liberty deceived both Thompson and Hines. The encouraging reports from Hines to Thompson had helped create the illusion that success would follow.

Three months after the failure, Thompson still refused to accept reality. In his letter to Benjamin of December 3rd, he maintained: "The feeling among the masses is as strong as ever. They are true, brave, and I believe, willing and ready, but they have no leaders. The large bounties paid for treachery, added to the large military force stationed in those states, make organization and preparation almost an impossibility."[180]

Commissioner Thompson was rapidly confirming that he was an easy mark when it came to money. He well knew that the Confederacy was in dire straits and that chances had to be taken; that said, he dispensed money with little vetting to disreputable people touting outlandish schemes.

Thompson confessed that on one occasion a person approached him supposedly sent from Secretary Benjamin in Richmond. The person demanded $10,000 to purchase weapons but did not have the requisite orders. After being refused, he then requested $3,000 to travel back to Richmond to obtain a copy of the orders. Thompson trustingly provided him with $3,000, and that was the last he or the gold was seen.[181]

Holcombe had reported to Canadian authorities on his arrival. Thompson did likewise, promising to obey Canadian laws. He in turn advised Hines and others that Canada's neutrality must be respected. They were also advised diplomatic means were to be attempted first before resorting to more drastic measures.

Thompson repeatedly told them that if guerilla warfare was deemed necessary "to carefully avoid all transgressions of the laws of war as observed by open belligerents, and to neither command nor to permit the destruction of private property." According to Hines this was not possible. He rather caustically opined, "the obstinate, unimaginative Thompson was not the man to make a band of hard-riding raiders who knew what the torches of Sherman's men were doing to their own homes, obey such a restriction."[182]

HARDENING ATTITUDE

By July, however, Thompson's attitude had begun to change during the planning stages of the Northwest Conspiracy. His report to Richmond stated, "Though intending this a western confederacy and demanding peace, if peace is not granted, then it shall be war." He continued, "If Lee can hold his own in front of Richmond, and Johnston defeat Sherman in Georgia prior to the election, it seems probable that Lincoln will be defeated. Nothing less, however can accomplish this end."[183]

Of course this was wishful thinking. Atlanta soon fell, shaking the crumbling Confederacy anew. Sherman began his infamous fiery march to the sea. Grant was tightening a merciless noose around Richmond in spite of valiant efforts by its defenders. Thompson ended the report with these alarming words, "In short nothing but violence can terminate the War."[184] Frustrated with endeavors to stop the war through political means, he intended to give the North a taste of what the South was enduring.

The mood among the Confederate hierarchy in Richmond had changed dramatically shortly before Thompson's mission to Canada. An audacious attack on Richmond, the Kilpatrick-Dahlgren raid, was the impetus for a hardening of attitude toward the conduct of the war, especially involving noncombatants. The South, particularly the tidewater area, still clung to a semblance of chivalry, although this ideal was rapidly eroding. The documents found on Union Colonel Ulric Dahlgren, 21 year-old son of the famous Admiral John Dahlgren, served to usher in a further collapse of gentlemanly warfare.

Brigadier General Judson Kilpatrick, widely known as "Kill-cavalry" for his reckless behavior, glory seeking, and lack of regard for his men, was in charge of a two-pronged attack on the Confederate capitol. He had gone over the head of his superiors to gain approval for this venture, probably receiving the go ahead from Secretary of War Stanton. Colonel Dahlgren was the cavalry leader of the smaller leg of the attempt, ostensibly to free the Union prisoners on Belle Isle and in Libby Prison.

The raid, though meticulously planned, went wrong almost from the beginning. Undertaken in late February and March 1864, the weather did not cooperate. Snow and rain slowed the advance, requiring changes in plans. An almost undefended Richmond was alerted with home guards and scattered groups of regulars responding to the clarion call. During the ensuing encounter, pitting a group of primarily home guards against Dahlgren's Union troopers, the brave, one-legged Colonel Dahlgren was killed. (He had lost his leg at Gettysburg.)

His death was not the end of this saga as three documents were found on Dahlgren's body. One document, the address composed to be read to released Union prisoners, urged them to "destroy and burn the hateful city; and do not allow the Rebel leader Davis and his traitorous crew to escape." The accompanying instructions specified that Richmond "must be destroyed and Jeff. Davis and Cabinet killed." In the notebook he added that the murders must be carried out "on the spot."[185]

The North vigorously denied that the documents were genuine, claiming that they were forgeries concocted to elicit support from European countries. In the South, newspapers printed the documents in full. Photographs were taken of the evidence and forwarded to General George Meade, Commander of the Army of the Potomac, along with a formal protest. Universally, there was no doubting the authenticity by southerners, who were further incensed by the North's absolute refusal to acknowledge any responsibility.[186]

Virgil Carrington Jones, author and expert on guerilla warfare in Virginia, concluded that the documents found on Dahlgren were real, not fabrications, in his pioneering book on the raid, *Eight Hours before Richmond*.[187] Although still contested, other researchers have tended to agree with his learned opinion. Even General Meade confided to his wife that contrary to his reply disavowing the sanctioning or authorizing of these acts by anyone in the Federal government, he had serious suspicions. He wrote her, "I regret to say Kilpatrick's reputation, and collateral evidence in my possession, rather go against this theory" (of disavowal.)[188]

It really did not matter if the documents had been altered or not. The Confederate hierarchy certainly believed them to be real and was aghast. An incensed Confederate Secretary of War James Seddon favored retaliating by summarily executing some of the prisoners captured in the failed raid.[189] Cooler heads prevailed, but a stark realization took hold that the generally accepted rules of war had changed. The Richmond *Dispatch* expressed the southern position succinctly by stating "that these Dahlgren papers will destroy, during the rest of this war, all rose-water chivalry; and that Confederate armies will make war after and upon the rules selected by their enemies."[190]

Neither did anyone in the South forget that Kilpatrick's cavalry speedily responded to Dahlgren's death by punishing the people of King and Queen Court House where Dahlgren had been "ambushed." The entire village was burned save for one dwelling, and citizens were hauled away as captives.[191] Undeniably, a new phase had begun in an already savage civil war.

PEACE INITIATIVE

To better understand the Canadian mission, one needs to recognize that several of the multiple attempts to influence the outcome of the war were occurring simultaneously. Some were peace efforts where Jacob Thompson could utilize his political skills and relationships with northern Democrats, while others involved guerilla warfare. The personnel necessary to carry out the clandestine operations were not trained as a unit or schooled in covert actions. Discipline for the volunteers proved to be impossible at times. They were brave but also reckless and impulsive.

Plots were planned hastily with little vetting or rehearsal. Central control proved impossible as approvals and orders originated from varying sources. Security of planning as well as implementing missions was an ongoing headache. Union agents almost invariably infiltrated preparations, made easier by Thompson's trusting and lax attitude regarding secrecy. Jacob Thompson excelled at many things, but being an effective spy was not one of them.

This was espionage, of course, so historians will never manage a full accounting of every secret mission. Most of the Confederate records were purposely destroyed, leaving the story to be told primarily by the victors. If it all seems confusing, it is because it is. And all these initiatives were compressed into the little over half a year that Thompson led the mission.

Various plots were constantly presented to Thompson, beginning as soon as he arrived in Canada. He was directly involved with some of these, indirectly with others, and some were concocted without his knowledge or approval. One plan with his indirect involvement was the Niagara Peace Initiative. Thompson certainly wanted to influence the 1864 presidential election, hoping that a Democrat victory would result in a negotiated peace.

With Thompson's knowledge but without his approval, Clay, Holcombe, the master manipulator George N. Sanders, and one other contrived a peace initiative. In order to show his displeasure, Thompson even resorted to dispatching Cleary to implore them not to use his name in any negotiations.[192] To succeed, they needed an eminent and respected intermediary from the North; ultimately, soliciting the well-known newspaper publisher Horace Greeley, who had previously denounced Jacob Thompson as a traitor. The Confederate operatives informed Greeley that they were authorized by Jefferson Davis to negotiate a peace settlement.[193]

Although skeptical of their power to fully negotiate on behalf of the Confederacy, Greeley wrote Lincoln to let him know he had been contacted by Confederate agents in Niagara Falls, Canada. He then proceeded to pressure Lincoln into agreeing to a meeting. Greeley, encouraged by Lincoln's support, went to Niagara Falls and met with the agents on the Canadian side of the border.[194]

George N. Sanders, arriving from Europe unannounced and unasked, quickly ingratiated himself to Clay and Holcombe after receiving a cold shoulder from Jacob Thompson. Ever the wheeler-dealer, he proceeded to essentially take over the peace initiatives with no authority except that obtained from the cover of Clay and Holcombe. How he managed to inveigle himself into this position of leadership without any authority or orders is almost unfathomable—but he accomplished it in short order.

Clay had moved his headquarters to St. Catherines, 15 miles from Niagara Falls, which offered a more leisurely lifestyle away from the frenetic pace of Thompson. He remained physically weak, irritable, and homesick. At this point the two commissioners were running dual operations at cross-purposes on occasion. Really, there were three operations as Sanders had his own agenda in his self-appointed role.[195]

With his personality and health, Clay was no match for the manipulative, charming, and willful Sanders, who had spent many years honing his art. Even though he recognized Sanders was a conniver, Clay was unable to control him. Later, Sanders showed little respect for Canada's neutrality in promoting the fateful St. Alban's Raid.

Hines and his military second in command, Captain John B. Castleman, clashed with Sanders from the outset. According to Castleman, Sanders was "strong, visionary, persistent." He further stated that the persuasive, smooth talking Sanders had "obtained control of Mr. Clay and Mr. Holcombe and might get anyone in trouble by his active brain and tireless scheming."[196] Captain Hines candidly summed up George Sanders, "In my long life, I have known no counterpart to this man. He was a constant menace to the interests for which the commissioners were responsible."[197]

Commissioner Thompson did not listen to Sanders and, tellingly, did not participate in the ruse he carried out with Clay and Holcombe. Jacob Thompson bluntly declared of Sanders, "He came from Europe to do what he says he did not know we were entrusted to do and he has gone on to do it. There is such a thing as spoiling broth by having too many hands in it."[198]

In a letter to Jefferson Davis, Sanders criticized Thompson because he "would not enter into my views; he had no confidence in political movements; he believed in nothing but stirring up rebellion and revolution in the Northwest."[199] The scheming Sanders attempted to get Lincoln's stance on a peaceful end to the war. He then planned to circulate this opinion confirming Lincoln's intransigence to peace at the upcoming Democratic convention in Chicago, hoping to get a commitment to peace from the party.

After several meetings, the Confederates finally admitted that they were not empowered to deal for Davis but only wished to get Lincoln's position on a peaceful conclusion to the war. Greeley belatedly revealed Lincoln's bottom line, "embracing the restoration of the Union and the abandonment of slavery."[200] Sanders and his cohorts had their answer and used it to label Lincoln as a warmonger, who had no intention of compromise to stop the bloodshed.

This fiasco did serve to embarrass the Lincoln administration and was a propaganda coup for the Confederates. Newspapers in both the North and South disparaged Lincoln and Greeley for not disclosing Lincoln's preconditions for peace. The tide of public opinion in the war weary nation turned against the President with cabinet members even conspiring against him as they thought he would lose the upcoming election.[201]

Though Jacob Thompson did not personally participate in the peace conference, he did become directly involved in the conference that followed in mid-August. Jeremiah Black, who served with Thompson in the Buchanan administration, came to Toronto with a peace feeler. As so many things in these confusing times, there are multiple versions of the meetings between Thompson and his friend Black.

Black ostensibly told Thompson that he came at the request of Secretary of War Edwin Stanton. The Secretary of War, Thompson's old adversary in the Buchanan administration, did not believe that Lincoln could win reelection. He wanted Thompson's thoughts on a peaceful settlement with slavery left intact.[202]

Thompson was adamant that independence must be a part of peace terms much to the dismay of Hines and Castleman, who both realized the current grim state of the Confederate armies. Perhaps, Black offered the best chance of a brokered settlement to the typically sensible Jacob Thompson. The two friends had developed a mutual trust while serving together in the cabinet. Black eventually persuaded Thompson to slightly modify his rigid stance.

Appreciating Black's evaluation and the gravity of the South's situation, Thompson told Black that with assurances of the rights of the seceded states to control their own affairs, reunion might be possible. Each state in this proposal could determine "what shall be the legal relations between black and white races."[203] Black's opinion was that if an agreement could be reached on this requirement, the seceded states would rejoin the Union.

Upon his return, Judge Black reported to Stanton that the South desired peace but would not concede "any right to regulate their domestic affairs by State authority." Black felt a four to six month truce to allow for negotiations would be productive. He obviously thought the chances of peace were good and recommended obtaining the official position of the Confederate government in Richmond.[204]

The irascible Stanton was irate. He had already been chastised and embarrassed over the negative publicity he had received in the northern press from the meeting. He harshly responded, "Your recent interview with Mr.

Thompson… clearly proves that the rebel leaders… will accept no peace but upon the terms of absolute independence." Then he denied ever approving the quest.[205]

Black, stunned by Stanton's scorn, retorted, "you very unequivocally expressed your wish that I would… go and see Mr. Thompson…. You repeated it not less than three times." This attempt at a peaceful reunion had concluded as a result of Stanton's total change of heart, but Thompson and others in Canada did not know it.[206]

The visit with Judge Black left Thompson with the impression that a settlement might be reached. Elated, he conferred with Clay, who, although practically estranged, approved of the plan to present a report of the meetings to the Confederate ministers of Great Britain and France. The "remarkable change" in the political outlook in the United States, and the Republican fear of losing the upcoming presidential election excited Thompson. He fervently hoped the revelation about the election would induce the European powers to intercede.

Holcombe was appointed to travel to London with Thompson's letters to James Mason and John Slidell, Confederate ambassadors to Great Britain and France. Nothing came from this attempt as Holcombe was shipwrecked, never making it to England. The letters finally arrived in London four months later after Lincoln's re-election made it a nonissue.[207]

Thompson's letters to the ministers is revealing as to his thoughts and hopes at the time: "Judge Black visited me in Toronto, delegated by Mr. Stanton to do so, and stated to me that Mr. Stanton was convinced of the present prospect of Mr. Lincoln's overthrow in November, and of the necessity of something being done…. Mr. Stanton does not believe that anything except a determined favorable turn in military affairs will prevent the defeat of the Republican Party at the next election…. I am given to understand that a proposition will be considered which will secure us in all our rights, present, and prospective."[208]

Confederate prisoners at Camp Douglas.
One in five would die while incarcerated.

ATTEMPTS TO RELEASE PRISONERS

Thompson had not given up on springing Confederate prisoners held in the Great Lakes area. The failure of plans to break soldiers out of prison with the help of Copperheads stuck in his craw. He was now determined to act without them. An intriguing plan to rescue 2,000 Confederate officers from Johnson's island in Lake Erie had been presented to him by Confederate Captain Charles Cole and Acting Master of the Confederate Navy John Yates Beall.

They proposed to capture the Michigan, a Union ship armed with 14 guns guarding the prison, and use it to free the captives. Actually, the idea of wreaking havoc with the Michigan, the only Union gunboat on the Great Lakes, had been presented earlier to Richmond authorities by Beall. It had been rejected then out of fear of violating Canadian neutrality.[209] Thompson liked the plan and sent Cole to learn the ins and outs of harbor schedules and security. As part of his mission, Cole pretended to be a wealthy Philadelphia banker in order to become familiar with officers and sailors of the Michigan. Armed with $4,000 from Thompson, he was accompanied by a prostitute, Annie Brown, who posed as his wife.

After hosting several elaborate dinners replete with expensive wines, Captain Cole was invited aboard the Michigan. Soon he was a daily guest at Johnson's Island prison as well as on the Michigan. He was able to not only reconnoiter the island but also to pass messages to the prisoners regarding the planned action.[210]

Now it was Beall's turn. He and twenty Confederates stationed in Canada would seize the American steamboat Philo Parsons at Detroit. They would proceed to Sandusky, Ohio, capture the Michigan, and release the prisoners at nearby Johnson's Island. Thompson, true to form, lavished money on the spendthrift Cole. He also gave $25,000 to Beall for the operation.[211]

Castleman wrote years later, "There was no military achievement which promised results so important, because at that time and for the then immediate future the destructive agencies of an unopposed gunboat was inestimable." Once again, Union spies were one step ahead of the plotters. They alerted officials that something was in the works as they followed Cole through his Great Lakes inspections.[212]

The daring, though impractical, plot began in earnest when a Confederate operative boarded the Philo Parsons in Detroit. He persuaded the captain to make an unscheduled stop on the Canadian side of the lake to pick up Beall and another recruit. At the next stop a group of young men boarded lugging an old trunk. The trunk was opened, the arms it contained distributed, and Beall took over the ship.[213]

The Philo Parsons made haste for Middle Bass Island, some ten miles from Johnson's Island. There they took on wood for fuel and released passengers and crew. While this was transpiring, the Island Queen, another lake steamer, appeared unexpectedly. A brief skirmish followed before Beall and crew commandeered the ship with its cargo of unarmed Union soldiers headed home. Beall directed the ship to the U. S. side of the lake where the passengers, including twenty-six Union soldiers, and crew were put ashore. The Island Queen was then taken into deep water and intentionally sunk.

Captain Beall and his men on the Philo Parsons steered to a safe vantage point while awaiting the signal from Cole on the Michigan that was scheduled for 9:00 P. M. The signal never came. Cole had asked the officers of the Michigan to another one of his festive dinners intending to ply them with drugged wine, thereby making the task of capturing the ship feasible. Alas, he and the plot had been unmasked. He was arrested as a spy even as

Beall and associates moved closer, observing the crew positioned to repel an attack. The Philo Parsons backed away and was scuttled.[214]

A Union detective posing as a patent medicine salesman had been planted at the prison. He had overheard enough of the plot from prisoners to realize that a breakout involving the Michigan was planned. Naturally, he alerted the military, forcing Beall, under pressure from his own men, to abort the mission. Once again, Confederate espionage was thwarted by Union infiltrators. It was becoming a recurring theme in the doomed Canadian operations.[215]

Thompson admonished Cole about the necessity of obeying the neutrality of the British provinces (Canada) before approving the plan to capture the Michigan. This requirement proved to be nearly impossible to follow as the action had been initiated from Canadian soil. Perhaps, Thompson was actually trying to lure the British into the war. It did serve to increase Anglo-American tensions, while leaving Canadians increasingly aggravated at Confederate operations using their borders as cover.

Undaunted, on November 1, 1864, Thompson bought the speedy steamer Georgian in Toronto. His report to Richmond stated his objective was "to have a boat on whose captain and crew reliance could be placed, and on board of which arms could be sent to convenient points for arming such vessels as could be seized for operations on the Lakes" Now that Thompson and staff were being constantly watched, his plan to use the ship was worthless. A frustrated Thompson wrote Secretary of War Benjamin that, "The bane and curse of carrying out anything in this country is the surveillance under which we act. Detectives, or those ready to give information, stand at every corner. Two or three can not interchange ideas without a reporter."[216]

Thompson and the Confederates were becoming ever more desperate. The effort to bring the war to American cities on the Great Lakes would almost assuredly violate Canadian neutrality and even leave Thompson facing prison time or extradition. He obviously weighed the options and took the risk. This operation galvanized Canadian authorities to challenge Confederate violations of Canadian neutrality laws.[217]

Sure enough, an informer reported Thompson's plan to arm the Georgian, thereby bringing the war and its terror to the North. Ultimately, the ship was not outfitted and its intended mission was never carried out; however, Confederate efforts on the Great Lakes did have one positive effect.

A hue and cry went up to the White House for more ships and soldiers to defend the Lakes and port cities. These troops were drawn from Grant in his ongoing struggle with Lee in the Richmond area. Even with his vast numerical superiority, Grant was not happy about releasing soldiers for border defense. This led him to disdainfully write General Dix, "It seems to me that you and General Butler ought to be able to take care of Jake Thompson and his gang."[218]

More Plots

Many of these fanciful intrigues, plots, and brainstorms of plots were overlapping, creating a crazy stew of espionage that seldom amounted to anything worthwhile. With Clay in Montreal and Thompson in Toronto, cooperation was almost wholly lacking. Too, orders were sent from Benjamin and Seddon in Richmond directing some of the actions with some dispatches even going directly to the operatives, bypassing the commissioners.

George N. Sanders, conniving and pushy as ever, took the opportunity to essentially take over the Montreal operations as he held sway over commissioners Clay and Holcombe. Sanders became so bold that he asked Hines and Castleman to rob banks in Niagara and Buffalo, which they adamantly refused to do and duly reported the request to Thompson.[219]

There were also escaped Confederate prisoners in Canada who remained after participating in the various efforts to release those incarcerated in northern prisons. Jacob Thompson ordered these escapees to leave Canada and return home. Many refused. They wanted to strike a blow against the North to avenge the perceived sufferings and cruelties inflicted upon them and the South. It was in this spirit that the raid on St. Albans, Vermont, was perpetrated on October 19, 1864.

The raid on St. Albans, fifteen miles south of the Canadian border, consisted of robbing the three banks in town followed by a wild shoot-out along with setting fire to several structures, which caused limited damage. One person died in the melee, with the bank heists netting $208,000. Outraged and frightened, the residents of the United States close to the border called for an invasion of Canada.

On learning of the attack, John B. Jones, a Confederate War Department clerk in Richmond commented, "A war with England would be our peace." While Confederate leaders longed for an international incident to save the cause, the St. Albans raiders, former prisoners all, viewed their efforts as "retaliation for the recent outrages in the Shenandoah Valley and elsewhere in the Confederate States," according to their leader, Lieutenant Bennett H. Young.[220]

Most of the raiders made good their escape to Canada. An international incident ensued as the United States threatened to forcefully retrieve the marauders from across the border. The British garrison was alerted to resist this intrusion, which was partially defused when the U. S. eventually backed down.

Later, the extradition hearing against Lieutenant Young clearly proved that Sanders devised the St. Albans raid. While Commissioner Clay knew of the plan and tentatively approved of it, Sanders forged the final order. Jacob Thompson disavowed any prior knowledge of this raid and the official transcript of the hearing substantiated his claim.[221]

Thompson was appalled and admonished Clay for approving the raid. In a defensive mode, Clay was disingenuous in his reply, denying any prior knowledge of the plan. Writing Judah Benjamin, Clay admitted he sanctioned Young's mission, while giving him instructions to "destroy whatever was valuable, not to stop to rob; but after firing a town he could seize and carry off money or treasury notes." Not surprisingly, this raid is still attributed by some to Jacob Thompson despite unambiguous evidence to the contrary.[222]

Several other schemes did pass muster with Thompson. The South was suffering the horrors of total war with its brutal, morale-sapping waves of death, hunger, and homelessness. As their cause waned, calls for retaliatory attacks on northern civilians increased. Jacob Thompson got the message and rapidly organized an attack on Chicago to correspond with the presidential election on November 8th. Release of Confederate prisoners held in the area was also on the agenda. Yet again, the ever- present Union agents uncovered his plans. The conspirators were identified and arrested before any planned mischief could be implemented. It had become laughingly easy to penetrate the Confederate plotters in Canada.[223]

The focus on prisoners was high priority with efforts in their behalf beginning even before Jacob Thompson was sent to Canada. First, the Confederacy needed them in the worst way to help fill the ranks of its diminishing armies. Second, southern authorities were aware of the often dreadful conditions in the prisons.

Once the decision was made by the Union to curtail prisoner exchanges, it put pressure on prisons and prisoners, North and South. That conclusion, though wise strategically, wrote the death warrant for many on both sides. While the notorious Andersonville prison has been rightly depicted as an absolute hellhole in the destitute South, northern prisons have tended to escape the same scrutiny. They were no models of enlightened punishment either.

At Camp Douglas prison, an inspection in October 1863, found filthy clothing and unwashed inmates. Three hydrants supplied all water for 7,100 prisoners plus the guards. The barracks were in pitiful condition. Another inspection revealed that of 6,085 prisoners, 1,200 had no blankets, while being cramped together in buildings made for 4,500. The location of the camp was swampy and poorly drained with "sanitary facilities beyond description."[224]

After improvements, the mortality and morbidity rates improved but remained appallingly high. In the warm temperatures of September 1864, 123 died with 1,357 on the sick list. Winter was approaching in soon to be cold Chicago, where health problems would be exacerbated. And this was in the Union, which had a functioning economy producing adequate food and clothing.[225]

Thwarted at every turn, frustrated no end, and miserable from persistent eye problems, Thompson stubbornly persevered. The welfare of his wife and son behind enemy lines caused constant worry. In letters home he asked about the status of friends in Oxford and must have been distressed over their plight as well as his own. He was well aware that by agreeing to become a spy in far-off Canada, he had brought this on himself. As a consequence his life had changed forever; however, he intended to stay the course until the end.

On October 30th at the same time that the Chicago conspirators were in place, eight Confederate operatives arrived in Manhattan. There they met with New York Copperheads to gain their support. Thompson felt New York was ripe for an uprising based on the anti-war sentiments of the populace, including the mayor, along with the recent bloody draft riots.

The Confederates used letters of introduction from Jacob Thompson to authenticate themselves. Like in Chicago, an informant predictably divulged the plans; hence, the attack was delayed. The conspirators lost their enthusiasm after Lincoln's re-election, but Thompson encouraged them to continue.[226]

After the election, New York returned to normal. The troops added during the scare were returned to Grant. This time, instead of trying to take over the city, the Confederates proposed to burn it, in effect returning fire for fire in the wake of the burning of Atlanta and Sherman's scorched path to the sea. Greek fire was obtained and on November 25th at 8:00 P. M. the arson commenced. Nineteen hotels and several theaters were set on fire. Between the sluggish action of the tainted Greek fire and improper techniques used to set it, all fires were extinguished in a few hours. The city had been saved from burning, but terror had finally come to the North.[227]

The New York plot had been betrayed by Godfrey J. Hyams of Arkansas, who had introduced himself to Thompson on arrival in Toronto, claiming to have escaped from Johnson's Island prison in 1863. Thompson had been warned by Hines not to trust this stranger, but did not heed the admonition. Benefiting from Thompson's gullibility, Hyams brazenly attended the initial planning session for the Lake Michigan-Johnson's Island raid. Godfrey Hyams sold this critical information to Union authorities for $70,000 in gold.

Then he hung around Toronto and Thompson, obtaining the essence of the planned New York action. This agent for hire proceeded to report these details to Union authorities, including the involvement of twenty-five local Copperheads. Hymans was thus able to stymie the initial raid, but not the second. The City had let down its guard after Lincoln's reelection, making the second attempt possible.[228]

Events like this led John B. Castleman to assess Thompson's weaknesses in running the Canadian mission. Jacob Thompson, he wrote, was "unable to realize many men were not as honorable as he." This appraisal is very telling as Castleman dealt with Thompson on a day-to-day basis planning operations. He further concluded that the Confederate operation in Canada would have worked better if Thompson alone represented the Confederacy.

Castleman thought Clay was completely out of sync with Thompson, resulting in a lack of accord. Also, he thought both Clay and Holcombe were totally under the influence of George N. Sanders, whom he deemed wild and reckless.[229] If true, these flaws in the command structure were bound to end in failure.

Captain Hines, the other operative working closely with Thompson, recalled, "… Messrs. Thompson and Clay found it impossible to agree. Mr. Thompson was a man of sterling integrity, of undoubted ability, and large political experience. Unluckily he was inclined to believe much that was told him, trust too many men, doubt too little, and suspect less. He was, of course, often imposed upon and his subordinates were kept in continual apprehension lest he compromise their efforts by indiscreet confidences."[230]

Hines agreed with Castleman's assessment of the relationship between Clay and Thompson: "The differences of opinion which almost immediately developed between the two and the almost absolute impossibility of concession from either—each insisting on his own course—greatly impaired the usefulness of both."[231]

Desperate attempts to somehow alter the course of the war continued unabated. An attack had been carried out in the fall on steamboats moored at St. Louis. Greek fire was again employed and met with the same limited success as at New York. In December 1864, a poorly planned scheme to capture a train transporting Confederate officers, including several generals, from Johnson's Island to Fort Lafayette, New York, was undertaken. This attempt too failed, and the intrepid Beall from the Philo Parsons takeover was himself captured. Thompson had definitely been enthusiastically involved in devising this debacle.[232]

While it seemed that nothing worked as envisioned by Jacob Thompson, some things not involving military action or guerilla tactics did bear fruit. He and Confederate agent Beverly Tucker concocted a plan to have cotton shipped to Canada where it was traded for bacon. This bacon subsequently made its way clandestinely through the lines to help feed hungry Confederate soldiers.[233]

Thompson also brazenly attempted to devalue U. S. currency in a plan favored by Judah P. Benjamin. A former Nashville banker, John Porterfield, was appointed to manage this effort in order to create financial panic in the North. Thompson initially gave him $50,000 to carry out the mission. Porterfield set up shop in New York where he and associates bought gold and transported it to England where it was exchanged for sterling notes. These notes were used to purchase more gold and the process continued.[234]

Naturally, the transactions resulted in a loss of money from operations and shipping costs. A total of $25,000 had been consumed by the time $5,000,000 of gold had been exported. Others had been persuaded to join the scheme with the result that, as Thompson noted in his official report, it was "showing a marked effect." At this point the Federals stepped in and arrested one of the associates for exporting gold. Porterfield escaped back to Canada with the remaining $25,000 where he continued to buy gold through contacts in New York.[235]

Clay and Thompson, the alienated commissioners, actually had a conference in which they agreed to utilize northern newspapers to promote peace. The *New York Daily News* was selected as the instrument. Ex-mayor of New York Fernando Wood and his brother, both noted Copperheads, owned the paper, making it an obvious choice. Jacob Thompson forwarded $25,000 to the paper for editorials promoting peace. The *New York Daily News* followed through with a concerted barrage of articles expressing the need to end the war.[236]

Ongoing Peace
Initiatives

Many prominent northerners met with Jacob Thompson during his time in Canada. He had been chosen to head the Canadian mission in large part because of his contacts resulting from his years in Congress and in the Buchanan administration. Thompson and his associates are known to have had conferences with the following: "former Governor Washington Hunt of New York; Senator Charles R. Buckalew and former Secretary of State Jeremiah Black, both of Pennsylvania; former Governor and Senator John B. Weller of California; Congressman and former Mayor Fernando Wood of New York; Washington McLean, publisher of the *Cincinnati Enquirer*; New York State Democratic Chairman Dean Richmond; and Governor Horatio Seymour of New York."[237]

Surely, there were others lost to history plus the ongoing conversations with the Copperhead leaders involved in the Northwest Conspiracy. Thompson's best weapon was his power of persuasion and he was using every ounce of it to somehow salvage the steadily worsening situation in the South.

These were meetings with Democrat politicians, Confederate and Union, who shared a common past and who still agreed on certain issues. They had formerly been personal and political friends. It was imperative that Thompson keep the names of the conferees secret. He informed Secretary of State Judah P. Benjamin that he employed "extreme caution" with the records of these meetings. He continued, "I have so many papers in my possession which, in the hands of the enemy, would utterly ruin and destroy very many of the prominent men of the North." He was true to his word as he burned his papers before leaving Canada. Benjamin did likewise.[238]

Despite their long record of abject failure and ineptitude, the Copperheads again approached Thompson after the Democratic convention. They wanted money to help elect the peace Democrat candidate, James C. Robinson, governor of Illinois. Thompson, after getting written assurances that, if elected, Robinson would support the Copperhead movement including giving access to the state's arsenals, agreed to furnish gold. Initially, $20,000 was sent, followed by nearly another $30,000 in incremental contributions. He remained an easy touch.[239]

Thompson was still cautiously optimistic that the Copperheads would revolt. Hinds and Castleman warned him against giving more gold, but he stubbornly refused to listen. Again money was essentially wasted. Some of the Copperhead leaders were apparently skimming a large portion of the Confederate gold provided to them.

Thompson continued to believe that the best chance of stopping the war was through the Northwest Conspiracy. That meant dealing with some men of questionable character. Too, he had to feel that the Copperheads were better at politics than their already proven military deficiencies. Plus, he was rather bull-headed.[240]

Jefferson Davis wrote of the Northwest Conspiracy, "The aspect of the Peace party was quite encouraging, and it seemed that the real issue to be decided in the presidential election of that year was the continuance or cessation of the war. A commission of three persons, eminent in position and intelligence, was accordingly appointed to visit Canada, with a view to negotiate with such persons in the North as might be relied on to aid the attainment of peace."[241]

In another communication, Davis noted that Jake Thompson was sent to Canada "mainly to confer with men of the Northwest, and if practicable to bring that section into friendly relations with their natural allies in the agricultural South." With that goal Thompson faithfully tried to comply with the wishes of his commander, although often his blind trust in certain people was misguided.[242]

Another weird plot has been often ascribed to Jacob Thompson. This one involved a purported attempt at bioterrorism by Dr. Luke Blackburn, a Confederate sympathizer originally from Kentucky. At the time of the Civil War, he lived and practiced medicine in Natchez, Mississippi, and had been sent to Canada by Mississippi governor John Pettus to procure essential supplies through the blockade. Dr. Blackburn had a notable reputation as a humanitarian with expertise in treating yellow fever.[243]

He traveled to Bermuda from Canada at the request of the British government to help with a yellow fever outbreak there. While there, he allegedly saved clothing and bedding from yellow fever victims, placing the materials thus obtained in trunks. His plan according to later testimony was to ship the infected clothing to cities along the east coast of the United States, spreading disease and panic.[244]

Double agent Godfrey Hyams, the ubiquitous spy, had been recruited to help him. Hyams testified at the Lincoln assassination trial that he did not participate in the heinous attempt after first agreeing to do so, while indicting Blackburn as the mastermind with Thompson as financier. W. W. Cleary, commission secretary, admitted to knowing Dr. Blackburn and Hyams, and was aware of a possible plot, but swore that Thompson did not fund it. Blackburn had acted on his own, if at all.[245]

Blackburn was tried in Canada for violation of its neutrality laws and acquitted because of lack of evidence that the contaminated trunks were ever in Canada. The United States did not investigate further, electing to forego trying him. It is hard to believe that a person so dedicated to saving lives throughout his career could countenance the killing of innocent people by germ warfare. For instance, in 1867 following a yellow fever outbreak in New Orleans, Dr. Blackburn appealed to President Johnson for permission to travel to New Orleans to assist in the epidemic there. With Reconstruction still in effect, his request was denied, but Blackburn went anyway, helping those in need.

His selfless deeds were repeated many times, often without remuneration and always with significant personal risk, wherever yellow fever appeared. He returned to Kentucky in 1872 and was elected governor in l879. His popularity had soared from his dedication to treating patients in western Kentucky during the terrible epidemic of 1878.

About the bioterrorism claims, Blackburn remained silent, only once declaring the accusations were "too preposterous for intelligent gentlemen to believe."[246] The attempts, if real, were doomed, since yellow fever, a viral disease, is transmitted by mosquitoes. This was unknown at the time. It would have to wait for the trailblazing research of Walter Reed and others in the early 20th century.

Meanwhile, Thompson had been linked to this "plot" through the testimony of Hyams, who claimed Thompson supplied money to Blackburn for his endeavor. While this could be true, Judge Advocate General Joseph Holt was in the process of procuring witnesses to implicate Confederate leaders including Thompson—many of whom were soon found to be perjurers. It is not known if Hyams remained on the Federal payroll when making his claims.

Here we are again faced with the question of innocence or guilt of Thompson. Was there a diabolical plot and if so, did Thompson approve and finance it? There are no clear answers. What is clear, however, is that the mood in the United States immediately after the War was extremely hostile toward Confederate officials with "witnesses" willing to swear to most anything, especially when bribed. For his part, Thompson had become more vindictive as events unfurled, making it more believable that he would stoop to this level. More than 150 years later, we are left peering into the fog of history, guessing at the truth.

END OF MISSION

The Confederate guerilla war continued, creating ever more tension in Canada. Multiple incursions across the border by Confederates in Canada, and the United States' threats of retribution nearly led to war. The release of the St. Albans raiders by Canada was the proverbial straw that nearly broke the camel's back. While cooler heads ultimately prevailed, Canada began efforts to appease the United States by expelling Thompson. After all, he had been embroiled in multiple covert activities, both real and imagined.[247]

For most of his adult life, Jacob Thompson had been accustomed to success. He had been a Cabinet officer, a heavyweight in Congress, advised presidents, picked candidates, become a backroom wheeler dealer, made a killing as a frontier lawyer, performed well in combat. It must have been a bitter pill to swallow when he had to admit his failure as a peacemaker and spy.

Yet, in his letter to Benjamin of December 3rd previously quoted, Thompson soberly acknowledged his lack of success. But he also defended his efforts. He wrote, "I have relaxed no effort to carry out the objects the Government had in sending me here. I had hoped at different times to have accomplished more, but I still do not think my mission has been altogether fruitless. A large sum of money has been expended in fostering and furthering these operations and it now seems to have been to little profit. But in reviewing the past I do not see how it could have been avoided, nor has it been spent altogether in vain. The apprehensions of the enemy have caused him to bring back and keep from the field in front at least 60,000 to watch and browbeat the people at home."[248]

Thompson realized that his leadership of the Canadian mission needed to end. He had been sent to broker a deal for peace using his contacts with northern Democrats. That had failed with the mission now completely a military one; hence, his request to be relieved. Thompson apparently intended to briefly stay in Canada to assist with the legal matters that had arisen from the mission. He again advised the remaining Confederates in Canada to return home, giving travel allowances when asked.[249]

A few days later Brigadier General Edwin Lee, cousin of Robert E. Lee, arrived in Toronto to relieve Thompson. The letter Lee presented Thompson from Benjamin lauded his efforts while continuing with "From reports which reach us from trustworthy sources, we are satisfied that so close espionage is kept upon you that your services have been deprived of value which is attached to your further residence in Canada. The President thinks, therefore, that as soon as the gentleman arrives who bears this letter…that you transfer to him as quietly as possible all of the information that you have obtained and the release of funds in your hands and then return to the Confederacy."[250]

In retrospect, perhaps it had not been such a good idea to make a well-known and easily recognizable congressman a spy.

USING HIS
LEGAL EXPERTISE

The abrupt dismissal surprised Thompson as he believed he had an important role in defending those Confederates jailed in Canada and the United States. Therefore, he briefed Lee but did not leave. Thompson's version was that authorities in Richmond asked him to assist in aiding the many Confederate prisoners awaiting trial as spies.[251] Given Thompson's propensity to strictly follow orders, his recollection is certainly believable.

Thompson proceeded to energetically defend those troubled Confederates with all means at his disposal. He gave money for legal expenses of the St. Albans raiders even though he had not approved of their incursion. Clay and Holcombe had both left Canada by this time, so Thompson felt it his duty to assist in the defense of the raiders. To prove these men were soldiers rather than spies, he requested their commissions from Jefferson Davis.

The extradition trial commenced with the defense claiming the raiders were Confederate soldiers and had not violated Canadian laws. Thompson attended at least one of lengthy hearings, oddly with George Sanders. Eventually, the Canadian judge ruled in favor of the raiders.[252]

An incensed U. S. Consul John Potter wrote to Secretary of State Seward that the verdict "was cheered most vociferously both in the courtroom and in the street…. The decision removes all barriers to similar outrages and their repetition is now highly probable." The prisoners were then promptly rearrested and charged with breaching the new Canadian Neutrality Act. Before they could be tried under Canadian law, the war ended, and they were released.[253]

In an attempt to save the brave John Beall from hanging, Thompson wrote Confederate Secretary of the Navy Stephen Mallory, who duly forwarded Beall's commission along with an affidavit reading "that Jefferson Davis had authorized everything that Thompson and his men had done." Beall had in all probability followed orders and certainly was an intrepid Confederate officer; however, the effort was to no avail. He was hanged as a spy.[254]

After the confrontation with the United States, Canadian authorities added their investigators to the large contingent of U. S. agents trying to suppress Confederate activity across the border. In early January, 1865, Lieutenant Sam B. Davis, a Confederate courier was given messages from Thompson to deliver to Richmond. In spite of extra care and stealth, Davis was apprehended in Newark, Ohio, with the dispatches hidden in the lining of his clothing. He was rapidly convicted of treason and sentenced to hang.[255]

Thompson quickly wrote to Abraham Lincoln, his old colleague from the House of Representatives. He explained that Lieutenant Davis was indeed a Confederate officer, not a spy, and was carrying messages at Thompson's request about the looming trial of another officer. The missive to Lincoln concluded, "You have a right to retain him as a prisoner of war, but I declare on my honor he is not a spy." Lieutenant Davis was subsequently released on order of President Lincoln.[256]

Yet another Confederate on trial received assistance from Thompson. Acting Master Bennett Burley had been found guilty of piracy in a Canadian court for his part in the Philo Parsons incident. The decision to extradite him to the United States was appealed. Thompson furiously fired off a letter to James Mason, Confederate minister to the United Kingdom. He wrote, "I think you will agree with me that in this case not only is a great outrage about to be perpetrated on a citizen, but a great wrong is to be done and an insult offered to the Confederate States." Thompson asked Mason to pressure British authorities to have Burley released.[257]

Jefferson Davis also became involved in this case after Thompson wrote him also seeking help. In support of Burley, Davis opined that the Michigan-Philo Parsons prisoner rescue attempt "was a belligerent expedition ordered and undertaken under the authority of the Confederate States of America and that the Government of the Confederate States of America assumes the responsibility for answering for the acts and conduct of any of its officers engaged in said expedition, and especially of the said Bennett G. Burley, an Acting Master of the Confederate States Navy."[258] He further echoed Thompson's statement that the participants had been ordered to maintain the neutrality of Canada, including obeisance to their laws.

An order came from London on February tenth to free Burley. The persistence of Thompson had struck a chord somewhere. The big Scot, appropriately named Burley, later returned to the British Isles where he became a Member of Parliament.[259]

Thompson had become more bellicose over time as he realized the South was being destroyed and that peace efforts were futile. He even concocted a foolhardy scheme for military operations that he sent to the War Department. His proposal was so far-fetched that it could not possibly succeed. The pressures of being an unproductive commissioner seemed to have caused the once pragmatic Thompson to become irrational.

With the Confederacy collapsing, Thompson devised his final unrealistic plan. He would take the remaining gold at his disposal to purchase a schooner. The idea of utilizing a ship in some fashion apparently resonated with him. After outfitting, the ship would then transport Confederates in Canada to the Rio Grande.[260]

Agents of the Sons of Liberty in Portland, Maine, bought the schooner Canadian Eagle for Thompson, and a captain was hired. The Canadian Eagle was taken to St. Johns, New Brunswick to be prepared for its mission. As had become the norm, provost marshals in Portland found out about the plan and alerted Canadian authorities. The Sons of Liberty agents were apprehended and acknowledged that the ship was "to help the Rebels in Canada to escape."[261]

The U. S. War Department issued an urgent alert to search for the schooner and to "arrest all the Rebels aboard." Thompson's description was attached to the bulletin: "His eyelids are greatly inflamed, so that his eyes are often nearly closed."[262] This is a recurring reference to his eye condition while in Canada. He was noted in meetings as constantly dabbing his "sore eyes" which undoubtedly caused him much misery. With the Union navy patrolling the Maine coast looking for it, the Canadian Eagle never left port.[263]

Union General A.J. "Whiskey" Smith, who ordered
Oxford burned, including the home of
Jacob and Kate Thompson.

THE HARD HAND OF WAR

As these events were unfolding in Canada, Kate Thompson was intimately involved in a harrowing war of her own. The bold, intimidating Confederate General Nathan Bedford Forrest attempted to both control north Mississippi and strike Sherman's supply lines as the Union army advanced inexorably toward Atlanta. With "that devil Forrest" having a real and psychological impact, General William Tecumseh Sherman ordered General A. J. Smith out of Memphis to destroy his nemesis.

Smith cautiously approached Forrest's headquarters in Oxford. The Confederates fiercely resisted but ended up retreating through Oxford, similar to what had happened two years prior. On August 9, 1864, Union soldiers again occupied Oxford. They wasted little time in "robbing and plundering indiscriminately men, women, children, and negroes."[264] The Thompson home was looted anew with furniture ruined and carted away. Forrest returned with reinforcements and Smith retreated north to Abbeville, leaving Oxford temporarily to the Confederates.

After daily skirmishes for two weeks, the Yankees again advanced on Oxford from nearby Abbeville with an overwhelming force. Meanwhile, Forrest had employed one of his favorite tactics—he divided his army. Of course, this made Oxford vulnerable and it was retaken on August 22st. Then, Forrest led a daring night raid on Memphis, the hub of Union activities. Forrest even famously rode his horse into the lobby of the Gayoso Hotel, nearly capturing a sleeping Union general.

Within a couple of hours of re-entering Oxford, Smith received orders from Memphis commanding his return. Forrest and his men had destroyed a significant part of the vast Memphis supply depot. It was apparently at this point that General Smith, on learning of the situation in Memphis, lost his temper and decided to burn the Square at Oxford along with the homes of leading citizens.

He had to be embarrassed at letting Forrest outwit him once again, which probably led to the egregious and rash decision to torch the town, earning him the undying contempt of local residents. For these deprecations he forever earned the sobriquet of "Whiskey" Smith. Whether he was drunk or not is open to speculation, but he was definitely enraged.

The Thompson home was once more targeted, this time by order of General Smith. A detail headed by Captains Burns and Hough was sent to burn two properties, Thompson's Home Place and the buildings of the University of Mississippi a short distance away.[265]

At Burns' order, Kate Thompson was forced from her home yet again. But Sally, her daughter-in-law, presented a sticky problem. She had given birth, remained weak and was still confined to her bed. Even soldiers turned hard and bitter by years of war could not bring themselves to make this bedridden woman march herself outside. Instead, they picked up the bed with Sally still in it and carried it outside. They would show not even this modicum of mercy to the house.

As the Thompson ladies and a few slaves watched helplessly, soldiers torched the stately home, an unmistakable message to the hated Jacob Thompson. To add insult, a Yankee soldier grabbed two treasured paintings that Kate had evacuated from the house. He vengefully tossed them into the conflagration. One of the paintings was a portrait of her only child Macon that had been completed shortly before his facial disfigurement. The Union soldiers cheered wildly as the house was consumed by fire.[266]

In his memoir, Captain Burns confessed more than a little regret at this flagrant act of spite. "It was the hardest fighting against nature I had to do during the war," he acknowledged.

Writing home to Iowa, a Union soldier revealed what the torching detail felt about Jacob Thompson, their real target: "The splendid mansion of Jacob Thompson, rebel Secretary of the Interior, with its gorgeous furniture, went up in crackling flames, a costly burnt offering to the 'Moloch of treason.'"[267]

After completing the first part of their orders, the troop rode to the nearby campus of the University of Mississippi. Captain Burns and Captain Hough took one look at the tree-shrouded campus and its graceful buildings and summarily decided to disobey their orders. They rationalized that it was just too beautiful to burn and besides, the buildings were of no real strategic importance to the Confederates.[268]

Other Oxford locations did not fare as well. Houses of prominent citizens were ransacked and burned including the home of James Brown, where Grant had established his headquarters in 1862. The greatest destruction occurred on the Oxford Square, which was entirely consumed by fire. The courthouse, Masonic lodge, two large hotels, and at least 34 businesses all went up in smoke. Oxford was left in ruins. *The Chicago Times* correspondent wrote of the scene: "Where once stood a handsome little country town now only remained the blackened skeletons of the houses, and smouldering ruins."[269]

Howard T. Dimick in his "Motives for the Burning of Oxford, Mississippi," concluded that it was due to the worst instincts of warfare. "There was apparently no need for Federal occupation of the town on that day except for the premeditated purpose of burning it," he wrote. "The burning of Oxford resulted from the cumulative hatred and frustration caused by the alleged Fort Pillow massacre and the failure of the Federal expeditions to eliminate Forrest as a military factor in Mississippi and Tennessee. It is probable that hatred of Jacob Thompson acted as an additional motive."[270]

Jacob and Kate had extreme difficulty communicating long distance through enemy lines; however, in a November 13th letter to Kate, he confirmed that eventually he learned of the burning by reading "Yankee newspapers."[271] Kate moved into the home of her mother at Woodson Ridge eight miles from Oxford. It was a sad, grim time for the former social star of Washington. In fact, Dorothy Oldham in her 1930 Masters thesis stated that Kate considered Jacob dead at some point since she had not received any message from him.[272]

Kate Thompson. Her expression reflects
personal hardship and grief

KATE'S ESCAPE THROUGH ENEMY LINES

While Kate struggled with the loss of her home, Jacob had been labeled the "espionage mastermind" by the Canadian government and it was in the process of expelling him.[273] He truly had overstayed his welcome. With north Mississippi the scene of almost constant fighting and Union occupation since his departure for Canada, Jacob Thompson had been unable to reliably contact his wife. Now it became imperative.

Out of desperation, Thompson selected Mrs. Loring, a French-Canadian, to travel from Montreal to Oxford and bring back Kate. She was promised $5,000 for completion of this most trying mission. Both of the journeys, to and fro, had to go through enemy territory—her one advantage was her sex. Her disadvantage—and it was a huge one—was her connection to Jacob Thompson, who could scarcely breathe without being observed by spies. Before she could even start the arduous trip, the Union consul was tipped off that she was in the employ of the now infamous Jacob Thompson, hired to escort his wife to a reunion with him in Canada.[274]

Thus begins the fantastical story recounted by Dorothy Oldham and based upon a Montreal newspaper's published interview with the intrepid Mrs. Loring. After being warned that her initial plans had been uncovered, Mrs. Loring took another route, traveling from Montreal to Cairo, Illinois. She used the guise of a northern lady in search of an aunt in Mississippi as she boarded a steamboat for Memphis. From there she made her way to Panola County, Mississippi, adjacent to Lafayette County, where she was temporarily stranded.[275]

The bold Mrs. Loring next approached Union officials, requesting safe transportation to Oxford, eventually paying $100.00 for a passport, which amounted to a blatant inducement. When she finally reached Oxford, Mrs. Loring could not locate Kate, who unbeknownst to her, was still residing at her mother's country home on Woodson Ridge. After being informed that an emissary from Jacob sought her, Kate hurried to town. Mrs. Loring then delivered Jacob's message and papers that she had secretly brought through Union lines.[276]

After disposing of the papers, the ladies prepared for the return journey. Kate had been such a highly visible figure before the war that she was forced to disguise herself. Following Jacob's instructions, Kate carefully concealed a bank note in her corset. This note, payable in pounds, was reportedly for a large sum realized from cotton sold in Liverpool. They found it necessary to bribe Union officials more than once on the seventy-five mile trip from Oxford to Memphis. The next leg was to Cairo by steamboat. Great care was taken to embark and disembark at night to avoid detection.[277]

Proceeding northward from Cairo, the number of inspections increased and so did the scrutiny. The ladies were searched seemingly at every turn. Enduring these nerve-racking and demeaning experiences, Mrs. Loring and Mrs. Thompson made it safely to Canada. Their arrival, it turned out, came at an especially turbulent time—occurring nearly simultaneously with the surrender of General Lee, the assassination of President Lincoln, and the frenzied search for the supposed perpetrators of the assassination, which included Jacob Thompson.[278]

ASSASSINATION

The precise chronological sequence of events becomes somewhat murky at this point. Robert E. Lee surrendered his army at Appomattox on April 9, 1865, followed by Lincoln's assassination on April 14th. On that day, Lincoln held his final cabinet meeting and later after work Charles A. Dana, Assistant Secretary of War and head of intelligence, found the President still at his office. Dana informed Lincoln that Jacob Thompson was due to arrive in Portland, Maine, shortly to make passage to England. Secretary of War Edwin Stanton had told Dana to have Thompson arrested, then reconsidered and asked Dana to get Lincoln's approval.[279]

The President replied, "Well, no, I rather think not. When you have an elephant by the hind leg, and he's trying to run away, it's best to let him run." Thompson would have made his escape compliments of the President, but that evening John Wilkes Booth changed it all. Abraham Lincoln had been shot while attending a play and was soon to die.[280]

In the wee hours of April 15th, Stanton rescinded Lincoln's order allowing Jacob Thompson's passage to Europe. An all points bulletin was quickly issued for Thompson's arrest. Stanton had diligently been collecting information on him since early in the war, and he now believed that Confederate leaders, including Thompson, had been involved in a plot to kill Lincoln.[281]

The assassination and subsequent events changed Thompson's plans. He dared not enter the United States. Despite suspicion that he had been involved, he reportedly was outraged and stunned at the assassination.[282]

A week later, while Booth and some associates were still being pursued, Thompson became a hunted man with a price on his head. His old adversary, now Judge Advocate General Joseph Holt, issued a report to Secretary of War Edwin Stanton, also an adversary from Buchanan administration days, officially naming Thompson as a conspirator in the assassination of Abraham Lincoln.

Impetuously, Thompson's initial reaction was to go to Washington in an attempt to clear his name. Friends talked him out of this precipitate undertaking, arguing that with the ugly mood in the Capital, he was doomed to fail. At the very least he would be risking arrest. At the worst, he might face execution for plotting to kill the President. Eventually realizing his grave predicament, he went into hiding in Canada to avoid capture by bounty hunters.[283]

As these events transpired, Kate Thompson and her trusty guide Mrs. Loring had crossed the border into Canada. They joined Jacob in Windsor. He had arrived from Montreal in the company of a quasi-friend, a former blockade-runner named Trufent. Once again, Jacob Thompson had trusted the wrong man.

Trufent secretly hoped to obtain the reward money for Thompson's arrest. He approached Mrs. Loring with a plan for her to detain the Thompsons long enough to allow Federal detectives time to capture Jacob. For doing this, Trufent promised to split the bounty money with her. Mrs. Loring agreed to help, becoming his supposed ally.[284]

At the first opportunity, she informed Jacob of the plot. The grateful Thompsons were able to avoid Trufent, making it to Halifax, Nova Scotia. Though barely ahead of the agents summoned by Trufent, the Thompsons boarded the steamship Asia bound for England.[285] It had been another nerve-racking adventure for a man who sometimes tended to trust too much.

By any realistic analysis of his work in Canada, he had failed to achieve the results the Confederacy had hoped for. Probably no one in his position could have altered the outcome of the war, but his sheer lack of spying skills compromised many operations. That coupled with the ever-increasing counter-espionage of the Federals assured repeated failure. Thompson also was saddled with the irritable and easily influenced Clay, an even worse choice than he was. The end result was predictable.

Certainly, Thompson reflected on his time in Canada, trying to rationalize his role in Confederate defeat. Being both pragmatic and proud, he had to find his place in a world turned upside down. He now knew the sad fate of his home and the town he had done so much to organize and promote. His letters reveal his deeply felt compassion for many friends now rendered destitute. Too, he had to ponder the circumstances of his only son Macon plus the rest of his family in the devastated war zone.

Finances apparently were the least of his immediate worries. While obviously concerned with the vast land holdings he had transferred to Macon before departing for Canada, he had other resources. In addition to the note brought from Oxford by Kate, he had deposits in Liverpool and London. Thompson had been able to amass considerable wealth from agriculture and from the generous dowry received at marriage. He probably began the transfer of assets to England after the Panic of 1857, continuing until the advent of war.[286]

Conspiracy To Convict

Within a week of the assassination Holt "found what he expected to find" without proper vetting of informers or thorough investigation. On April 24th, Stanton publically announced, "This Department has information that the President's murder was organized in Canada and approved at Richmond." The names of the conspirators per Holt were Jefferson Davis, Jacob Thompson, Clement C. Clay, Beverly Tucker, George Sanders, and William C. Cleary. All except Jefferson Davis were part of the Confederate Canadian mission.[287]

The proclamation that President Andrew Johnson signed and submitted on May 2nd read:

"Whereas it appears from evidence in the Bureau of Military Justice that the atrocious murder of the late President, Abraham Lincoln, and the attempted assassination of the Hon. William H. Seward, Secretary of State, were incited, concerted, and procured by and between Jefferson Davis, late of Richmond, Va., and Jacob Thompson, Clement C. Clay, Beverley Tucker, George N. Sanders, William C. Cleary, and other rebels and traitors against the Government of the United States harbored in Canada:

"Now, therefore, to the end that justice may be done, I, Andrew Johnson, President of the United States, do offer and promise for the arrest of said persons, or either of them, within the limits of the United States, so that they can be brought to trial, the following rewards." The reward for Jefferson Davis was $100,000 and $25,000 each for Jacob Thompson and the others except $10,000 for William C. Cleary.[288]

The *New York Times* lengthy headline of May 4, 1865, screamed: "THE ASSASSINS; IMPORTANT PROCLAMATION BY PRESIDENT JOHNSON. MR. LINCOLN'S MURDER PLANNED BY LEADING

TRAITORS. MOST OF THESE TRAITORS ARE HARBORED IN CANADA. JEFFERSON DAVIS IS THE HEAD OF THE ASSASSINS. HE IS AIDED BY JACOB THOMPSON, CLEMENT C. CLAY, BEVERLEY TUCKER, AND GEORGE N. SANDERS."[289]

Thaddeus Stevens, a leader of the Radical Republicans and a fierce opponent of slavery and the South, on learning of the accusation of high Confederate officials exclaimed: "They are public enemies and I would treat the South as a conquered country and settle it politically upon the policy best suited for ourselves. But I know these men, sir. They are gentlemen, and incapable of being of being assassins."[290]

Jacob Thompson angrily responded to the President's proclamation. The sensitive and ever combative Thompson was not about to acquiesce in silence. He wrote, "I aver upon honor that I have never known, or conversed, or held communication, either directly or indirectly with Booth… or with any of his associates, so far as I have seen them named. I knew nothing of their plans. I defy the evidence in the Bureau of Military Justice…" Referencing the calling card Booth had left for Andrew Johnson at the Kirkwood House, Thompson continued, "I know there is not half the ground to suspect me than there is to suspect President Johnson himself."[291]

In an attempt to vent his anger and frustration, Jacob wrote Jeremiah Black from Halifax, Nova Scotia, on July 6, 1865, stating, "the vindictiveness of our old colleagues at Washington knows no bounds. Holt & Stanton knew as well as I did that to connect my name with the assassination of Lincoln was an outrage."[292] His defiant attitude is akin to his reaction to allegations of personal fraud in the Indian Trust Fund case.

There was absolutely no doubt that Booth killed Abraham Lincoln. By the time of the proclamation Booth was dead and buried. Was there a grand conspiracy as imagined and promoted by the mean and vindictive Joseph Holt, the once congenial southern Democrat? Did Confederate officials conspire with Booth to kill Lincoln? Holt's pointing the finger at Jacob Thompson was no big surprise. They had been antagonists in the Buchanan administration, and Holt was now in a position to exact his revenge.

A contemporary of Holt described him: "[He] was the meanest man of his time. He was both unscrupulous and ambitious and the smartest man I ever knew." Joseph Holt with the backing of the powerful Federal government had the will and the means to ruin Thompson. Undoubtedly, that was his intention.[293]

The initial evidence against Thompson was a receipt for a currency exchange found among Booth's possessions issued by the Ontario Bank of Montreal where Thompson maintained an account of Confederate funds.[294] Later evidence would show that Booth stayed at St. Lawrence Hall in Montreal on October 18, 1864. This was then the base of operations of Jake Thompson and other Confederates in Canada. Did Booth converse with Thompson or others about his cockamamie plan to capture Lincoln and take him to Richmond? Did they talk about an assassination plot?

While certainly feasible, no proof exists that Booth sought approval and support from Thompson for his dark intentions. Thompson later vehemently disavowed any connection with Booth, and no reliable evidence has been found to refute his word. Holt and his cohorts plus numerous investigators since have unsuccessfully attempted to link the two.

Booth's eight co-conspirators were tried in a military court, zealously presided over by Holt with assistance from Special Judge Advocate Colonel Henry Burnett and Special Judge Advocate John A. Bingham. The trial began in haste even while some of the defendants were still attempting to find legal counsel. Making it even more difficult for the defense attorneys, Holt dispensed with an opening statement, thus keeping them in the dark. This could not happen in a civilian court but with Holt and a military trial, it did. Other cohorts of Booth were allowed to go free as Holt pursued his obsession of indicting Confederate officials including Thompson.[295]

On the stand George Atzerodt, one of the accused, lied about aspects of the murder conspiracy but did not implicate Jefferson Davis or Jacob Thompson, even though the prosecution tried to elicit a connection to them. He stated that he "knew nothing at all" of a Confederate conspiracy.

Judge Advocate Bingham, prosecuting at the trial, hammered the grand conspiracy theory so vigorously that all eight defendants were found guilty instead of three or four being acquitted as widely predicted. He discounted the kidnap plot and declared that the intent was murder from the outset.[296] Reflecting the blood lust rampant in the North following a long and exhausting conflict, Bingham in his closing remarks boldly proclaimed, "Jefferson Davis is as clearly proven guilty of this conspiracy as John Wilkes Booth." By extension the guilt applied to Jacob Thompson and the other Canadian operatives.[297]

Bingham did appear to be on firm ground in his accusations as witness after witness implicated the accused Confederate officials including Jacob Thompson. The trial began with the jury hearing secret testimony at Holt's orders. All involved were also sworn to secrecy. The prosecution initially tried to prove that the Confederate government engaged in a pattern of "uncivilized warfare" that ultimately ended with the Lincoln assassination. Several incidents presented as proof had been undertaken with Thompson's approval. According to Michael Kauffman in his splendid book *American Brutus*, "To Joseph Holt, it was one enormous plot."[298]

Richard Montgomery, a Union spy, testified early in the trial that he knew most of the Confederate leaders in Canada. He declared that Thompson informed him in January 1865 of a plot to kill Union leaders. Montgomery said that while Thompson supported the plan, he awaited approval from Richmond before taking action. Montgomery further swore that Thompson met with Booth in Montreal and that after the assassination Thompson was crestfallen that Seward and Andrew Johnson had survived.[299]

Later in the trial, Montgomery was recalled to testify specifically about Thompson. He stated that Thompson either directed or knew of all Canadian generated terrorist activities, including the St. Albans raid and the New York arson. The testimony continued with a recounting of Thompson's alleged support of the effort to spread yellow fever to the North via infected clothing. He even tied Thompson to a plan to poison New York City's drinking water.[300] The prosecution was doing its best to demonize Thompson.

The next day General Grant was called to testify specifically about Jacob Thompson's role in the government of the Confederacy. Holt made clear his overarching intent to convict Thompson, even though he was not on trial and not in the country. Grant's testimony rehashed his encounters with Thompson, but did nothing to implicate him in the Lincoln assassination.

Another witness, Dr. James B. Merritt, part of a large contingent of southerners then in Canada, testified that Lincoln's assassination was a popular topic of conversation among Confederates in Canada. He stated he heard George N. Sanders talk about Booth and George Surratt, another alleged conspirator, having approval from Jefferson Davis to kill Lincoln. Merritt also testified that he heard Clay contend, "he thought the ends justified the means." [301]

After repeated complaints by defense lawyers to President Johnson, General Grant, and General Comstock, a member of the military commission, the secrecy ceased. The badgering of witnesses and the attempt to blend Booth's actions with Confederate "atrocities" in order to obtain the desired result would now be exposed to the northern public. Holt's plan was to gain convictions by conflating the two different subjects, thus provoking the commission into a verdict without adequate proof of individual guilt. [302]

The trial progressed in a deliberate manner until some two weeks in when Holt's "best" witness," Sandford Conover, testified. In 1864 he had been a reporter for the *New York Tribune*, filing anonymous articles from the South on supposed conspiracies against Lincoln. Assuming the alias of James Watson Wallace, he allegedly traveled to Montreal in October 1864, where he was able to meet various Confederate officials. Conover stated that while there he was told of plots to terrorize the North. He further testified that Jacob Thompson actually recruited him to participate in a plan under Booth's lead to kill Lincoln and other prominent officials. [303]

Conover alleged that sometime after April 6, 1865, Thompson received approval from Richmond for the scheme to kill Lincoln. Upon reading the letter delivered by courier, Thompson purportedly said, "This makes the thing all right." Then, according to Conover, after Lee's surrender with accompanying wild rejoicing in the North, William C. Cleary told Jacob Thompson that the "rebels would put the laugh on the other side of their mouth in a day or two." With that damning testimony, Sandford Conover had methodically implicated Thompson, Cleary, Davis, and Booth. He had made the government's case, placing Thompson at the center of a far-reaching plot to kill Lincoln and fellow Washington politicians.[304]

But Sandford Conover was an inveterate liar. So were Montgomery and Merritt. Even while the trial droned on, the *Montreal Evening Telegraph* broke the story that a local man claimed to be the real Sandford Conover. The star witness of the trial was impersonating him. This accusation proved to be true—the witness was in actuality named Charles Durham. An affidavit was sent from the paper to the court and placed in the record. Amazingly, the testimony of Conover/Durham was allowed to stand.[305]

Soon after the once secret proceedings of the trial became available, Canadian newspapers reported that the sum total of their testimony had been "cooked to order." Dr. Merritt was not a physician and his testimony totally fabricated. Conover/Dunham had several aliases and once had even been employed as a Confederate spy. Montgomery was also discredited over stating that he had talked with Thompson in Montreal after Thompson had previously vacated the city, making it impossible All this had been documented and widely published before the end of the trial.[306]

Following the exposure of Conover, Montgomery, and Merritt by the Canadian press as perjurers and imposters, newspapers in the United States reprinted the articles. The final blow for Conover was a letter he sent to Thompson, which was published in several papers. Remember, he had testified that he had become a friend and associate of Thompson in 1864. Conover began his letter, sent to Thompson on March 20, 1865, with "Although I have not had the pleasure of your acquaintance…" This letter in his own hand refuted the entire scenario since he could not have known Thompson in the fall of 1864 and winter of 1865.[307] The trial as regards Jefferson Davis and the Canadian operatives had almost become a joke.

The verdict was a foregone conclusion. In his closing statement, lead prosecution attorney John Bingham concisely summed up his position: "Surely no word further need be spoken to show that John Wilkes Booth was in this conspiracy; that John Surratt was in this conspiracy; and that Jefferson Davis and his several agents named, in Canada, were in this conspiracy."[308]

Four of the accused conspirators actually on trial were given the death sentence including the first female to be hanged in the United States. Three others were sentenced to life at hard labor. By this time Jefferson Davis and Clement Clay both languished in prison under dreadful conditions. Jacob Thompson had the good fortune to have escaped to Europe, hopefully beyond the reach of Holt and Stanton.

After the trial as appeals were being heard, questions arose about witnesses and verdicts. Joseph Holt amazingly still stubbornly pursued his theory of the grand conspiracy, referencing Conover/Durham (already proven to be a total fraud) and several other witnesses. When challenged by the House of Representatives Judiciary Committee investigating the assassination, Conover found eight new "unimpeachable" witnesses who gave depositions. Under examination by the Committee, one frankly admitted under oath that the entire case against Jefferson Davis and the Canadian operatives was contrived. Conover had invented the whole story, subsequently coaching the other witnesses as to their testimony.[309]

The witnesses had been bribed by Conover to tell the carefully rehearsed tales that Holt and Stanton expected and needed them to tell. All eight of the new witnesses recruited by Conover were revealed to be perjurers. As this was unfolding, Conover quietly disappeared.

Stanton and President Johnson now realized that convictions of those accused in the May 2nd proclamation were unlikely. Only Judge Advocate General Holt persisted for debatable reasons. In November 1866 Conover was tracked down and put on trial for perjury before the Committee along with charges of coaching and paying witnesses. He was sentenced to ten years in prison for his part in this reprehensible conspiracy to convict.[310]

On November 24, 1865, Stanton cancelled the rewards for the capture of those named in the May 2nd edict still at large. This included Jacob Thompson. The wish of Secretary Stanton was that these fugitives not be apprehended and returned for trial. Dealing with the incarcerated Davis and Clay was quite enough of a headache. This did not mean that Thompson was free to come home—the reward was simply rescinded.[311]

Once more Jacob Thompson had been accused. Likewise, the evidence against him was not sufficient to pronounce him guilty; however, he was found guilty in the world of northern popular opinion as the northern press berated him as a traitor and terrorist in addition to being complicit in the Lincoln assassination. There was no doubt that he had become *persona non grata* in the United States.

Accusations Of Theft

When the Thompsons arrived in Europe, they soon made their way to Paris where they established themselves at the new, imposing Grand Hotel, conveniently located next to the glamorous opera house and merely a brisk walk from the world-famous Louvre. Their lifestyle in Europe for the next three years would contribute to the never-ending accusations that he had embezzled the remaining Confederate funds in Canada. No doubt Thompson had access to the funds, and, just as surely, his instructions from Davis required no accounting of expenditures. As he feared before accepting the mission to Canada, he was vulnerable to charges of fiscal wrongdoing.

The insinuations followed Thompson to Europe, but he was not alone. Disgruntled ex-Confederates also accused Judah P. Benjamin and Jefferson Davis of embezzlement. The evidence against Jacob Thompson ultimately proved stronger than that against the others. It didn't help that Thompson had already been stigmatized by the Indian Trust Fund scandal, leaving him wide open to this latest charge. Espionage itself naturally spawns suspicion, especially on behalf of a lost cause. This accusation, while plausible, remains questionable.[312]

In the summer of 1865, John Breckinridge, former Vice President of the United States and former Confederate general and secretary of war, reached London after a harrowing trip. A compatriot on part of this journey was Captain John Taylor Wood, the famed commander of the privateer Tallahassee. Wood traveled to Cuba where he separated from Breckinridge; hence, he went to Montreal. While there, at the request of Breckinridge, he sent a report on conditions in Canada.[313]

As part of the report he wrote, "I have met but few persons, Messrs. (Beverly) Tucker and (George N.) Sanders once; they complained bitterly of Mr. Thompson's conduct, of course, of which I know nothing. They say he has gone to Europe with $300,000." In fairness, this is the same wily George N. Sanders who was disparaged by Thompson and his primary operatives, Hines and Castleman. Breckinridge thought it prudent to investigate this serious charge.[314]

John Breckinridge met with little success in his attempt to establish if Thompson had retained part of the funds remaining in his control at the end of the War. The two met in Paris where Breckinridge gingerly inquired about missing money. Thompson was somewhat evasive according to Breckinridge, but they remained friends after the interrogation.

This delicate issue was put on hold until the arrival in London of former Secretary of State Judah P. Benjamin, who had made a nearly miraculous escape from pursuing Federal authorities. Soon after Benjamin was settled, Breckinridge conferred with him, explaining his suspicions of Thompson being less than forthcoming about the remaining Canadian funds. Benjamin assured Breckinridge that he would follow up.[315]

Benjamin subsequently explored the issue with Thompson, requesting him to "make up your account with the department [of state,] so that I may make use of our draft for £25,000 upon Fraser, Trenholm, & Company."[316] In his conversation Benjamin acknowledged the receipt of £103,000 from Thompson in March, 1865 as instructed. Jacob Thompson then grudgingly agreed to remit £12,000 to Fraser, Trenholm & Company as partial payment for an outstanding debt of the Confederacy. For so doing, Benjamin wrote him a receipt, "The payment now made is in full of all claims of the Confederate Government on account of the undersigned as secretary of state of said government against the said Jacob Thompson for money deposited in his hands as agent of said government."[317]

This issue seemed to have been put to rest, but as with so many things involving Jacob Thompson, that was not the case. On November 30, 1865, Benjamin wrote to Breckinridge and asserted Thompson had owed the defunct Confederate government £35,000. Benjamin further related that in the testy confrontation Thompson claimed he was entitled to the money he retained in compensation for his "burnt cotton."[318]

In addition, Thompson told Benjamin that he had set aside funds for the defense of the incarcerated Jefferson Davis. In July 1865 he indeed contacted Jeremiah Black, former secretary of state, to help Davis with his legal issues and promised to compensate him. As Benjamin, Breckinridge, and Thompson all knew, there was no way to pursue collection of any more money held by Thompson.

Any attempt to do so would only bring embarrassment to the former Confederacy. What's more, any funds obtained risked confiscation by the victorious United States government. Union agents were in Europe and elsewhere pursuing the presumed money trail and sending wildly differing reports to Washington. Their efforts ended in futility. If Jake Thompson absconded with a large sum, he hid it very well.

Breckinridge continued his suspicion and distrust of Thompson, penning in his diary, "It seems Thompson compromised with him [Benjamin] retaining a large sum." Benjamin had concluded his letter to Breckinridge by saying, "This is a most repulsive subject, and I would not have this letter communicated to any one in the world, except Mr. Davis, if he succeed in escaping from his present unfortunate condition."[319]

Jefferson Davis was released from prison on bail after two years, making six trips to London after the war. On each occasion he consulted and socialized with Judah P. Benjamin. They also maintained a trans-Atlantic correspondence by mail.[320]

Did Benjamin fail to tell Jefferson Davis of Thompson's perceived misappropriation and duplicity? Did Breckinridge? Either Davis was not apprised or did not care or did not believe the charges as he was later a frequent guest of the Thompsons in Memphis. In fact, he first met Jacob postwar in Canada, soon after his release from prison. Thompson, true to his word, was a benefactor of the financially struggling former president.[321] Jefferson Davis had a tendency to tenaciously stand by his friends; however, he was a stickler for absolute honesty.

The correspondence between Breckinridge, Benjamin, and other ex-Confederates came to light when published in *Civil War Times Illustrated* in its May 1970 edition. William C. Davis, the esteemed and prolific southern author, uncovered these letters while researching his biography of John C. Breckinridge. The Breckinridge family found the letters in an attic and gave Davis access. These revealing and potentially incriminating communications along with Breckinridge's diary provided the basis for his extremely critical article titled "The Conduct of Mr. Thompson."[322]

Of course, this was published nearly a century after the death of Thompson. One can easily conjure up images of Jacob rising to his own defense, but that was not to be. Perhaps his actions in this regard *were* indefensible. By his admission, he held back funds for his cotton being burned and for the legal defense of the incarcerated Jefferson Davis. However, Thompson may have believed that he was due that money as much as anyone else since the Confederate government ceased to exist.

Whatever his reasoning, the charges and insinuations that he retained an enormous sum are more speculative. The allegations are impossible to prove. An accurate accounting of the funds received and spent by the Canadian mission is unrecoverable. [323] The records maintained by Jacob Thompson were inadequate for proper auditing.

Much of the money in question was distributed to individuals involved in the Northwest Conspiracy and to murky clandestine operations still directed by him months after he had been ostensibly recalled. It is, of course, possible that complete records of these expenditures would have potentially exposed those involved, including Thompson, to trial as war criminals. If detailed accounting existed, Thompson likely destroyed it.

Thompson's confidante and dependable agent, Captain John B. Castleman, came to be in possession of the minute book of the Canadian mission. Castleman wrote, "These records, accounts, and letters came to me in chief part from and because of my intimacy with Jacob Thompson, a lovable man, to whom I was personally greatly devoted, and with whom I lived, studied and traveled for a time abroad, and in some part from Mr. Cleary, secretary to the Confederate commissioners.[324]

"In one instance three leaves have been cut from the 'Official Record' and in a few cases lines have been blotted out so as to entirely obscure what has been written, obviously and admittedly because these leaves and these lines were thought by the Confederate Commissioner Thompson to contain compromising records which in some cases would, if known, have furnished sufficient proof of the disregard of right of asylum, and good ground for extradition."[325]

Castleman and Thomas Hines were the closest and most trusted operatives of Jacob Thompson during the period of the Canadian mission. They carried out his orders and they delivered the monies as directed. These two later collaborated in composing several articles on their remembrances of the war. Neither ever suggested that they thought Thompson "embezzled" the remaining funds.

John C. Breckinridge and John *Breckinridge* Castleman were kin, Breckinridge being Castleman's uncle. Breckinridge either did not divulge his suspicions of Thompson to his nephew or Castleman did not give it credence. They certainly had occasion to discuss Thompson. Remarkably, Breckinridge was a tutor at Trinity College (later University of Toronto) after the war, while both Hines and Castleman were students there, studying French and law.[326]

Both of these reliable intimates had distinguished postwar careers after each graduated from law school. Hines was elected Chief Justice of Kentucky's Court of Appeals, serving two terms. Castleman never ran for public office but wielded major influence in Kentucky politics. He joined the army at the onset of the Spanish-American War, receiving the rank of colonel. During the brief fighting in Puerto Rico, he was cited for bravery. Upon his return from combat President William McKinley promoted him to brigadier general. Both men had shown themselves to be trustworthy, honest, and dependable through long service in the public eye.[327]

James Horan in his seminal 1954 book, *Confederate Agent*, about Thomas Hines and the Northwest Conspiracy, had this to say, "Thompson, who had been a wealthy man before the war, had his slaves and property confiscated and lived only modestly in later years." Thompson's postwar lifestyle in fact was modest only as compared to his prewar life. Horan further deduced that Thompson was "scrupulously honest."[328]

There were other accusers besides George N. Sanders, Beverley Tucker, and Clement Clay, who had doggedly remained in thrall to Sanders. Charles Friedrich Henningsen hated Jefferson Davis with a passion for not utilizing his self-perceived talents during the war. His comrade in hate was John T. Pickett, infamous for selling the "Pickett Papers" to the United States for $75,000. These papers were part of the archives of the Confederate State Department.

Pickett also had a gripe with Davis, having been recalled as an agent in Mexico and censured. Pickett believed Davis or his representative wrote a letter to the *Memphis Appeal* in 1872 belittling his service in Mexico and questioning the validity of a communication from Thompson to Benjamin included in the "Pickett Papers."[329]

Henningsen corresponded with Pickett in an obvious attempt to incite him even more by accusing Davis of receiving Confederate gold after the war. Their objective was to indict Davis directly and also through his allies.

Then Henningsen turned on Thompson commenting, "But all this pales before Jake Thompson's Colossal plunder—which he received for himself individually." Pickett contended "all three (Davis, Benjamin, and Thompson) treated me badly enough in my time, thus I am, albeit unintentionally, the instrument of the execution of a sort of poetic justice upon them...."[330] This bitter duo, out for their pound of flesh, were throwing mud and hoping some of it would stick.

Then there was the cantankerous Henry Foote. A longtime outspoken critic of Jefferson Davis, Foote had been a pre-war senator and governor of Mississippi (he successfully ran against Davis on the Unionist ticket.) He and Davis hated each other personally and politically, having resorted to a fist-fight while both were senators. The peripatetic maverick lived in Nashville during the War, serving in the first and second Confederate Congresses. While there he viciously maligned Davis and Benjamin, so it is little wonder that he continued his diatribe post-war in his book *Casket of Reminscences.*

According to Foote, "I know that I always expected him (Davis) and Mr. Benjamin to get rich by the war...." Their postwar meetings in London gave Foote all the impetus he needed to insinuate that they were both after Confederate money made from cotton stored in Liverpool.[331] Jacob Thompson was next in line to be charged.

"Some two hundred thousand dollars in gold, or more, were placed in the hands of Mr. Jacob Thompson for certain war purposes, which he took with him to Canada and deposited in the bank of Mr. Porterfield, (now a Nashville neighbor of mine of the greatest respectability.)" Porterfield, Foote wrote, told him Thompson had "drawn out all his money and taken it with him to England." This was the same Porterfield that functioned as a Confederate agent in New York City.

"Now what did Mr. Thompson do with that large sum? Did he and Mr. Davis divide it between them? Did the immortal Benjamin get his share…?" Then he further castigated Davis and the Democrats for ruining the South.[332] (Foote had switched to the Republican Party by this time.)

Jacob Thompson was interviewed about his remembrances of the deceased Foote in 1883. This was his chance to defend himself, but he demurred. Thompson answered, "Foote … was a regular skirmisher … in the Senate. He took all sides of all questions and never really had much weight. His learning, however, was wonderful, and no man of that day was more apt or accurate in a classical quotation." There was never a word of defense or any attempt to denigrate Foote.[333]

The publication of Bonner's *Child's History of the United States, Volume III, Great Rebellion* brought the accusations to a wider, essentially northern audience. The book recounts, "Mr. Thompson stole a million, ran away, and became a rebel general." Thompson took umbrage to this summary, writing his confidante and counselor Judge Black in late 1879, "what ought to be done to such a historian is to hunt him up and kick him." He explained his dilemma, "To reply to the article in the newspapers is what I cannot consent to do. To submit to such a slander in silence requires all the patience and philosophy I possess… The whole book is so full of falsehoods… I turn from it with great loathing and contempt."[334]

After asking Black's advice over the course to pursue, Thompson pondered his legacy. "I would like to leave behind me an irreproachable name—

as I know I have endeavored to square my whole life by the rules of honor, honesty, truth, fidelity to every engagement—to live a gentleman, a true friend, a patriot and Christian."[335] That was wishful thinking and not happening, no matter how much he desired it.

"The Greatest Scoundrel," an ominously titled article by Peggy Robbins published in the November/December, 1992 issue of *Civil War Times Illustrated* about Jacob Thompson, addressed this contentious accusation. "Questions about what happened to old Confederate funds continued to generate disputes between ex-Rebel officials and fuel suspicions Jake had helped himself to some… Ever buoyant, Jake Thompson still retained large real estate holdings and other negotiable assets… Without any ledgers to look over, modern Americans are left to conclude that historians who say he 'died a wealthy man' are correct, and that those who go on to link that wealth to 'money Thompson embezzled from the Confederacy' may be grievously wrong."[336]

Thompson's financial condition after the war did not necessarily result from pilfered Confederate funds. The Jackson, Mississippi *Clarion* proclaimed in its February 19, 1868 edition that he was "a millionaire, the richest man in the state." The article revealed that he had recently sold $80,000 of land in the Delta close by the Mississippi River. It also reminded the readers that his wife Kate was the only heir of "a very wealthy and prominent man." The census of 1870 reported real estate wealth of $150,000.[337] This did not totally reflect his holdings as some still remained in Macon's name.

As previously noted, he had prudently transferred titles of his real estate holdings to Macon before departing on the Canadian mission. Though losses incurred as a consequence of the war diminished his wealth, Jake Thompson did not become destitute.

He weighed in on this subject in a letter of July 1865 writing, "Before I left home I disposed of my entire large estate, what was available I brought with me."[338] Often forgotten in the eagerness to implicate him is that he was a smart businessman who knew how to make money. After his return from overseas, Thompson sold land and timber from his extensive Delta holdings, later branching out into railroads, banking, and insurance. Clearly the man had money. And the means to make more.

Kate Thompson addressed the issue of finances with Macon, writing from Florence, Italy, on October 21, 1865. "...with the Bonds I saved in my pettycoat—which will all be good-- & other means your Pa has—we will all be able to have enough for our little family to live comfortably upon the interest derived from the principal."[339] In 1870 she wrote Macon that Jacob returned to Paris "to get his money."[340]

This is all tantalizing but does not answer the essential question of the origin of this money. They definitely went to Europe with the bonds surreptitiously carried by Kate, which were reputedly augmented by bonds already held in Liverpool. Did the funds in Paris include significant monies taken from Canada at war's end?

Continuing Education, Pardon, and Return

On October 9, 1865, after becoming settled in Paris, Thompson wrote a letter to Judge Jeremiah Black stating, "In truth I never look upon any other country as my country. The graves of my ancestors are in the South for two hundred years and in defence of a flag of a common country they have shed their blood freely. Thus consecrated it is impossible to adopt another country as my country."[341] He was bitter over what had transpired but remembered all those years of service and devotion to the United States.

Several months later Thompson replied to a letter from William De-Lay, editor of the Oxford, Mississippi *Falcon*. This lengthy missive clearly projected his feelings about the current climate in the United States. Kate was leaving their grand tour of Europe to return to Oxford, "yearning to see the land we both have loved and love still." He could not accompany her, he wrote, not out of a fear of prosecution, but "because I felt there was no constitution or law in the South for the protection of my rights...[342]

"For I assure you, that with all her faults, I love my country. There is no other such country in the world... No, for good or evil the best country is in the United States and if there could only be security of person, property, and reputation it would be the most desirable country on earth." He advised that a petition currently circulating in Mississippi asking for a pardon from President Johnson was appreciated but would be to no avail. In his reply later printed in the *Falcon*, Thompson wanted his supporters "to remain and abide the fate and destiny of their country."[343]

Jacob Thompson took advantage of his exile in Europe to travel widely, absorbing local history, culture, and literature wherever he went. He began by learning the rudiments of French while in Paris. Accompanied by Kate, he toured Switzerland, then on to Rome and Naples. Next came Egypt and the Holy land, both of which impressed him greatly. The return trip took them to the Greek Isles, Venice, Vienna, Munich, Frankfort, Cologne, and Brussels. In the course of this journey, Kate had become homesick, anxious to see her son and mother, and she decided to visit them in Oxford.[344]

While sightseeing in Europe with Kate, Jacob wrote Macon a very informative letter from Naples in early 1866. In it he gave great insight into his current state of mind, advising Macon that "we must recognize the fact, however much we might desire otherwise and act accordingly. We have made our struggle and done all that brave and honorable men could do to maintain our cause but a greater force has defeated all our efforts and now it is part of true wisdom and sound philosophy to conform our conduct—to the inevitable logic of events…" Then he offered a sobering admission, "Somehow or in some way I had incurred for myself a mountain of prejudices which, during the war found opportunity to wreak and I hope, expend itself."[345]

Jacob further counseled his son: "I fear Mississippi, however, with her large population of free negroes will never be a country in which a family should be raised. In the resettlement of the people I foresee that Oxford with its University will become a prosperous village and property there will continue to enhance in value." He cautioned Macon that it no longer would be possible to make a living out of farming.

During their time in Italy, the Thompsons had an audience with the Pope. Jacob recounted the meeting to Macon in the same correspondence. "When I told him the Southern people reverenced his name on account of his sympathy with us in our struggle, he expressed himself gratified and said it was not God's will that we should prevail and therefore we ought to submit to the result cheerfully for our own good." This seemingly was Jacob's intent as well as his advice to Macon.[346]

After Kate's departure Thompson reconnected with John Castleman from the Canadian mission who had made his way to Europe after being released from prison and shivering through a cold Canadian winter. Castleman recounted, "The anticipated pleasure of meeting Honorable Jacob Thompson in Paris hastened me to the French capital where together we studied French, saw the sights and went nightly to the opera..." When the weather warmed, they embarked on a "grand tour" of Great Britain, including Ireland.[347]

The excursion began in London with all it had to offer. Proceeding to the Lake District, the two wartime companions lingered to read the works of the area's famous poets; hence, they went to Melrose Abbey in the Scottish borderlands to read the novels of Sir Walter Scott. They slowly advanced to Edinburgh, Stirling, and onward to the Highlands, stopping to read along the way. The poetry of Robert Burns was particularly pleasing to both of them. The journey concluded in Ireland but not before perusing the writings of Thomas Moore as they leisurely returned to Paris.[348]

Castleman professed to be "happy listener" during their two-month long cultural vacation. Since his vision was impaired, Thompson did all the reading. He "read aloud with ease and pleasure and emphasis," according to Castleman's account.[349] These scholarly journeys were consistent with Thompson's past. He remained always a man of action and a proponent of education. He was disinclined to wallow in self-pity and loathing, choosing to seize the opportunity presented.

After Kate returned to Oxford in the late summer of 1866, Jacob became increasingly restless and homesick. He had rented a house in Halifax, Nova Scotia sometime in 1867 to be closer to family and friends. Later in 1867, he accompanied his son Macon on a visit to Europe. By 1868 Jacob had relocated to Montreal to be within two day's train ride of Oxford. In Canada, Kate and her elderly mother joined him.

He frankly wrote his friend James Howry, a fellow Oxonian and member of the Board of Trustees of the University of Mississippi, "Sometimes I wish I were among you, then again I am glad I am away as I could do nothing to help anybody and could have no influence (not the least) in public matters."[350]

But he still yearned to return home. Thompson composed a letter to President Andrew Johnson on December 26, 1868, attempting to get the proclamation issued following Lincoln's assassination revoked. The straight-forward message read,

> *I was abroad when your proclamation was issued. Regarding it in the light of an edict of banishment, I have remained abroad ever since; and I feel I am honor bound to do so, until the proclamation is in some way revoked. I am convinced now that you must be fully persuaded that all the evidence on which it was originally based was a tissue of perjury or at all events, untrustworthy and unreliable.*
>
> *If you are not convinced, I have not a word more to say. I will endure to the end what I have patiently borne for near four years and wait until the truth can be manifest... (Moreover I swear to you before High Heaven, I never knew any one of the parties engaged in the assassination and never had any communication with any one of them or with any other person for them, directly or indirectly, either before or after the act...)*
>
> *My public career is ended. In adhering to the principles which I conscientiously believed to be right and true & in accordance with the teaching of the fathers, I have stranded my little boat.*[351]

Unbeknownst to Thompson on the day prior to posting this letter, President Johnson had issued on Christmas day an unconditional pardon to all Confederates with the exception of high-ranking officials. Even though technically the proclamation was not revoked for Thompson and the others named, in reality the sweeping pardon applied to them.[352] Jacob Thompson could return to the United States!

In the spring of 1869, Thompson arrived back in Oxford after an absence of five years. His return generated great excitement among students and locals alike. He was "greeted at the Oxford depot with a tremendous ovation, and Professor Lamar delivered an hour long address of welcome. At the end of the speech, as he and Thompson stepped into a waiting carriage, half a hundred students unhitched the horses and themselves drew the carriage on a triumphal journey through town to the Avent home where a brilliant reception and banquet were given in the former fugitive's honor."[353] His reputation at home had obviously not been tainted by the accusations repeated *ad nauseum*, primarily by the northern press.

Removal To Memphis

Although warned by his wife and others, Thompson was unprepared for the devastation and abject poverty in and around Oxford. He found his two sisters impoverished as well as many of his friends. Fortunately, his two brothers, John and William, had survived with their homes intact. Several former friends had perished in the war, which greatly affected him.[354]

Finally, Thompson viewed the ruins of his once beautiful and lavishly furnished home. Kate and Jacob initially decided to live in the three-room office Jacob utilized before the war. The gatekeeper's lodge had also survived the ravages of war. McDonald, the gardener, had been employed since the late 1840s and Jacob would not ask him to move in order that they could temporarily live there. Soon the Thompsons built a frame house on the site of Home Place, which they subsequently gave to their son Macon on their move to Memphis.[355]

On learning of the prior intentions of the Freedmen's Bureau to appropriate his property, Jacob became even more outraged at his world turned upside down. The bureau had been formed in 1865 in part to resettle former slaves and poor whites on abandoned or confiscated lands. While the Thompsons were abroad, the local bureau agent Charles Austin concocted a plan to confiscate two of their plantations, Clear Creek with 2700 acres and Home Place with 550 acres.

Of one of them Austin opined, it "is one of the best in the country. It contains a mansion house and is well provided with other buildings. A fine place this would be for a colony and a colony will be needed by the first of next year." The salvation for Jacob Thompson was the revelation that he had shrewdly transferred title of these lands to Macon before leaving on the Canadian mission.[356]

Also in the late summer of 1865, Charles Austin focused on establishing a school for former slaves in Oxford. The site he recommended was none other than that of the burned home of the Thompsons. Austin wrote, "On the Jacob Thompson place stands the walls of a brick building. The Freedmen think they can cover this and use it for a school house." Although the intent of a school was noble in conception, the attempted seizure of his property must have deeply troubled Jacob Thompson. In the end this property was not selected.[357]

The Thompsons did not reside long in Oxford. Every step they took through town passed places that reminded them of the war and its devastation. Reliving what once was at every waking moment took a toll on them.

Kate also preferred the entertainment opportunities that the much larger city of Memphis offered. Jacob needed the larger population for business connections. Neither could face the dire straits of so many of their friends, although they would continue to help both family and friends in Oxford from their new home in Memphis. McDonald followed them to Memphis, becoming coachman and butler. Most of the former slaves employed as house servants went also, continuing their same tasks, only now as free men and women.[358]

Kate remarked to Macon in mid-1870, "Your Pa seems to be like an india (sic) rubber ball, can stand any amount of squeezing."[359] Jacob had not only survived, he had regained his zeal for life, allowing him to resume the entrepreneurial strategies he so loved. Their rapid acceptance into Memphis society was an added bonus. Even though returning from exile a sick man, Jacob thrived in the postwar bustling Memphis environment.

Jake and Kate purchased a rather large home in Memphis, but it was not of the quality or size of their former magnificent home in Oxford. This recently acquired residence needed completely new furnishings since theirs had been destroyed or pilfered. The silver had been saved. Conscientious slaves had hidden it and retrieved it after the end of hostilities. Likewise, some of the china had been collected and stored by McDonald and was eventually moved to Memphis. This was essentially all that remained of their prewar home.[360]

Verbal attacks on Jacob Thompson were still in vogue in 1870, prompting Judge Jeremiah Black, though a strong Unionist, to reply to the latest denunciation, this time by Senator Henry Wilson of Massachusetts. Wilson used the opportunity of eulogizing Edwin Stanton to once again berate Thompson. Through a letter to the *Cincinnati Commercial* reprinted in the *Memphis Daily Appeal*, Judge Black gave "instructions" to Senator Wilson as follows:[361]

"It has been the fashion of loyal people to consign the ex-Secretary of the Interior to the most hearty and remorseless condemnation. Scarcely a word has been heard from the other side, while epithets and charges have been exhausted to prove that Mr. Thompson was a rascal and a poltroon... But perhaps the most extraordinary of your averments is that the Secretary of the Interior permits the robbery of trust funds... You could not possibly have believed this unless you perversely closed your eyes against the light of plain truth...

"A committee of Congress consisting of men opposed to the Secretary examined the evidence when it was fresh, and reported upon it. The correctness of their judgment has never been impugned. In the face of these recorded and well known facts you deliberately set down and write out, or get somebody to write out and publish to the world on your authority, the accusation that Mr. Thompson has committed an offense which should make him infamous forever. The force of mendacity can go no further.

"I admit that you are a loyal man in the modern sense of the word, and a Senator in Congress from a most loyal state; and it is equally true that Mr. Thompson was a rebel; that he was for years an exile from his home and country, pursued wherever he went by an Executive proclamation which put a price on his head. This gives you an immense advantage over him. But the fact is still true that no department of this Government was ever managed more ably or more faithfully than the Interior while he was at the head of it.

"You may have all the benefit of loyalty, and you may weigh him down with the huge burden of rebellion; nevertheless, his mental ability, good sense, and common honesty put him so immeasurably far above you, that you will never in this life get a horizontal view of his character."

The *Memphis Daily Appeal* added at the end of the article, "When any man who has been basely and continually belied gets such a vindication from one who knows the truth, and is both able and willing to testify to it, we feel that humanity owes the benefactor its gratitude… We congratulate Mr. Thompson, who now resides in Memphis, upon the annihilation of the worst scandal against an honest man."[362]

As soon as they were established in Memphis, the Thompsons tactfully assumed the care and education of several nieces and nephews whose families had been left penniless by the war. His brother Young died in the early postwar period, followed shortly by his wife. The orphans left after their deaths were incorporated into the growing Thompson household. All these children varying by age, sex, and personality required a strict, almost military, schedule. The Thompsons reportedly were very kind and nurturing, trying to make their lives as pleasant as possible.[363]

Jacob, ever the educator, often took the children to plays, especially those of Shakespeare. His only requirement was that they read the play before attending the performance. The Thompsons got a reprieve in the summer when the children returned home or stayed with relatives. They seized this opportunity to travel to the likes of Europe, Canada, Bermuda, and Cuba, often taking Kate's mother.[364] These vacations were sometimes made necessary to escape from yellow fever epidemics, particularly in 1878 when Memphis felt the full brunt of the mosquito borne illness.

By 1871 another tragedy confronted the Thompsons. Macon's medical condition had so worsened that they realized the end was near. As their only child, Macon was especially dear to their hearts. They brought him from Oxford to Memphis, striving to keep him comfortable. The end came on June 6, 1873, when Macon died at the young age of 33. Macon left behind a wife, Sarah Fox Thompson, and two daughters, Kate and Mamie. Later, the two girls were added to the Thompson's expanding menagerie.[365]

Thompson, his name still anathema in the North, became an issue in the 1872 presidential election between Horace Greeley and U. S. Grant. Grant's supporters distributed copies of a captured 1864 report from Jacob Thompson to Benjamin in which he disclosed the failed Niagara peace conference. Under the headline of "The Terrible Thompson," the long, inflammatory article strove to connect Greeley with Thompson, Clay, and Sanders. The article inferred that Greeley had been involved with traitors; therefore, he had their endorsement. Grant easily won the election, while Thompson acquired yet more infamy.[366]

In 1874 while on vacation, the Thompson's Memphis home caught fire sustaining $15,000 in damages. The circumstances of the fire were suspicious and there was speculation that arson was involved; however, nothing was proven and their insurance company paid the claim. The insurance report noted "the residence of Jacob Thompson set fire and partially destroyed, loss $15,000." The peace they sought still eluded them.[367]

Their life in Memphis was not all doom and gloom. On their return, the Thompsons bought another house, not as large as the first Memphis house, but more elegant.[368] Kate still enjoyed entertaining and they both took pleasure in the varied social events of Memphis. The *Memphis Appeal* of February 3, 1872, recounted "the most brilliant social event in Memphis history" on the visit of Alexis, the 22 year-old son of Czar Alexander II of Russia. A select greeting committee, comprised of elite Memphians, including Jake Thompson, met and entertained Alexis Romanov[369]

Jacob spent protracted time with friends rehashing the war. Often they met at his home for stag dinners to discuss campaigns, battles, and alternate outcomes in great detail. Their war experiences were vividly recounted as well as their detestation of Reconstruction.[370] Once Jefferson Davis came over expressly to discuss the battle of Shiloh with Jacob and compatriots.[371]

Davis visited frequently at times for pleasure and at times for business reasons as Jacob continued to aid him in his financial difficulties. According to Jacob Thompson's niece who resided with them during this time, well-known former Confederate guests in addition to Davis included Nathan Bedford Forrest, L. Q. C. Lamar, and Alexander H. Stephens, former vice-president of the Confederacy.[372]

The Confederate Relief and Historical Association of Memphis, formed "to engage in works of charity and benevolence, and to render succor and protection to the unfortunate and destitute," listed Jacob Thompson as one of its members. Second only to New Orleans, Memphis became home to numerous former Confederate leaders. Thompson had been proposed for membership by Jefferson Davis and Rev. J. Carmichael and was elected on April 28, 1870.[373]

His participation in this organization is quite logical except for the accusations of absconding with Confederate gold at the end of the war. He seemingly had no qualms over associating with former high-ranking Confederates, which appears odd if he did indeed take a fortune as critics claimed. His close relationship with former Confederate generals who comprised much of the faculty and staff of the University of the South is also counter-intuitive for the same reason.

Saving A University

The Episcopal Church, especially the newly established church affiliated University of the South at Sewanee, Tennessee, became very dear to Thompson after his relocation to Memphis. He and Kate joined Calvary Episcopal Church in Memphis, where he served on the vestry for many years, functioning as senior warden and teaching a young men's Bible class. He was a delegate to successive Diocesan Conventions, a deputy to the General Convention, and a member of the standing committee. His choice of Calvary is interesting since, before he got to Memphis, former Confederate officers had left Calvary to found St. Lazarus. Jacob rejected the obvious choice of St. Lazarus, opting for the congregation "where prayers were said for the President of the United States."[374]

Sewanee, or the University of the South, had been organized shortly before the Civil War at the behest of Episcopal dioceses from across the South. It was closed during the war and restarted shortly afterwards but experienced almost overwhelming financial problems in the postwar cash-poor South. Jacob Thompson was on the four-man executive committee for much of the period encompassing the gravest financial woes.[375]

In 1878 Jacob and another committee member were appointed trustees of mortgage and bonds "with authority to negotiate sale of same." Attempting to sell bonds, he traveled to New York on two occasions—both unsuccessful. Thompson and a Mr. McNeal finally agreed to personally guarantee one-third of the bonds, which did not work either. A mortgage company eventually came to the rescue.[376] Despite the old, lingering accusations of financial impropriety, Thompson was not shy about handling the money of others. Nor did he have any trouble getting people to trust him with it.

The first permanent academic structure on campus was completed in 1883, the Chemical and Philosophical Hall. Shortly after completion, the building was renamed Thompson Hall in honor of its primary benefactor, Jacob Thompson. It has since functioned as the medical school and later as the student union. Several years afterwards in the *History of the University of the South,* reviewing the year 1885, the author would note, "Suitable notice was taken of the death of Hon. Jacob Thompson, formerly secretary of the interior. Mr. Thompson was very much interested in the welfare of the University. He contributed largely to the erection of the Philosophical Hall, and by his will gave ten thousand dollars to the University."[377]

An interesting take on Jacob Thompson's relationship with Sewanee came from *Sewanee Sampler* by Arthur Ben and Elizabeth N. Chitty. They explained that in his will Jacob wrote, "I own $100,000 in the Bell Telephone Company in Washington City. I request my wife to transfer this stock to the Trustees of the University of the South... Should the stock not be valuable... I request her to turn over to the University $10,000." The board in its infinite wisdom took the $10,000.

The authors characterized this decision: "It is the fate of trustees—and boards thereof—to deviate from perfection. But when the Sewanee board of 1885 erred, it erred colossally. And if Jacob Thompson is not listed with such benefactors to education as John Harvard, John D. Rockefeller, Paul Tulane, and Leland Stanford, it is not his fault. He tried."[378]

Reestablishing Himself

While Thompson did not pursue his legal career in Memphis, he remained extremely active in the business world. He became involved in banking, insurance, and railroads, but agriculture, especially its scientific advancement, was his first love. This is made manifest by his being president of the Planters and Landowners Association[379] and additionally president of the Memphis Agricultural and Mechanical Society.[380] Jacob used his influence and positions to promote pet projects, attending meetings and speaking through the South.

He even had the audacity to write President Ulysses S. Grant in 1871 about meteorology as it pertained to agriculture. Addressing the President as Excellency, Thompson encouraged annual conferences for the betterment of meteorology in order to improve crop forecasts.[381] One can imagine the expression on the former general's face as he read this missive from a former enemy, if indeed he ever did read it.

Railroads, so essential to development, had intrigued Thompson since his days in Congress. Postwar he served as a trustee of the Mississippi Central Railroad Company[382] and as vice-president of the Selma, Marion, and Memphis Railroad.[383] At the National Railroad Convention held at St. Louis in 1875, Thompson chaired the committee on resolutions promoting the Texas-Pacific Railroad.[384] His railroad experiences were not all financially rewarding as the Selma, Marion, and Memphis Railroad headed by Nathan Bedford Forrest was chronically under-capitalized. Thompson again went to New York seeking funding and again was unsuccessful.

The Sholes' *Memphis Directory Guide Taxing District* of 1883, listed Jacob Thompson as vice-president and board member of the Manhattan Bank. The same directory identified him as president of the Shelby County

Building and Loan Association.[385] Thompson remained a large landowner, managing row crops and timber as well as land sales. He had managed to achieve financial success in these endeavors—no small feat in the postwar South, particularly at his age and health.

REVISITING AN
OLD SCANDAL

Jacob Thompson had managed to stay out of the national spotlight for a while, and by avoiding taking an active role in politics, it seemed reasonable that he could expect to remain in relative national obscurity. Or could he? He was such an easy mark—so vulnerable to further scorn and contempt. This time the accusation would prove to be totally political in an effort to deflect attention away from the corrupt Grant administration.

In 1876 the issue of the Indian Trust Fund, already adjudicated sixteen years prior, was revisited. Secretary of War William W. Belknap, serving in the Grant administration, had been impeached for malfeasance involving kickbacks and had resigned in order to escape conviction.

The argument he and his allies presented was that as he had resigned, he could not be impeached. Zachariah Chandler, Secretary of the Interior, argued that if Congress attempted to prosecute Belknap after his resignation, then Jacob Thompson should be likewise prosecuted. The rationale for bringing suit against Thompson was that he had resigned at the advent of the War, whether he had been subject to impeachment or not.[386]

This was party politics at its worst and Thompson was the scapegoat. The corrupt Grant presidency was adding yet another chapter. Secretary Chandler publically announced that Jacob Thompson had been guilty of illegally withdrawing Indian Trust Fund bonds and that he would be impeached if Congress claimed jurisdiction in the Belknap case. Immediately after being made aware of this new take on an old charge, Thompson boarded a train for Washington to defend himself.[387]

Through intermediaries, Thompson gained a meeting with Secretary Chandler where he (via friends) demanded Chandler publically retract the statements about his involvement in the Indian fund fraud. Secretary Chandler consented to issue the retraction but procrastinated in delivering it. Meanwhile, Thompson remained in Washington visiting L. Q. C. Lamar, awaiting the withdrawal of the charges. After several days of hearing nothing, Thompson again insisted on the promised retraction.[388]

Instead, Chandler reneged, filing a civil suit against Jacob Thompson for $2,000,000. This action did have its intended effect of providing cover for the sins of Belknap. It also subjected Thompson to more defamation by the northern press. The thinly veiled political witch-hunt was also meant to injure the Democrat party, while drawing attention away from widespread Republican corruption in an election year.[389]

Thompson pleaded his innocence and the case was continued on the docket during the presidential campaign. At the conclusion of the race, retiring Secretary Chandler quietly dismissed the suit at the expense of the government. The politically motivated trumped up charges in this instance were so patently false as to be ridiculous; however, this episode served to even further erode Thompson's already shattered reputation in the North.[390]

OPINIONS AND
COUNTER-OPINIONS

William S. Speer in his *Sketches of Prominent Tennesseans* provided a rare glimpse of Jacob Thompson near the end of his life when he interviewed him while researching his book, published in 1888. Speer noted that the aging Thompson was 5'11" with "his form somewhat attenuated and a little bowed with age." His manner of speaking "was eager and earnest, as well as closely argumentative, sparing in the use of ornamental diction… always very effective." The "impression conveyed was that he was a man of affairs, of culture and refinement, and in his careful but easy politeness and attention to his visitors a typical southern gentleman."[391]

Thompson died on March 24, 1885, after experiencing declining health since his arrival in Memphis. On March 26th he was buried with Episcopal rites at Elmwood Cemetery in Memphis. Jake was eulogized at the funeral as a "brilliant statesman" and "a friend to all classes."[392] Another memorialized him as, "a dear, good man, an excellent friend, sympathetic in nature, kind and generous, in manner dignified, commanding respect. He was remarkable in being never overbearing to inferiors."[393]

Jacob Thompson had not been lowered into the ground when still another furor started, again fueled by the relentless press. This time his long-time friend L. Q. C. Lamar bore the brunt of the attacks. Lamar had recently been appointed Interior Secretary, the post Thompson had left twenty-four years prior. On hearing of Thompson's death, Secretary Lamar ordered the flag to fly at half-mast over the Interior Department and closed the department for the day. He issued the directive on the 25th to be implemented on the 26th, the day of the funeral.

It should come as little surprise that Republican papers published castigating editorials about Jacob Thompson along with Lamar's decision to honor his memory. A *New York Tribune* writer stated, "It really begins to look as if the Confederates have captured the capital at last. The maimed veterans of the war must wait for their pensions while the officers and clerks of the Interior Department take a holiday to honor the memory of a conspirator and traitor, who gloried in breaking his oath of office and divulging Cabinet secrets to the South Carolina rebels."[394]

An editorial in the same paper derided Democrats for paying "tributes of affection even to a notorious thief if he was a rebel." Thompson's name could still stir up strong emotions in the North, but the real target of these Republican barbs was the Democrat party itself. Jacob Thompson had been stigmatized to the point that he could be used to dishonor a person, party, or cause. Some Democrat newspapers did come to Lamar's defense, but Thompson received no sympathy even in death from the northern press.[395]

By the time of his death, Jacob Thompson had received twenty-five years of opprobrium in editorials through which the populace above the Mason-Dixon line became indoctrinated to despise him. Perhaps he was deserving of the defamation to a degree, but he had no voice to defend himself. Typically in war, the victors write the histories and pass judgments. The American Civil War was no different.

The situation was dissimilar in the South, especially the Mid-South, where he was happily welcomed back after his exile. Even the accusations of stealing the remaining Confederate gold on leaving Canada did not appear to concern the local citizenry. Thompson resumed his social standing and was able to prosper in both new and old businesses.

Roy Franklin Nichols, writing in the Pulitzer Prize winning *The Disruption of American Democracy*, described Thompson pre-war as "a matter-of-fact, humorless, relentless, and ambitious self-made man who lived by careful calculation. He could be vindictive to the point of embracing questionable means of retaliation."[396]

The vindictive allegation is supported by an entry in James K. Polk's diary written during his presidency in which he concluded, "Mr. Thompson's conduct in this affair was vindictive and without excuse."[397] The affair concerned an attempt by Thompson to punish his nemesis Robert J. Walker, who had deprived him of a Senate seat, by undermining one of Walker's allies. This portrayal has real significance since President Polk and Thompson were friends as well as close political allies.

Addressing the vengeful nature of Thompson toward the close of his time in Canada, Amanda Foreman in her excellent and comprehensive work, *A World on Fire, Britain's Crucial Role in the American Civil War*, described him: "Thompson had become a bitter and vengeful man since his arrival in Canada; during his absence from home, Federal soldiers had burned his Mississippi plantation and assaulted his wife. Isolated from friends and family and surrounded by like-minded fugitives, Thompson turned his personal grievances into an excuse to inflict the greatest possible suffering on the North, and in particular on Northern civilians. Nothing, he complained to Clay, should distract the Confederates from delivering the message of violence."[398]

Another reason for his alleged spiteful behavior was the suffering of non-combatants in the South. He had witnessed the worsening conditions subsequent to the wanton destruction and theft of civilian property perpetrated by Sherman, Sheridan, and others including "Whiskey" Smith, who had ordered the destruction of Oxford. The resultant starvation, homelessness, and appalling poverty weighed heavily on his mind. Medicines were unavailable in the South due to the tightening blockade and southern prisoners were starving in the midst of plenty. Too, the incendiary Dahlgren papers had to be considered.

However, the humorless characterization of Nichols does not hold up to scrutiny. There are repeated instances of Thompson's dry sense of humor with Jeremiah Black declaring, "Howell Cobb of Georgia... and Jacob Thompson were particularly jolly."[399] Black should know as he was around both on a near daily basis in the Buchanan administration. More recently, John Boyko in his well-researched 2013 narrative of Canada's role in the

Civil War, described Thompson as "a smart, witty, ambitious and ruggedly handsome man..."[400] These widely differing takes on Jacob Thompson are frequent from authors old and contemporary.

Adam Mayers, who has written extensively on the Canadian mission, explained, "Jacob Thompson's guerilla war did not change the outcome of the conflict.... Yet for Canadians it served as a catalyst; a poignant reminder of the perils of existence so close to a large and unruly neighbor.... Coming as it did at a time when they had decided to secure their own future, it could be said that the final days of the embattled states of Dixie did in a small way help the Canadians form their own Dominion." Ironically, both Jefferson Davis and Jacob Thompson were in Canada in 1867 when the Confederation, Canadian style, took place.[401]

A lengthy article, "The 25 Most Influential Politicians, Civilians, Inventors, Spies & Soldiers of the Civil War (That you've probably never heard of,) appeared in the Winter 2013 issue of *The Civil War Monitor*. The magazine "polled leading historians—and ranked their picks—for the most influential people who never got their due." Jacob Thompson placed number ten on that list. About him they concluded: "Spy outfits, if they are any good, cover their tracks. By this measure at least, Jacob Thompson, the assumed head of the Confederate Secret Service in 1864 was very good."[402]

The historians polled confidently tied him to the effort to free the prisoners at Johnson's Island in Lake Erie. They too concluded that he probably was connected "to a more nefarious plot to burn down New York City." No judgment was forthcoming on the more improbable plots he has been accused of.[403]

Thompson's culpability in the New York arson had been revealed in a missive he wrote to Benjamin, found in the Pickett Papers. Thompson rebutted by explaining that he had given approval to burn the New York Navy Yard. He claimed that the letter in the Pickett Papers had been altered.

Jefferson Davis in response to the New York City burning charge defended Thompson by writing that "the letter purporting to have been written by Jacob Thompson is in whole, or at least, in every material part, a forgery. In no instance did the Confederate Govt. attempt or contemplate the burning of N. York or of any other City. Had it been practicable to destroy the Navy Yard, I should have considered it quite proper to do so, as we would have destroyed an arsenal or storehouse of supplies… [Thompson's] character sufficiently assures me that the design imputed to him has no foundation than the malice and disregard of truth on which other allegations against other Confederates have been built."[404]

The "Pickett Papers" possibly were altered, but there remains persuasive evidence that Jacob Thompson advocated more than the destruction of the Navy Yard. It is also possible that he authorized the burning of New York City without the knowledge of Jefferson Davis. Perhaps, the actual perpetrators expanded their role and neither Thompson nor Davis was being disingenuous.

The available information, however, indicates that Thompson was more involved in this plot than he admitted, while Davis was in the dark. It is not difficult to rationalize that Jake Thompson took an Old Testament approach to the arson—an eye for an eye, a tooth for a tooth, and a burning for a burning.

The article continued with a brief discussion of Lincoln's assassination "from which he (Thompson) cannot be fully cleared." The authors wonder what Thompson possibly did to encourage Booth. With the presumption of innocence until proven otherwise, it seems highly unlikely Thompson was involved directly or indirectly in this dastardly deed.[405] Holt, Stanton, and their cohorts could not gain a conviction as hard as they tried. Out of desperation, Holt bribed witnesses or was totally naive in his rush to convict Thompson and others. Speculation about Thompson and his possible complicity still persists 150 years later with no new revelations.

A reporter for the *Cincinnati Enquirer* interviewed Judge Cleary, Secretary of the Canadian mission, in 1882 regarding Thompson's possible connection with John Wilkes Booth. He unequivocally averred, "I am very certain that Colonel Thompson never saw Booth in Canada or had any communication with him…" As Thompson's secretary, Judge Cleary stated that he accompanied Thompson everywhere and knew of the comings and goings around him.[406]

The interesting take on the role of Jacob Thompson in the Civil War from *The Civil War Monitor* ended by asking the question, "Thompson's various plots may have been long shots, but how might history be written if he had succeeded?"[407] This is food for thought, but Thompson, a very capable administrator, proved to be ill suited for espionage. Too, the Confederacy was already reeling by the time of Thompson's appointment to Canada. In many respects, the war was already lost and its formal end was just a matter of time.

In perspective, there were multiple players and pieces partly responsible for the failure of the espionage and covert operations part of the mission. The lack of cooperation between the two mission heads as well as the scheming by Sanders undoubtedly played a role. Although Thompson had been given considerable independence, correspondence from the War Department was sent directly to Hines and others at times, bypassing Thompson. The difficulty of communications with Richmond, often taking weeks to get a reply also severely complicated operations. Perhaps, most important was the Union's ability to quickly adapt counter-espionage measures, stifling Thompson throughout his tenure.

Hines has been broadly criticized by some authors for being grossly overenthusiastic in his reports to Thompson on the Copperheads. This in turn helped create Thompson's confidence in the Copperhead movement, which fizzled into a nearly total lack of success. Hines lack of attention in encrypting dispatches allowed the United States Telegraph Office to rapidly break the cipher, compromising mission secrecy in addition to having to contend with the embedded spies.[408] The list could go on—the mission was truly mission impossible.

The renowned Pulitzer Prize winning Civil War historian Bruce Catton thought Thompson "was an experienced politician well fitted for his shadowy role." However, he acknowledged that the results achieved from beginning to end of the Canadian mission amounted "to nothing much more than a series of petty annoyances." Catton continued by elucidating the factors contributing to this lack of success.[409]

"Thompson had a wild, devil-may-care crowd at his command," he surmised. "Many of their operatives seem to have looked on the whole program as a glorified Tom Sawyer lark, with the sheer fun of conspiring and risking their necks offering a welcome outlet for restless spirits bored by the routine of ordinary army life." The second factor preventing success according to Catton was Union spies so effectively observed the mission "that it had little chance to accomplish anything very sensational."

The most crippling aspect of the mission occurred, Catton suggested, when looking at the "vast body of supposedly militant Northern Copperheads, they took them seriously." Utilizing the Copperheads was the primary charge given to Jacob Thompson by Jefferson Davis. It became evident to the North "that the war would not be lost because of revolt at home. The attempt to crush secession would not fail because of a second secession."[410]

Jake Thompson does deserve real credit for his significant role in the founding of the University of Mississippi. He did as much or more than any one person in that regard. After the war, he fulfilled a similar role at the University of the South, helping that institution survive and function in the postwar South. His sound advice, tireless efforts, and material support set the two universities on paths to success, evidenced by the fact that both are still thriving.

Arguably, the appraisal that would have most riled Jacob Thompson came from David Sansing, emeritus professor of history at the University of Mississippi and author of *The University of Mississippi: A Sesquicentennial History*. Sansing concluded his short biography of Thompson in the University sanctioned history by declaring, "In early 1865 Thompson fled to France with a large but undetermined amount of Confederate funds. After living 'in high style in the elegant Grand Hotel in Paris' for four years, Thompson returned for a brief stay in Oxford…"[411] This summary of his life after the Canadian mission is demeaning as well as problematic. It would have been especially galling to Thompson coming from a Mississippi author writing a history of the University that owed him so much.

The insinuation that staying in the Grand Hotel was made possible by utilization of Confederate funds he absconded with at War's end is unsupported by facts. The Thompsons had money, and they were not the only ex-Confederates at the hotel.

The Paris correspondent for the *New York Times* reported on August 18, 1865, "For the last week the court of the Grand Hotel has looked much as it did in the flourishing days of the Confederacy…. Messrs. Breckinridge, Helm, and Jacob Thompson have arrived there, and these, united to Mr. Slidell, and a host of other more or less distinguished representatives of the Confederacy, are holding council there and debating their affairs…."[412] How did these other southerners legitimately escape to Europe with financial resources enough to afford Paris and the Grand Hotel but not the Thompsons?

Slaves were an integral part of Jacob Thompson's life prior to the war. He was not just a slave-owner. He was a big slave-owner. His mentoring father-in-law, Peyton Jones, also had many slaves; additionally, Jake grew up in a household that owned slaves. Slave labor allowed him to rapidly accumulate wealth following the example of Peyton Jones. While not a "fire-eating" radical on the subject, Thompson spent his entire political career attempting to preserve and expand the institution that had helped make him wealthy.

A little insight into Thompson's treatment of slaves came from Lewis Mason, who managed his families' plantation, which adjoined the plantation of Thompson in Coahoma County. Mason liked Jake's "warmth"and determined to sell their land and slaves in Mississippi to Thompson when financial difficulties made it imperative in 1856. Lewis Mason from Virginia found the handling of slaves in Mississippi (as contrasted to Virginia) to often be less than satisfactory; however, in Jacob Thompson he found someone "like minded," reflecting his own more compassionate approach.[413] Though Thompson likely was more solicitous than most Mississippi slave-owners, his slaves were still enslaved.

Before leaving for Canada, Thompson employed an overseer known to be "strict" with slaves. He met with this overseer to give instructions and afterwards with his slaves. Pledging loyalty and promising to continue with their duties, the slaves satisfied Jacob that they could be trusted in his absence. But the overseer, now in total control with Jacob in Canada, quickly became cruel to the slaves, prompting many of the field hands to flee.[414]

Taking further advantage of the situation, he became infatuated with one of the house servants, and, on being rejected, beat her to death. He was also insolent to Kate Thompson, all the while embezzling plantation money—an all-around evil man. Jake knew nothing of this and nothing suggested that he intended any deviation from his usual caring but firm approach.[415]

Another vignette of Thompson and slaves comes from the W. P. A. Federal Writers Project in the 1930s. Joanna Thompson Isom's narrative recounted her birth shortly before the advent of the Civil War. Her mother, a Jacob Thompson slave, had died in childbirth. Immediately before her demise, the mother gave the infant girl to Macon Thompson. He promptly brought the three-hour old baby to his wife Sally. Joanna was raised in their home as a family member until at age fifteen she married Henry Isom in the Thompsons' parlor. Even though Joanna stated in the narrative that her father was of "Indian blood," it has been alleged that she was the child of Jacob or Macon. This, of course, is totally unsubstantiated, perhaps perpetuated by her surname of Thompson.[416]

In an 1881 interview by the *Washington Post* concerning the recent publication of *The Rise and Fall of the Confederate Government* by Jefferson Davis, Thompson was asked if the South wished for slavery again. He replied, "No sir (very positively) should a vote be taken to-morrow there would be an overwhelming sentiment against it. There were many people who were made poor by the loss of their slaves who would like to have their money value... Lincoln had no right to set all the slaves free without providing for compensating their owners. The slaves were private property and could not legally be taken away by force."[417]

Slavery is abhorrent to us all today and was fast becoming an anachronism at the time. Great Britain and France had previously outlawed the "peculiar institution." That said, Thompson was a man of his times in the South. Slavery was legal according to the U. S. Constitution with most mainline southern churches accepting it. It was also a vehicle to rapidly attain wealth. To possibly understand Thompson, one has to place him in his time period, not subject to today's mores. Surprisingly, he has been treated rather gently on this provocative topic.

The oft- repeated allegation of Thompson being a traitor is certainly realistic from a northern vantage point. If the South had won, he would by contrast be deemed a hero. His conduct in persuading North Carolina to secede while he served as a cabinet officer could be construed as treason. In his defense, Thompson amazingly had the approval of President Buchanan for this scheme. By his admission Thompson indirectly notified South Carolina authorities of the approach of the Star of the West as it attempted to resupply the forts in Charleston harbor. This disclosure did not alter a thing but was questionable since Thompson gleaned this information from his cabinet position.

Whether or not Thompson was a terrorist is also a matter of debate. He walked a fine line in Canada, keeping Canadian officials mollified to a point as he carried out espionage against the North. After ascertaining that the peace party was doomed without Confederate military victories, Thompson became more aggressive.

Benjamin ordered certain of the plots from Richmond, but Thompson had been given great flexibility to act independently. In his defense, Thompson did not have total control of the many fugitive Confederate soldiers and sympathizers in Canada. Some of them launched impetuous operations without his knowledge. Too, Clement Clay and his allies were hatching plots independently of Thompson.

In response to accusations of terrorism, the Pulitzer Prize winning northern industrialist and historian James Ford Rhodes surmised, "But there was not a word or a thought that looked to any violation of the rules of war as they exist among civilized nations … Was it not strange, however, that those that burned Atlanta, Jackson, Columbia, and a score of Southern towns, besides a belt of country in South Carolina forty miles wide, should assume that the Confederate government would retaliate in kind."[418]

Thompson has been accused repeatedly of involvement in the larceny of the Indian Trust Fund though he was categorically cleared by a Congressional investigation at the time of discovery. The same charge in 1876 against him from the Grant administration was purely political. That this almost certainly false accusation has persisted to the present demonstrates the negative depiction of Jacob Thompson emanating from wartime propaganda.

The accusation of taking Confederate money from Canada to Europe at war's end will never be definitively answered. Thompson did disclose that he retained £10,000 for his cotton destroyed by Union forces and for Jefferson Davis' legal defense. He also promptly followed through by retaining counsel for the then imprisoned Davis. Thompson's wealth after the war is commonly used as proof that he kept the allegedly considerable remaining funds of the Canadian mission. No one now alive really knows if the large sum of money even existed at that time or if Thompson did actually take it. This accusation will in all probability remain one of the mysteries of history.

Jacob Thompson and General Albert Pike, an Arkansan of many talents, in a current theory stand accused of collaborating in hiding Confederate gold toward the conclusion of the war as part of a conspiracy of Freemasonry and the Knights of the Golden Circle, a secret peace society. This could explain where the remaining Confederate money in Canada went at war's end instead of into Thompson's pocket. However, this whole theory remains dubious. Albert Pike apparently did cross paths with Jacob Thompson in Canada and perhaps saw him at some point in Europe postwar, but any other significant connection between the two is lacking.

The inference is that they were bonded through Masonry along with several leaders of western civilization in a vast conspiracy, which led them to conceal available monies in anticipation of a later uprising. While Pike was very active in Freemasonry, specifically Scottish Rites, Thompson definitely was not. Jacob had joined a Lafayette County, Mississippi lodge in 1842 but never became a zealot.

A letter from Thompson in Halifax, Nova Scotia, to James Howry in Oxford on May 4, 1868, affirmed his weak Masonic ties. "There is one favor I would ask of you as a Mason... I would like for you to grant me a regular certificate of membership in the Oxford Lodge so I might enter the Lodges in Montreal. I do not wish even in this to accept any thing as a favor and you know I am not bright (in Masonry.)"[419] Further, he told William S. Speer in an interview shortly before his death that he had not attended a lodge in twenty years.[420] Does this remotely sound like someone deeply involved in a Masonic plot with worldwide implications?

Remarkably, new accusations like the Masonic plot are still being added to Thompson's ledger. Some merit study and review; most are so outlandish that even a cursory glance leads to their rejection. Guilt by association is impossible to disprove. Jacob Thompson knew John Surratt, a Confederate courier, who was questionably involved in Lincoln's assassination, as well as other unsavory characters. After all, he was in charge of a spy mission. Also, he was a postwar friend and business associate of Nathan Bedford Forrest, serving as a pallbearer at his funeral.

Jacob Thompson knew and was on friendly terms with many if not most northern Democrat politicians. He was selected to head the Canadian mission principally because of these connections. Are these politicians guilty since they were once allies and friends of Thompson? Without corroborating evidence of collaboration for wrongdoing, these associations and friendships are just that—associations and friendships.

Finally, Joseph Holt felt compelled to take one more shot at his hated rival. In 1883 he composed a "Reply of J. Holt to certain calumnies of Jacob Thompson." Calumny was a popular word at the time meaning making false statements in an attempt to ruin one's reputation. Today it is commonly referred to as slander.

In it he forcefully responded to the perceived character assassination carried out by Thompson beginning before the Civil War. The venom in his pen readily came across as he wrote, "It will be observed that Mr. Thompson dominates every scene in which he appears, bestriding it like a Colossus, after the fashion of the interviewed of our day, who so magnify their own proportions and so dwarf surrounding persons and things as to sorely try public credulity and public patience as well."[421]

The twenty page diatribe continued: "The heart of the country has been found large enough and magnanimous enough to forgive these services

(Thompson's) against its flag, but, of course, they were too brilliant to be forgotten."[422] With this much pent-up anger, credibility is given to Holt's devious actions at the assassination trial.

This vicious verbal attack when he and Thompson were both in their 70's leaves little doubt that he would do almost anything to undermine Thompson. He was a sad, bitter man, who had his chance to convict Thompson and others, but failed, arguably by the revelation of his own decision to promote perjury. While Thompson rightly had a dislike of Holt, he evidently did not harbor anything like the animosity of his former employee.

LEGACY

Thompson's legacy was primarily shaped by the Civil War, principally by the Canadian espionage mission. Without Canada, Thompson might be merely a footnote of history. The carping of the northern press on other subjects involving him would not have been nearly as pronounced if not for his Canadian activities. Neither would there be an accusation of complicity in the Lincoln assassination nor a charge of theft of Confederate funds.

Perhaps a street in his beloved Oxford would have been named for him or a building at the adjacent university would have borne his moniker. Alas, that did not happen. He was caught up in the maelstrom of a bitter civil war, attempting to do his duty as he understood it. Worse for him, he had no real forum to attempt a rebuttal of the charges leveled at him, whether real or spurious.

Was he perfect? No! Could he be scheming and vengeful? Yes! Was he a victim of propaganda? Yes, somewhat. He remained an easy target for Republicans to use as a whipping boy whenever a diversion was needed. He was a human being, good and bad, placed in an impossible situation, and his flaws came to the forefront.

To put his misdeeds in perspective, Sherman destroyed more property and as a result killed more civilians in one hour than Thompson did in his entire life. Ironically, Sherman is generally considered a hero (in the North) while Thompson has been labeled the consummate villain. On the other hand, Thompson had a very positive impact on numerous lives through his civic undertakings and his diligent assistance to two nascent southern universities.

The person who arguably researched Jacob Thompson's personality more than anyone else was Philip Gerald Auchampaugh, PhD of New York, who was Professor of History at State Teacher's College, Duluth, Minnesota. In his book *James Buchanan and His Cabinet on the Eve of Secession*, published in 1926, he explained Thompson's postwar reputation: "The most attractive member of Buchanan's Cabinet was Jacob Thompson… His unpopularity in the North was due to the fact that it fell his lot to be the agent of the Confederate Government in Canada during the war. In that capacity it was his duty to try and co-operate with those in the North opposed to the continuation of the war." [423]

Auchampaugh concluded, "Thompson was a man who has never received due notice. A most pleasing personality, he had a very cool head, and could play a difficult role with little friction. Winning, able, persuasive in argument, affectionate, and warm hearted, he melted opposition rather than destroyed it. The deep mutual regard between Secretary [Thompson] and President [Buchanan] is very apparent in the correspondence which forms a vivid and very full narrative of their relations in the critical days of the period." [424]

Today, Jacob Thompson has nearly faded from memory. What vague memories remain are aroused by the occasional article in Oxford newspapers and Civil War magazines. The monument at his grave in Memphis' Elmwood Cemetery is impressive. There his wife Kate and son Macon are also buried. Other close family members are interred under old cedar trees in a wrought iron enclosed plot of St. Peter's Cemetery. Jacob had reserved this prime location when he donated the land for the cemetery.

On the 200th anniversary of his birth, Jacob Thompson had a "birthday party" in Oxford replete with cake and official pronouncements. Dr. Carolyn Ross, who had diligently researched his life for several years, organized this event in 2010. Unfortunately, she died before the completion of her manuscript. Dr. Ross did manage in this and other ways to keep his memory alive at least temporarily, if only in Oxford.

Historical markers in Leasburg, North Carolina, and Oxford, Mississippi, are dedicated to him. The marker in Leasburg is located very near the site of the house where he was born. In Oxford, a marker commemorates Home Place, the Thompson's elegant home on Old Taylor Road, burned in 1864 by order of Union General A. J. "Whiskey" Smith. The house constructed by Thompson on his postwar return to Oxford was erected on the site of the burned house. This house, which still survives, was soon given to son Macon when Kate and Jake moved to Memphis. The Gatekeeper's lodge too has endured and both properties have been extensively restored.[425]

A tablet at the University of North Carolina honors Jacob Thompson and recounts highlights of the life of its distinguished graduate. Thompson Union at the University of the South (Sewanee) is named for Jacob, as he was the leading contributor to its construction. In 1869, Macon Thompson constructed Thompson House on the square in Oxford, apparently with Jacob's approval and money. The hotel has recently been saved from demolition and lovingly refurbished, still bearing the name Thompson House, although now serving primarily as law offices.[426]

Oddly enough, a lake in South Dakota originally titled Dry Woods Lake by local Indians, was renamed Lake Thompson for Jacob Thompson, Secretary of the Interior. This beautiful lake, once completely dry, naturally filled in the 1980s and has been designated as a National Natural Landmark.[427] Thompson's association with what later became South Dakota was likely due to his involvement with Indian issues in the area during his tenure as Interior Secretary.

Even more unusual, a revenue cutter with a displacement of 50 tons, launched in 1857, had been dubbed the Jacob Thompson. Seven cutters, uniformly built, had been constructed in that same time period and were individually named for each member of the initial Buchanan cabinet. The Jacob Thompson first was assigned to patrol the Great Lakes. On the advent of the Civil War, it was moved to the Atlantic and stationed at Newport, Rhode Island, with her title surprisingly unchanged. In 1870, the schooner Jacob Thompson (still the same name) was sold for merchant service. Steam powered vessels were rapidly replacing sailing ships.[428]

Jacob Thompson became Jason Compson in the fertile imagination of William Faulkner. Actually, there were two Jasons in his writings, both of whom have commonalities with Jake Thompson. Jason Compson I was involved in politics and was an early settler in Oxford (referred to as Jefferson in Faulkner's books.) Faulkner places Jason II in the battle of Shiloh, like

Jacob, and describes him as "the most powerful, popular, and successful of the family in North Mississippi."

To make it even more complex and convoluted, the Compson family home is located at the corner of 13th and Buchanan on Faulkner's map of his fictitious Yoknapatawpha. This was in reality the former home of William Thompson, Jacob's brother and law partner.[429] The large, imposing William Thompson house is being painstakingly restored while the undeveloped property on the site of Jacob Thompson's Home Place has been approved for a small subdivision directly across the street from William Faulkner's Rowan Oak.

Jacob Thompson will live on in the timeless writings of William Faulkner as the patriarch of a once influential, aristocratic family now in decline. Faulkner's words that could easily pertain to Jake still resonate: "I think that no one individual can look at truth. It blinds you. You look at it and you see one phase of it. Someone else looks at it and sees a slightly awry phase of it. But taken all together, the truth is what they saw though nobody saw the truth intact."

EPILOGUE

While walking with my dog through the grounds of the modest L. Q. C. Lamar house, I found myself reflecting on how the lives of Lamar and Thompson compare. The parallels were quite evident before the Civil War and startlingly different afterwards. Both had been trained as lawyers upon graduation from colleges in their home states, and both migrated to the Oxford, Mississippi area after their schooling.

Lucius Lamar and Jake Thompson were Democrats and both were elected to the U. S. House of Representatives. Remarkably, both served as Secretary of the Interior. Though separated in age by fifteen years, they became friends and political allies in Oxford with higher education and opposition to the abolition of slavery being common passions.

The two became acquainted through their association with the newly established University of Mississippi. Lamar taught mathematics while Thompson worked relentlessly as the first chairman of the Board of Trustees. After his return from Europe following the war, Thompson devoted his time and money to improving the struggling University of the South at Sewanee. Education remained at the forefront with both men, but politics required most of Lamar's time in later life.

Lamar was the more fervent on slavery, ultimately writing the Mississippi Ordinance of Secession. Thompson assisted him by reviewing the document and suggesting changes. Thompson's real role regarding slavery consisted of attempting to influence President Buchanan as well as being outspoken during his tenure in Congress. Lamar, the former college professor now Congressman, surprisingly was one of the principals in the infamous Keitt-Grow brawl on the floor of Congress during debate on the controversial Lecompton Constitution of Kansas. Preservation of slavery, naturally, was at the heart of this sectional scuffle. Thompson for his part managed to avoid physical altercations.

At the advent of secession, the likenesses continued as Lamar and Thompson resigned their posts in the U. S. government. Thompson's departure was significantly more high profile as he was a Cabinet member. His name already carried a negative connotation in the North. Both returned to Oxford, helping to organize and equip local units in preparation for the conflict to come. Though neither had military experience, the parallels extended with Lamar becoming an officer early on and Thompson later doing likewise.

Soon the parallels would diverge dramatically as they were asked to fill very different positions by the Confederate government. Lamar was appointed ambassador to Russia while Thompson was tapped to head the Canadian mission. From this point their political lives took separate tracks.

Lamar, the rabid fire-eater, would rise above his past to become the "Pragmatic Patriot." He served as U. S. Congressman, Senator, Cabinet member, and Justice of the United States Supreme Court. Towns, counties, and streets in multiple states bear his name. John F. Kennedy would later extol Lamar's virtues in his Pulitzer Prize winning biography of eight politically courageous Americans.

By contrast, Thompson was tainted forever, largely from his role as commissioner to Canada. The two friends and fellow Oxonians with so many similarities prewar were starkly contrasted postwar—one a hero and the other a villain. Arguably, this resulted in no small part from the vicissitudes of war and its aftermath. How Thompson's life would have been different if he had not veered into espionage at Jefferson Davis' request. We will never know.

ENDNOTES

1   Dorothy Zollicoffer Oldham, *Life of Jacob Thompson, Masters Thesis* (University of Mississippi, June 1930), 4-5.

2   Ibid.

3   "Caswell County Family Tree, Nicholas Thompson Genealogy and Will," http//www.rootsweb.com.

4   Oldham, *Jacob Thompson*, 5-10.

5   Ibid.

6   P. L. Rainwater, "Letters to and from Jacob Thompson," *The Journal of Southern History,* Vol 6, No 1 (Feb 1940), 99.

7   J. F. Bivins, "The Life and Character of Jacob Thompson," *Historical Papers of the Trinity College Historical Society 1-7* (Duke University) 83-84.

8   Oldham, *Jacob Thompson*, 1.

9   J. F. H. Claiborne, *Mississippi as a Province, Territory, and State: with Notices of eminent citizens* (Power and Barksdale, Jackson, MS 1880), 447.

10   Ibid.

11   Charles J. Kappler, "Treaty with the Chickasaw 1832," *Indian Affairs: Laws and Treaties 7* (Govt. Printing Office, 1904), 356-364.

12   Oldham, *Jacob Thompson,* 24.

13   Claiborne, *Mississippi as a Province*, 448.

14   Ibid.

15   Thomas Prentice Kettell, *The United States Democratic Review, Vol 26* (Langtree and O'Sullivan, New York, 1880), 80,

16   Robert Wernick, "The Debts We Never Repaid," *American Heritage 1* (1964), 3.

17   Claiborne, *Mississippi As a Province*, 448.

18   Oldham, *Jacob Thompson*, 31-32.

19   Ibid, 34.

20   Claiborne, *Mississippi As a Province*, 449.

21   Clyde Wilson, "Macon, Nathaniel," *NCPedia,* http//www.ncpedia/ biography/macon-nathaniel-0.

22   *Mississippi Intelligencer* (Brandon, MS, June 4, 1839.)

23   *Congressional Globe*, January 23, 1841.

24   Jack Mayfield, "The Organization of Lafayette County—February 9, 1836," http://hottytoddy.com/2013/03/11.

25   Oldham, *Jacob Thompson*, 35-36.

26   P. L. Rainwater, *Letters to and from Jacob Thompson*, 96.

27   Ibid.

28   Jacob Thompson Property Ledger (1854-56), Carolyn Ross Collections, Jacob Thompson, *University of Mississippi Libraries, Archives, and Special Collections* (Oxford, MS.)

29   Oldham, *Jacob Thompson*, 67.

30   Ibid, 39-41.

31   *Congressional Globe, Vol 8, #31, June 23, 1840, 480.*

32   Claiborne, *Mississippi as a Province*, 450.

33   Stephen Enzweiler, *Oxford in the Civil War: Battle for a Vanquished Land* (The History Press, Charleston, S. C., 2010), 26.

34   Claiborne, *Mississippi as a Province, 450-451.*

35   William Edmunds Benson, *A Political History of the Tariff 1789-1861* (Xlibris Corporation, 2010), 110.

36   Claiborne, *Mississippi as a Province, 453.*

37   James K. Polk, Wayne Cutler, editor, *The Correspondence of James K. Polk, Vol 7, Jan-Aug, 1844* (Vanderbilt Press, Nashville, TN, 1989), 212.

38   Claiborne, *Mississippi as a Province, 451-452.*

39   Ibid, 453.

40   Rainwater, *Letters to and from Jacob Thompson,* 104.

41   Kettell, 26.

42   Claiborne, *Mississippi as a Province,* 454.

43   Robert E. May, *John A. Quitman: Old South Crusader* (L. S. U. Press, Baton Rouge, LA, 1994), 210.

44   Dunbar Rowland editor, *Mississippi: Comprising Sketches of Towns, Events, Institutions, and Persons, Vol II* (Southern Historical Publishing Association, Atlanta, GA, 1907), 497

45   Ibid.

46   *Congressional Globe, Vol 15* (February 2, 1846.)

47   Jacob Thompson, "Increase of the Army Speech," *Congressional Globe* (Jan 9, 1847), 154.

48   Robert W. Merry, *A Country of Vast Designs: James K. Polk, the Mexican War, and the Conquest of the American Continent* (Simon and Schuster, New York, N. Y., 2009), 340-341.

49   Kettell, 78-82.

50   Ibid, 79.

51   Ibid, 80.

52   Ibid, 82.

53 Lynette Boney Wrenn, *A Bachelors Life: The Diary of Dr. Elijah Millington Walker, 1849-1852*, (University of Tennessee Press, Knoxville, TN, 2004), 52, 132.

54 Westley F. Busbee, *Mississippi: A History*, (Harlan Davidson Inc., Davidson, N. C., 2005.), 101-102.

55 David G. Sansing, *The University of Mississippi: A Sesquicentennial History* (University Press of Mississippi, Jackson, MS, 1999), 22

56 Ibid, 31.

57 Ibid, 69.

58 Michael de L. Landon, *The University of Mississippi School of Law: A Sesquicentennial History* (University Press of Mississippi, Jackson, MS, 2006), 16.

59 Enzweiler, *Oxford in the Civil War*, 31.

60 Ibid, 29-32.

61 Ibid.

62 Carolyn Ross manuscript (unfinished), *The University of Mississippi Libraries, Archives, and Special Collections* (University, MS.)

63 Ibid.

64 Edward Mayes, *Lucius Q. C. Lamar: His Life, Times, and Speeches* (Publishing House of the Methodist Episcopal Church South, Nashville, TN, 1896), 56.

65 Enzweiler, *Oxford in the Civil War*, 21.

66 Oldham, *Jacob Thompson* (quoting Mrs. Katherine Thompson Andrews, great niece of Jacob Thompson), 63.

67 Carolyn Ross manuscript (unfinished.)

68 Cleo Hearon, "Mississippi and the Compromise of 1850," *Publications of the Mississippi Historical Society, Vol 14* (Oxford, MS, 1913), 56.

69 John Caldwell Calhoun, *The Papers of John C. Calhoun 1848-1849, Vol 26* (University of South Carolina, Columbia, S. C., 2001) 225-243.

70 *Oxford Constitution* (Oxford, MS, March 22, 1851.)

71 Carolyn Ross Collections, "Letter from Jacob Thompson to Aunt Rebecca," March 16, 1849 (The University of Mississippi Libraries, Oxford, MS.)

72 Claiborne, *Mississippi as a Province*,454.

73 James B. Murphy, *L. Q. C. Lamar: Pragmatic Patriot* (Louisiana State University Press, Baton Rouge, LA, 1973), 17.

74 William S. Speer, *Sketches of Prominent Tennesseans* (A. B. Tavel, Nashville, TN, 1888), 23.

75   Edward McPherson, *A Political Manual for 1870* (Philip and Solomons, Washington, D. C., 1870), 564.

76   William C. Davis, *Jefferson Davis: The Man and His Hour* (Harper Collins, New York, 1991), 118

77   Jefferson Davis, James T. McIntosh, editor, *The Papers of Jefferson Davis, Vol 2* (Louisiana State University Press, Baton Rouge, LA, 1974), 102.

78   William J. Cooper, Jr., *Jefferson Davis, American* (Alfred A. Knopf, New York, 2000), 183.

79   Ross Collections (The University of Mississippi Libraries, Oxford, MS.)

80   Cooper, Jr., *Jefferson Davis, American*, 274.

81   William Edward Dodd, *Jefferson Davis* (G. W. Jacobs, Philadelphia, PA, 1907), 153-154.

82   *Proceedings of the Democratic National Convention June 1-5, 1852 at Baltimore* Washington, D. C., 1852), 50.

83   *Memphis Appeal* (Memphis, TN, March 8, 1857.

84   Roy Franklin Nichols, *The Disruption of American Democracy* (The Macmillan Company, New York, 1948), 79.

85   Claiborne, *Mississippi as a Province*, 455-456.

86   Mary J. Windle, *Life in Washington and Here and There* (Philadelphia, PA, J. B. Lipincott and Co., 1859), 237.

87   Ibid, 268.

88   Mary Boykin Chestnut, C. Vann Woodward editor, *Mary Chestnut's Civil War* (Yale University Press, New Haven, CT, 1981), 22.

89   Nichols, *The Disruption of American Democracy*, 149-151.

90   Oldham, *Jacob Thompson*, 55, 68.

91   Rachel A. Shelden, *Washington Brotherhood: Politics, Social Life and the Coming of the Civil War* (University of North Carolina Press, Chapel Hill, N. C., 2013), 179.

92   Philip Gerald Auchampaugh, *James Buchanan and His Cabinet on the Eve of Secession* (Lancaster Press, Lancaster, PA, 1926), 52.

93   Will Bagley, *South Pass: Gateway to a Continent* (University of Oklahoma Press, Norman, OK, 2014), 203.

94   John D. Unruh, Jr., *The Plains Across: The Overland Emigrants and the Trans-Mississippi West 1840-1860* (University of Illinois Press, Champaign, IL, 1993) 44.

95   Conrad Kalmbacher, *Secession and the U. S. Mail, The Postal Service, The South, and Sectional Controversy* (Author House, Bloomington, IN, 2013), 73-74.

96   "The Seceders Sustained; Meeting at Memphis, Tennessee: Letter from Secretary Thompson," *The New York Times, June 7, 1860.*

97   Nichols, *The Disruption of American Democracy*, 313.

98   Ibid, 298.

99   Ibid, 361.

100   Michael Taylor, Herman Hattaway, and Ethan Sepp Rafuse, editors, *The Ongoing Civil War: New Versions of Old Stories* (University of Missouri Press, Columbia, MO, 2004), 64.

101   Joel Williamson, *William Faulkner and Southern History* (Oxford University Press, Oxford, England, 1993), 127.

102   James Buchanan Henry, *The Works of James Buchanan Comprising His Speeches, State Papers, and Private Correspondence, Vol 12* (J. B. Lipincott Company, Philadelphia, PA, 1911), 165.

103   Ibid.

104   Auchampaugh, *James Buchanan and His Cabinet*, 120.

105   Ibid, 118-119.

106   Charles B. Dew, *Apostles of Disunion: Southern Secession Commissioners and the Causes of the Civil War* (University of Virginia Press, Charlottesville, VA, 2001) 31.

107   Ibid.

108   "Letter of Jacob Thompson to the Governor of North Carolina," http://www.civilwarcauses.org/thompson.htm.

109   Dew, *Apostles of Disunion*, 30.

110   Auchampaugh, *James Buchanan and His Cabinet*, 118-119.

111   Ibid.

112   Ibid, 131.

113   Ibid, 138.

114   Ibid, 131.

115   Ibid, 116.

116   Nichols, *The Disruption of American Democracy*, 424.

117   Ibid, 424-425.

118   Ulrich B. Phillips, editor, *The Correspondence of Robert Toombs, Alexander H. Stephens and Howell Cobb, Vol II* (American Historical Association, Washington, D. C., 1913), 532.

119   Henry Alden, Thomas Wells and Lee Hartman, editors, *Harpers Magazine, Vol 25* (June to November 1867), 367.

120   Auchampaugh, *James Buchanan and His Cabinet*, 117.

121   E. Merton Coulter, *William Montague Browne: Versatile Anglo-Irish American* (University of Georgia Press, Athens, GA, 1967), 36.

122   Frank Windham, editor, "The Letters of Kate Thompson to Mary Ann Cobb, 1858-1861," *Journal of Mississippi History 50/3* (Jackson, MS, 1988), 187-188.

123   Ibid, 192-197.

124   Ibid, 197-198.

125   Coulter, *William Montague Browne*, 77.

126   Horace Greeley, *New York Daily Tribune, January 9, 1861*, 4.

127   Ross, manuscript (unfinished.)

128   Oldham, *Jacob Thompson*, 77.

129   Ross manuscript (unfinished.)

130   Elizabeth Leonard, *Lincoln's Forgotten Attorney: Judge Advocate General Holt* (University of North Carolina Press, Chapel Hill, N. C., 2011), 130.

131   Claiborne, *Mississippi as a Province*, 458.

132   "Mississippi Units by County of Origin 1861-1865," http://www.humphreys1625.homestead.com

133   Windham, *The Letters of Kate Thompson*, 190.

134   Jefferson Davis, Lynda Lasswell Crist, editor, *The Papers of Jefferson Davis, Vol 7, 1861* (Louisiana State University Press, Baton Rouge, LA, 1992), 327.

135   Ibid.

136   Robert W. Dubay, *John Jones Pettus, Mississippi Fire-Eater* (University Press of Mississippi, Jackson, MS, 1975), 115-116.

137   "Report of Colonel Jacob Thompson, C. S. Army, Aide-de-Camp to General Beauregard," http://www.civilwararchive.com/Research/1862/shilohcsa2.htm, 2-4.

138   Winston Groom, *Shiloh, 1862* (The National Geographic Society, Washington, D. C., 2012), 332.

139   Christopher Dickey, "The Confederate Spymaster Sleeping with the Enemy," *The Daily Beast* (May 8, 2016.)

140   Larry J. Daniel, *Shiloh: The Battle That Changed the Civil War* (Simon and Schuster, New York, N. Y, 1997), 196, 215.

141   Groom, *Shiloh, 1862*, 349.

142   "Report of Gen. P. G. T. Beauregard, C. S. Army, Commanding Army of the Mississippi, at the Battle of Shiloh (Pittsburg Landing), Corinth, Miss., April 11, 1862," http://www.civilwarhome.com.beau.html.

143   Claiborne, *Mississippi as a Province*, 459.

144   Enzweiler, *Oxford in the Civil War*, 79

145   Ibid, 81.

146   Ibid, 82-83.

147   Ibid, 89-90.

148   Ibid.

149   Ulysses S. Grant, *Personal Memoirs of U. S. Grant* (Charles L. Webster and Co., New York, N. Y., 1885), 273.

150   Ibid.

151   John C. Pemberton, *Pemberton, Defender of Vicksburg* (University of North Carolina Press, Chapel Hill, N. C., 1942), 148.

152   Ibid, 161.

153   Timothy B. Smith, *Champion Hill: Decisive Battle for Vicksburg* (Savas Beatie LLC, New York, N. Y., 2004), 121.

154   "Report of Lieut. Gen. Pemberton to Gen. S. Cooper, Adjt & Inspector General, Aug. 25, 1863," (Published by Order of Congress, 1864.)

155   Claiborne, *Mississippi as a Province*, 460.

156   "Letter from General Chalmers to Jacob Thompson, December 15, 1863," http://www.civilwar-online.com/2013/12/december-15-1863-james-r-chalmers-to.html.

157   Crist, *Papers of Jefferson Davis, Vol 10*, 123-124.

158   *Official Records, War of the Rebellion*, Series 2, Vol. 3, 174.

159   Ibid, 319.

160   *Lafayette County Mississippi Deed Book K,* (Oxford, MS.)

161   Crist, *Papers of Jefferson Davis, Vol 10* (123-124.)

162   Adam Mayers, *Dixie and the Dominion: Canada, the Confederacy, and the War for the Union* (The Dunburn Group, Toronto, Canada, 2003), 26.

163   Crist, *Papers of Jefferson Davis, Vol 10*, 154.

164   James D. Horan, *Confederate Agent: A Discovery in History* (Crown Publishers Inc., New York, N. Y., 1954), 81.

165   Pierce Butler, *Judah P. Benjamin* (George W. Jacobs and Co., Philadelphia, PA, 1906), 347.

166   Mayers, *Dixie and the Dominion*, 28-29.

167   Horan, *Confederate Agent*, 81-83.

168   Mayers, *Dixie and the Dominion*, 26-27.

169   Ibid, 52.

170   Ibid, Preface.

171   John Boyko, *Blood and Daring: How Canada Fought the American Civil War and Forged a Nation* (Vintage, Canada, Toronto, Canada, 2013), 163.

172   Ibid, 163-164.

173   Donald E. Markle, *Spies and Spymasters of the Civil War* (Hippocrene Books, New York, N. Y., 2004), 51-52.

174   Horan, *Confederate Agent*, 88.

175   Adam Mayers, "Confederacy's Canadian Mission: Spies Across the Border," *Civil War Times, June 2001.*

176   Horan, *Confederate Agent*, 94.

177   Claiborne, *Mississippi as a Province*, 461-462.

178   Mayers, "Spies across the Border," 3.

179   Thomas Hines, "Northwest Conspiracy," *The Southern Bivouac, Vol II, #1* (B. F. Avery & Sons, Louisville, KY, June 1886), 506.

180   Mayers, *Dixie and the Dominion*, 60.

181   Horan, *Confederate Agent*, 298.

182   Ibid, 86.

183   Hines, "Northwest Conspiracy," 507.

184   Ibid.

185   Virgil Carrington Jones, *Eight Hours Before Richmond* (Henry Holt and Company, New York, 1957), 100-101.

186   Ibid, 107, 107, 113, 124-126.

187   Ibid, 136-141.

188   Ibid, 128.

189   Ibid, 109-110.

190   Ibid, 110.

191   Ibid, 121.

192   Hines, "Northwest Conspiracy," 502.

193   Boyko, *Blood and Daring*, 165-166.

194   Ibid, 166-167.

195   Mayers, *Dixie and the Dominion*, 66.

196   Frank van der Linden, *The Dark Intrigue: The True Story of a Civil War Conspiracy* (Malloy Inc., Ann Arbor, MI, 2007), 131.

197   Mayers, *Dixie and the Dominion*, 63.

198   Frank van der Linden, *The Dark Intrigue*, 131.

199   Ibid, 132.

200   Ibid, 138.

201   Boyko, *Blood and Daring*, 168-169.

202   Horan, *Confederate Agent*, 109-110.

203   Ruth Ketring Nuermberger, *The Clays of Alabama: A Planter-Lawyer-Politician Family* (University of Alabama Press, Tuscaloosa, AL, 2005), 251-252.

204   Ibid.

205   Ibid.

206   Ibid.

207   Horan, *Confederate Agent*, 109-112.

208   Hines, "Northwest Conspiracy," 509.

209   Hines, *Confederate Agent*, 156.

210   Boyko, *Blood and Daring*, 170-171.

211   Ibid, 170.

212   John B. Castleman, *Active Service* (Courier Journal Printing Co., Louisville KY, 1917), 161.

213   Horan, *Confederate Agent*, 159.

214   Boyko, *Blood and Daring*, 171-172.

215   Markle, *Spies and Spymasters*, 54.

216   *Official Records, War of the Rebellion, Series I, Vol 43, pt. 2,* 930-936.

217   Mayers, *Dixie and the Dominion*, 132, 135.

218   Boyko, *Blood and Daring*, 190.

219   Castleman, *Active Service*, 136.

220   Mayers, *Dixie and the Dominion*, 111, 113.

221   Horan, *Confederate Agent*, 248-249.

222   Mayers, *Dixie and the Dominion*, 114-115.

223   Boyko, *Blood and Daring*, 186.

224   *Official Records, War of the Rebellion, Series II, Vol VI,* 372-373.

225   *Official Records, War of the Rebellion, Series II, Vol VII, 954.*

226   Boyko, *Blood and Daring,* 187-188.

227   Ibid, 188.

228   Horan, *Confederate Agent*, 157, 220-221.

229   Castleman, *Active Service*, 133.

230   Hines, "Northwest Conspiracy," 502.

231   Ibid.

232   Horan, *Confederate Agent*, 230-231.

233   Boyko, *Blood and Daring,* 179.

234   Horan, *Confederate Agent*, 89.

235   Ibid.

236   Ibid, 94.

237   Frank van der Linden, *Dark Intrigue,* 134.

238   Ibid, Preface XI.

239   Castleman, *Active Service*, 168-174.

240   Horan, *Confederate Agent*, 136.

241   Jefferson Davis, *Rise and Fall of the Confederate Government, Vol. 2* (D. Appleton & Co., New York, 1881), 611.

242   Lynda Lasswell Crist, editor, *Papers of Jefferson Davis, Vol. 13* (LSU Press, Baton Rouge, LA, 2012), 236.

243   Nancy Baird, *Luke Pryor Blackburn: The Good Samaritan* (Western Kentucky University, Bowling Green, KY, 1974), 10

244   Ibid, 11-12.

245   Matthew W. Lively, "Yellow Fever Plot of 1864 Targeted Lincoln & U. S. Cities," www.civilwarprofiles.com/yellow-fever-plot-of-1864-targeted-lincoln-u-s-cities, (July 13, 2014.)

246   Ibid.

247   Boyko, *Blood and Daring*, 224-227.

248   *Official Records, Series I, Vol 43, pt. 2, 930-936.*

249   Boyko, *Blood and Daring*, 227.

250   Ibid, 227-228.

251   Claiborne, *Mississippi as a Province*, 463.

252   Mayers, *Dixie and the Dominion*, 204-205.

253   Ibid.

254   Boyko, *Blood and Daring*, 228.

255   Ibid.

256   Ibid, 228-229.

257   Ibid, 229.

258   Ibid 229-230.

259   Horan, *Confederate Agent*, 251.

260   Ibid, 264.

261   Ibid.

262   *Official Records, Series II, Vol. VM,* 519.

263   Ibid.

264   Don Doyle, *Faulkner's County: The Historical Roots of Yoknapatawpha* (University of North Carolina Press, Chapel Hill, N. C., 2001), 246.

265   Stephen Enzweiler, "Union Memoir Details Oxford Burning on Aug. 22, 1864" (*Oxford Citizen, Thursday Aug. 21, 2014*), 5.

266   Oldham, *Jacob Thompson* 103.

267   Doyle, *Faulkner's County*, 248.

268   Enzweiler, "Union Memoir Details," 5.

269   Doyle, *Faulkner's County*, 248.

270   Howard T. Dimick, "Motives for the Burning of Oxford, Miss." (The Journal of Mississippi History, Vol VIII, July 1946), 119-120.

271   Carolyn Ross Collections, "Letter from Jacob Thompson in Toronto to wife Kate, November 13, 1864 (University of Mississippi Libraries, University, MS.)

272   Oldham, *Jacob Thompson*, 102.

273   "Jacob Thompson Congressman, Secretary of the Interior, Pirate of the Great Lakes," www.fulkerson.org/thompson.html

274   Oldham, *Jacob Thompson*, 98.

275   Ibid, 99-101.

276   Ibid, 101-102.

277   Ibid, 104-105.

278   Ibid, 105-106.

279   Charles A. Dana, *Recollections of the Civil War* (D. Appleton & Co., New York, 1913), 273-274.

280   Ibid.

281   Michael W. Kauffman, *American Brutus: John Wilkes Booth and the Lincoln Assassination* (Random House, New York, N. Y., 2004), 71.

282   Claiborne, *Mississippi as a Province*, 464.

283   Ibid, 463.

284   Oldham, *Jacob Thompson*, 107.

285   Ibid, 108.

286   Stephen Enzweiler, "Our History: Postwar years were a double-edged sword for Thompson," http://oxfordcitizen.com, (March 3, 2015), 3.

287   William Hanchett, *The Lincoln Murder Conspiracies* (University of Illinois Press, Urbana, IL, 1983), 63-64.

288   Ibid, 64.

289   *The New York Times, May 4, 1865.*

290   Pierce Butler, *Judah P. Benjamin* (George W. Jacobs & Co., Philadelphia, PA, 1906), 347.

291   Kauffman, *American Brutus,* 336-337.

292   "Letter from Jacob Thompson to Jerry Black, July 16, 1865" (Manuscript Division of Library of Congress, D2.)

293   Seymour J. Frank, "The Conspiracy to Implicate the Confederate Leaders in Lincoln's Assassination," *Mississippi Valley Historical Review 40* (1954), 629-630.

294   Hanchett, *The Lincoln Murder Conspiracies*, 44.

295   Kauffman, *American Brutus*, 340-341.

296   Ibid, 342-343.

297   Hanchett, *The Lincoln Murder Conspiracies*, 71.

298   Kauffman, *American Brutus,* 342.

299   Ibid.

300   Boyko, *Blood and Daring*, 251-252.

301   Hanchett, *The Lincoln Murder Conspiracies*, 71.

302 Kauffman, *American Brutus*, 344.

303 Hanchett, *The Lincoln Murder Conspiracies*, 72.

304 Kauffman, *American Brutus*, 350.

305 Boyko, *Blood and Daring*, 253-254.

306 Kauffman, *American Brutus*, 364.

307 Hanchett, *The Lincoln Murder Conspiracies*, 73.

308 Boyko, *Blood and Daring*, 254.

309 Ibid.

310 Hanchett, *The Lincoln Murder Conspiracies*, 74-81.

311 Ibid, 75.

312 Eli N. Evans, *Judah P. Benjamin: The Jewish Confederate* (The Free Press, New York, N. Y., 1988), 369-370.

313 William C. Davis, "The Conduct of Mr. Thompson," *The Civil War Times Illustrated, Vol IX, #2* (May 1970), 5.

314 Ibid.

315 Ibid, 7.

316 Ibid, 7.

317 Castleman, *Active Service*, 202.

318 Davis, "The Conduct of Mr. Thompson," 43.

319 Ibid, 43-44.

320 Evans, *Judah P. Benjamin*, 370-371.

321 Oldham, *Jacob Thompson*, 125-126.

322 Davis, "The Conduct of Mr. Thompson," 4.

323

324 Castleman, *Active Service*, 144.

325 Ibid.

326 Mayers, *Dixie and the Dominion*, 132.

327 Horan, *Confederate Agent*, 288-290.

328 Ibid, 298.

329 Browne, *Versatile Anglo-Irish American,* 270-276.

330 Ibid, 276.

331 Henry S. Foote, *Casket of Reminiscences* (Chronicle Publishing, Washington, D. C., 1874), 151.

332 Ibid.

333 *New York Times, July 21, 1883 from the New Orleans Times-Democrat.*

334 Jacob Thompson, "Letter from Thompson to Jeremiah Black, Nov. 27, 1879" (Dickinson College Archives and Special Collections, Carlisle, PA.)

335 Ibid.

336   Peggy Robbins, "The Great Scoundrel," *Civil War Times Illustrated, Vol 31, #5* (Cowles Media Co., Harrisburg, PA, Nov./Dec. 1992), 60.

337   Lynda Lasswell Crist, *The Papers of Jefferson Davis, Vol 14* (Louisiana State University Press, Baton Rouge, LA, 2015), 2.

338   Ibid.

339   Catherine Thompson, "Letter to son Macon, October 21, 1865" (Museum of the Confederacy, Eleanor S. Brockenbrough Library, Richmond, VA.)

340   Catherine Thompson, "Letter to Macon, May 26, 1870" (Ross Collections, University of Mississippi Libraries, University, MS.)

341   Jacob Thompson, "Letter to J. Black, mailed from Paris, France, October 9, 1865" (Stanford University Libraries Special Collections, Stanford, CA, MISC 1815.)

342   Rainwater, "Letters to and from Jacob Thompson," 104-106.

343   Ibid.

344   Castleman, *Active Service*, 199-200.

345   Jacob Thompson, "Letter to Macon from Naples, Italy, Jan. 12, 1866" (Museum of the Confederacy, Eleanor S. Brockenbrough Library, Richmond, VA.)

346   Ibid.

347   Castleman, *Active Service*, 199-200.

348   Ibid.

349   Ibid.

350   Rainwater, "Letters to and from Jacob Thompson," 106-110.

351   Paul H. Bergeron, editor, *The Papers of Andrew Johnson, Vol 15, Sept. 1868-Apr. 1869* (University of Tennessee Press, Knoxville, TN, 1998), 336.

352   Hanchett, *The Lincoln Murder Conspiracies*, 89.

353   Allen Cabaniss, *The University of Mississippi: Its First Hundred Years* (University and College Press of Mississippi, Hattiesburg, MS, 1971), 2.

354   Oldham, *Jacob Thompson*, 11.

355   Jack Mayfield, "Oxford's Olden Days: The Gardener's Home— The Gatekeeper's Lodge, http//www.hottytoddy.com/2015/03/16 (March 16, 2015.)

356   Doyle, *Faulkner's County*, 261-262.

357   Ibid, 267.

358   Oldham, *Jacob Thompson*, 121-122.

359 Catherine Thompson, "Letter to Macon, May 26, 1870, (Ross Collections, University of Mississippi Libraries, University, MS.)

360 Oldham, *Jacob Thompson*, 120.

361 Jeremiah Black, "Letter to *Cincinnati Commercial* reprinted in *Memphis Daily Appeal,* June 14, 1870.

362 Ibid.

363 Oldham, *Jacob Thompson*, 121-122.

364 Ibid, 123.

365 Ibid, 126.

366 Horan, *Confederate Agent*, 289.

367 *Insurance Journal: A Monthly Review of Fire & Life Insurance, Vol II* (Hartford, CT, 1874), 164.

368 Oldham, *Jacob Thompson*, 123.

369 *Memphis Appeal* (Memphis, TN, February 3, 1872.)

370 Oldham, *Jacob Thompson*, 125-126.

371 Crist, editor, *The Papers of Jefferson Davis, Vol 13, xiv.*

372 Oldham, *Jacob Thompson*, 125-126.

373 James Harvey Mathes, *The Old Guard in Gray: Researches in the Annals of the Confederate Historical Association* (Press of S. C. Toof & Co., Memphis, TN, 1897), 200-201.

374 Paul R. Coppock, "Mid-South Memoirs: A North Carolina Boy Who Made Good In Mississippi," *The Commercial Appeal* (Memphis, TN, Jan. 15, 1978.)

375 George R. Fairbanks, *History of the University of the South at Sewanee, Tennessee* (H. & W. B. Drew Co., Jacksonville, FL, 1905), 163-190.

376 Ibid, 177-178, 190.

377 Ibid, 238, 242.

378 Arthur Ben and Elizabeth N. Chitty, *Sewanee Sampler* (Proctor's Hall Press, Sewanee, TN, 1978), 141-142/

379 *Southern Farmer, Vol 5* (Memphis, TN, Jan. 1871), 268.

380 C. W. Howard, editor, *The Plantation, Vol 2, #46* (Atlanta, GA, Dec. 18, 1871), 721.

381 John Y. Simon, editor, *The Papers of U. S. Grant, Vol 22* (Carbondale, IL, 1998), 425.

382 *The Commercial and Financial Chronicle, Vol 28* (William B. Dana & Col, New York, N. Y., Mar. 15, 1879), 277.

383 Henry Varnum Poor, *Manual of the Railroads of the United States for 1872-1873* (H. V. & H. W. Poor, New York, N. Y., 1872), 564.

384   *Proceedings of the National Railroad Convention in St. Louis, MO, Nov. 23, 24, 1875*, 102.

385   *Sholes' Memphis Directory Guide Taxing District, Shelby Co., Tenn., Vol. 10* (1883), 13-14.

386   Claiborne, *Mississippi as a Province*, 465.

387   Oldham, *Jacob Thompson*, 116.

388   Claiborne, *Mississippi as a Province*, 465.

389   Ibid.

390   Ibid, 466.

391   Speer, *Sketches of Prominent Tennesseans*, 25.

392   Jim Woodrick, "Jacob Thompson," http//www.andspeakingof-which.blogspot.com, August 12, 2012, 3.

393   Bivins, "The Life and Character of Jacob Thompson," 91.

394   Edward Mayes, *Lucius Q. C. Lamar*, 478.

395   Ibid, 479.

396   Nichols, *The Disruption of Democracy*, 91.

397   James K. Polk, *The Diary of James K. Polk During His Presidency (1845-1849), Vol. 1* (A. C. McClung and Co., Chicago, IL, 1910), 240.

398   Amanda Foreman, *A World on Fire, Britain's Crucial Role in the American Civil War* (Random House, New York, N. Y., 2010), 663.

399   Mary Black Clayton, *Reminiscences of Jeremiah Sullivan Black* (Chrisian Publishing Co., St. Louis, MO, 1887), 106.

400   Boyko, *Blood and Daring*, 160.

401   Mayers, *Dixie and the Dominion*, 224.

402   "The 25 Most Influential Politicians, Civilians, Inventors, Spies, & Soldiers of the Civil War (That you've probably never heard of)," *The Civil War Monitor, Vol. 3, #4* (Bayshore History LLC, Margate, N. J., Winter 2013), 29, 38.

403   Ibid, 38.

404   Crist, editor, *The Papers of Jefferson Davis, Vol. 14* (April 22, 1885 letter from Davis to William Preston Johnston.)

405   "The 25 Most Influential," 38.

406   "Judge Cleary's Account of the Persecutions Endured by Leading Confederates After the Close of the War," *The Cincinnati Enquirer*, June 29, 1882.

407   "The 25 Most Influential," 38.

408   Robin W. Winks, *The Civil War Years: Canada and the United States* (McGill-Queen's University Press, Montreal, Canada, 1998), 277.

409   Bruce Catton, *A Stillness at Appomattox* (Doubleday & Co., Inc., Garden City, N. Y., 1954), 291.

410   Ibid, 291-292.

411   Sansing, *The University of Mississippi*, 31.

412   *New York Times*, published September 11, 1865.

413   Daniel W. Crofts, *Old Southampton: Politics and Society in A Virginia County, 1834-1869* (University Press of Virginia, Charlottesville, VA, 1992), 33.

414   Oldham, *Jacob Thompson*, 83.

415   Ibid, 102.

416   Isom, Joanna Thompson, *The Federal Writers Project of the Works Progress Administration for the State of Mississippi, slave narratives*, US Genweb African-American Griot Project, www.rootsweb.ancestry.com/~aagriots.

417   "Interview with Jacob Thompson on publication of Jefferson Davis' book *Rise and Fall of the Confederate Government*," *New York Times* from *Washington Post* (June 10, 1881), 3.

418   Butler, *Judah P. Benjamin*, 348.

419   Rainwater, "Letters to and from Jacob Thompson," 109.

420   Speer, *Sketches of Prominent Tennesseans*, 24.

421   Joseph Holt, "Reply of J. Holt to certain calumnies of Jacob Thompson," (Washington, D. C., 1883), 4.

422   Ibid, 19.

423   Auchampaugh, *James Buchanan and His Cabinet*, 115.

424   Ibid.

425   Mayfield, "Oxford's Olden Days: Jacob Thompson's Gardeners Home."

426   "Thompson House," http://www.tollisonlaw.com/about/thompson.house.

427   "Lake Thompson Recreation Area," http//gfp.sd.gov/state-parks/directory/lake-thompson.

428   Florence Kern, *The United States Revenue Cutters In the Civil War* (Allied Enterprises, Bethesda, MD, 1976), 9: 2-7.

429   Arthur F. Kinney, "Faulkner's Families," *A Companion to William Faulkner*, edited by Richard C. Moreland (Blackwell Publishing, Malden, MA, 2007), 190.

BIBLIOGRAPHY

Auchampaugh, Philip Gerald, *James Buchanan and His Cabinet on the Eve of Secession* (Lancaster Press, Lancaster, PA, 1926.)

Bagley, Will, *South Pass: Gateway to a Continent* (University of Oklahoma Press, Norman, OK, 2015.)

Baird, Nancy, *Luke Prior Blackburn: The Good Samaritan* (Western Kentucky University, Bowling Green, KY, 1974.)

Baker, Jean H., *James Buchanan* (Henry Holt and Co., New York, 2004.)))

Ballard, Michael B., *Pemberton: A Biography* (University Press of Mississippi, Jackson, MS, 1991.)

Bearss, Edwin Cole (The Campaign for Vicksburg, *Vol. I-III* (Morningside House Inc., Dayton, OH, 1985.)

Ben, Arthur and Chitty, Elizabeth N., *Sewanee Sampler* (Proctor's Hall Press, Sewanee, TN, 1978.)

Benson, William Edmunds, *A Political History of the Tariff 1789-1861* (Xlibris Corporation, Bloomington, IN, 2010.)

Bergeron, Paul H., editor, *The Papers of Andrew Johnson, Vol. 15* (University of Tennessee Press, Knoxville, TN, 1998.)

Bettersworth, John K., *Mississippi in the Confederacy as they saw it* (Kraus Reprint Co., New York, 1970.)

Boyko, John, *Blood and Daring: How Canada Fought the American Civil War and Forged a Nation* (Vintage Canada, Toronto, 2013.)

Busbee, Westley F., Jr., *Mississippi: A History* (John Wiley & Sons, Chichester UK, 2015.)

Butler, Pierce, *Judah P. Benjamin* (George W. Jacobs & Co., Philadelphia, PA, 1906.)

Cabaniss, Allen, *The University of Mississippi: Its First Hundred Years* (University and College Press of Mississippi, Hattiesburg, MS, 1971.

Calhoun, John Caldwell, *The Papers of John C. Calhoun 1848-1849, Vol. 26* (University of South Carolina, Columbia, S. C., 2001.)

Castleman, John B., *Active Service* (Courier Journal Printing Co., Louisville, KY, 1917.)

Catton, Bruce, *A Stillness at Appomattox* (Doubleday & Co., Inc., Garden City, NY, 1954.)

Chesnut, Mary Boykin, *The Unpublished Civil War Diaries* (Oxford University Press, New York, 1984.)

Chesnut, Mary Boykin, *Mary Chesnut's Civil War* (Yale University Press, New Haven, CT, 1981.)

Claiborne, J. F. H., *Mississippi as a Province, Territory and State: with notices of eminent citizens* (Power and Barksdale, Jackson, Mississippi, 1880.)

Clayton, Mary Black, *Reminiscences of Jeremiah Sullivan Black* (Christian Publishing Co., St Louis, MO, 1887.)

Commercial and Financial Chronicle, Vol. 28 (William B. Dana & Co., New York, 1879.)

Cooper, William J., Jr., *Jefferson Davis, American* (Alfred A. Knopf, New York, 2000.)

Coulter, E. Merton, *William Montague Browne: Versatile Anglo-Irish American* (University of Georgia Press, Athens, GA, 1967.)

Cozzens, Peter, *The Darkest Days of the War: The Battles of Iuka and Corinth* (The University of North Carolina Press, Chapel Hill, NC, 1997.)

Crist, Lynda Lasswell, editor, *The Papers of Jefferson Davis, Vol. 7, 1861* (Louisiana State University Press, Baton Rouge, LA, 1992.)

Crist, Lynda Lasswell, editor, *The Papers of Jefferson Davis, Vol. 10* (Louisiana State University Press, Baton Rouge, LA, 1999.)

Crist, Lynda Lasswell, editor, *The Papers of Jefferson Davis, Vol. 13* (Louisiana State University Press, Baton Rouge, LA, 2012.)

Crist, Lynda Lasswell, editor, The Papers of Jefferson Davis, Vol. 14 (Louisiana State University Press, Baton Rouge, LA, 2015.)

Crofts, Daniel W., *Old Southampton: Politics and Society in a Virginia County, 1834-1869* (University Press of Virginia, Charlottesville, VA, 1992.)

Cutler, Wayne, editor, *The Correspondence of James K. Polk, Vol. 7, Jan-Aug 1844* (Vanderbilt Press, Nashville, TN, 1989.)

Dana, Charles A., *Recollections of the Civil War* (D. Appleton & Co., New York, 1913.)

Daniel, Larry J., *Shiloh: The Battle That Changed the Civil War* (Simon & Schuster, New York, 1997.)

Davis, Burke, *The Long Surrender* (Random House, New York, 1985.)

Davis, Jefferson, *Rise and Fall of the Confederate Government, Vol. 2* (D. Appleton & Co., New York, 1881.)

Davis, William C., *Breckinridge: Statesman, Soldier, Symbol* (Louisiana State University Press, Baton Rouge, LA, 1974.)

Davis, William C., *Jefferson Davis: The Man and His Hour* (Harper Collins, New York, 1992.)

Dew, Charles B., *Apostles of Disunion: Southern Secession Commissioners and the Causes of the Civil War* (University of Virginia Press, Charlottesville, VA, 2001.)

Dodd, William Edward, *Jefferson Davis* (C. W. Jacobs, Philadelphia, PA, 1907.)

Doyle, Don, *Faulkner's County: The Historical Roots of Yoknapatawpha* (University of North Carolina Press, Chapel Hill, NC, 2001.)

Dubay, Robert W., *John James Pettus, Mississippi Fire-Eater* (University Press of Mississippi, Jackson, MS, 1975.)

Enzweiler, Stephen, *Oxford in the Civil War: Battle for a Vanquished Land* (The History Press, Charleston, SC, 2010.

Evans, Eli N., *Judah P. Benjamin: The Jewish Confederate* (The Free Press, New York, 1988.)

Fairbanks, George R., *History of the University of the South at Sewanee, TN* (H. & W. B. Drew Co., Jacksonville, FL, 1905.)

Foote, Henry S., *Casket of Reminiscences* (Chronicle Publishing, Washington, DC, 1874.)

Foreman, Amanda, *A World on Fire, Britain's Crucial Role in the American Civil War* (Random House, New York, 2010.)

Grant, Ulysses S., *Personal Memoirs of U. S. Grant* (Charles L. Webster & Co., New York, 1885.)

Groom, Winston, *Shiloh, 1862* (The National Geographic Society, Washington, DC, 2012.)

Hamilton, Holman, *Prologue to Conflict: The Crisis and Compromise of 1850* (University Press of Kentucky, Lexington, KY, 1964.)

Henry, James Buchanan, *The Works of James Buchanan Comprising His Speeches, State Papers, and Private Correspondence, Vol. 12* (J. B. Lipincott Co., Philadelphia, PA, 1911.)

Hooker, Charles E., *Confederate Military History, Vol. 7, Mississippi* (Confederate Publishing Co., Atlanta, GA, 1899.)

Horan, James D., *Confederate Agent: A Discovery in History* (Crown Publishers Inc., New York, 1954.)

Howell, H. Grady, Jr., *Going to Meet the Yankees: A History of the "Bloody Sixth" Mississippi Infantry C. S. A.* (Chickasaw Bayou Press, Jackson, MS, 1981.)

Jones, Virgil Carrington, *Eight Hours before Richmond* (Henry Holt and Company, New York, 1957.)

Kalmbacher, Conrad, *Secession and the U. S. Mail, The Postal Service, The South, and Sectional Controversy* (Author House, Bloomington, IN, 2013.)

Kauffman, Michael W., *American Brutus: John Wilkes Booth and the Lincoln Assassination* (Random House, New York, 2004.)

Kern, Florence, *The United States Revenue Cutters in the Civil War* (Allied Enterprises, Bethesda, MD, 1981.)

Kettell, Thomas Prentice, *The United States Democratic Review, Vol 26* (Langtree & O'Sullivan, New York, 1850.)

Kinney, Arthur F., Richard C. Moreland, editor, *A Companion to William Faulkner* (Blackwell Publishing, Malden, MA, 2007.)

Landon, Michael de L., *The University of Mississippi School of Law: A Sesquicentennial History* (University Press of Mississippi, Jackson MS, 2006.)

Leonard, Elizabeth, *Lincoln's Forgotten Attorney: Judge Advocate General Holt* (University of North Carolina Press, Chapel Hill, NC, 2011.)

Linden, Frank van der, *The Dark Intrigue: The True Story of a Civil War Conspiracy* (Malloy Inc., Ann Arbor, MI, 2007.)

Markle, Donald E., *Spies and Spymasters of the Civil War* (Hippocrene Books, New York, 2004.)

Mathes, James Harvey, *The Old Guard in Gray: Researches in the Annals of the Confederate Historical Association* (Press of S. C. Toof & Co., Memphis, TN, 1897.)

May, Robert E., *John A. Quitman: Old South Crusader* (Louisiana State University Press, Baton Rouge, LA, 1994.)

Mayes, Edward, *Lucius Q. C. Lamar: His Life, Times, and Speeches* (Publishing House of the Methodist Episcopal Church South, Nashville, TN, 1896.)

McIntosh, James T. editor, *The Papers of Jefferson Davis, Vol. 2* (Louisiana State University, Baton Rouge, 1974.)

McPherson, Edward, *A Political Manual for 1870* (Philip and Solomons, Washington, DC, 1870.)

McPherson, James M., *Battle Cry of Freedom* (Oxford University Press, New York, 1988.)

Merry, Robert W., *A Country of Vast Designs, James K. Polk, the Mexican War, and the Conquest of the American Continent* (Simon and Schuster, New York, 2009.)

Murphy, James B., *L. Q. C. Lamar: Pragmatic Patriot* (Louisiana State University Press, Baton Rouge, LA, 1973.)

Nichols, Roy Franklin, *The Disruption of American Democracy* (The Macmillan Company, New York, 1948.)

Nuermberger, Ruth Ketring, *The Clays of Alabama: A Planter-Lawyer-Politician Family* (University of Alabama Press, Tuscaloosa, AL, 2005.)

Oates, Stephen B., *The Approaching Fury: Voices of the Storm 1820-1861* (Harper-Collins Publishers Inc., New York, 1997.)

Oldham, Dorothy Zollicoffer, *Life of Jacob Thompson, Masters Thesis* (University, MS, 1930.)

Pemberton, John C., *Pemberton, Defender of Vicksburg* (University of North Carolina Press, Chapel Hill, NC, 1942.)

Phillips, Ulrich B., editor, *The Correspondence of Robert Toombs, Alexander H. Stephens and Howell Cobb, Vol. 2* (American Historical Association, Washington, DC, 1913.

Polk, James K., *The Diary of James K. Polk During His Presidency (1845-1849), Vol. 1* (A. C. McClung and Co., Chicago, IL, 1910.)

Poor, Henry Varnum, *Manual of the Railroads of the United States for 1872-1873* (H. V. & H. W. Poor, New York, 1872,)

Potter, David M., *The Impending Crisis: America Before the Civil War, 1848-1861* (Harper Perennial, New York, 2011.)

Rand, Clayton, *Men of Spine In Mississippi* (The Dixie Press, Gulfport, MS, 1940.)

Rowland, Dunbar editor, *Mississippi: Comprising Sketches of Towns, Events, Institutions and Persons ...*, *Vol. 2* (Southern Historical Publishing Association, Atlanta, GA, 1907.)

Sansing, David G., *The University of Mississippi: A Sesquicentennial History* (University Press of Mississippi, Jackson, MS, 1999.)

Sheldon, Rachel A., *Washington Brotherhood: Politics, Social Life and the coming of the Civil War* (University of North Carolina Press, Chapel Hill, NC, 2013.)

Simon, John Y., editor, *The Papers of U. S. Grant, Vol. 22* (Southern Illinois University Press, Carbondale, IL, 1998.)

Smith, Timothy B., *Champion Hill: Decisive Battle for Vicksburg* (Savas Beattie LLC, New York, 2004.)

Speer, William S., *Sketches of Prominent Tennesseans* (A. B. Tavel, Nashville, TN, 1888.)

Starr, Stephen Z., *Colonel Grenfell's Wars: The Life of a Soldier of Fortune* (Louisiana State University Press, Baton Rouge, LA, 1971.)

Swanberg, W. A., *First Blood: The Story of Fort Sumter* (Charles Scribner's Sons, New York, 1957.)

Taylor, Michael, Hattaway Herman and Rafuse, Ethan S., editors, *The Ongoing Civil War: New Versions of Old Stories* (University of Missouri Press, Columbia, MO, 2004.)

Unruh, John D., Jr., *The Plains Across: The Overland Emigrants and the Trans-Mississippi West 1840-1860* (University of Illinois Press, Champaign, IL, 1993.)

Williams, T. Harry, *P. G. T. Beauregard: Napoleon in Gray* (Louisiana State University Press, Baton Rouge, LA, 1955.)

Williamson, Joel, *William Faulkner and Southern History* (Oxford University Press, Oxford, England, 1993.)

Windle, Mary J., *Life In Washington and Here and There* (J. B. Lipincott & Co., Philadelphia, PA, 1859.)

Winks, Robin W., *The Civil War Years: Canada and the United States* (McGill-Queen's University Press, Montreal, Canada, 1998.)

Wrenn, Lynette Boney, editor, *A Bachelor's Life In Antebellum Mississippi: The Diary of Dr. Elijah Millington Walker, 1849-1852* (The University of Tennessee Press, Knoxville, TN, 2004.)

Wynne, Ben, *Mississippi's Civil War: A Narrative History* (Mercer University Press, Macon, GA, 2006.)

PERIODICALS, NEWSPAPERS, LETTERS, ETC.

Bivins, J. F., "The Life and Character of Jacob Thompson," Historical Papers of the Trinity College Historical Society, Duke University.

Black, Jeremiah, "Letter to *Cincinnati Commercial* reprinted in *Memphis Daily Appeal,* June 14, 1870.

Congressional Globe, June 23, 1840.

Congressional Globe, Vol. 15, February 2, 1846.

Congressional Globe, January 9, 1847.

Coppock, Paul R., "Mid-south Memoirs: A North Carolina Boy Who Made Good In Mississippi," *The Commercial Appeal*, Memphis, TN, January 15, 1978.

Davis, William C., "The Conduct of Mr. Thompson," *The Civil War Times Illustrated, Vol. IX, #2, May 1990.*

Dickey, Christopher, "The Confederate Spymaster Sleeping With The Enemy," *The Daily Beast, May 8, 2016.*

Dimick, Howard T., "Motives for the Burning of Oxford, Mississippi," *The Journal of Mississippi History, VIII, July 1946.*

Enzweiler, Stephen, "Union Memoir Details Oxford Burning on Aug. 22, 1864," *Oxford Citizen, Thursday, August 21, 2014.*

Enzweiler, Stephen, "Our History: Postwar years were a double-edged sword for Thompson," *Oxford Citizen, March 3, 2015.*

Frank, Seymour J., "The Conspiracy to Implicate the Confederate Leaders in Lincoln's Assassination," *Mississippi Valley Historical Review 40, 1954.*

Greeley, Horace, *New York Daily Tribune, January 9, 1861.*

Hearon, Cleo, "Mississippi and the Compromise of 1850," *Publications of the Mississippi Historical Society, Vol. 14, Oxford, MS, 1913.*

Hines, Henry, "The Northwestern Conspiracy," *Southern Bivouac, Vol. II, #1, June 1886.*

Holt, Joseph, "Reply of J. Holt to Certain Calumnies of Jacob Thompson," Washington, DC, 1883.

Howard, C. W., editor, *The Plantation, Vol. 2, #46, Atlanta, GA, December 18, 1871.*

Insurance Journal: A Monthly Review of Fire & Life Insurance, Vol. II, Hartford CT, 1874.

Kappler, Charles J., "Treat with the Chickasaw 1832," *Indian Affairs: Laws and Treaties 7* (Government Printing Office, 1904.)

Memphis Appeal (Memphis, TN, March 8, 1857.)

Memphis Appeal (Memphis, TN, February 3, 1872.)

Mississippi Intelligencer (Brandon, MS, June 4, 1839.)

New York Times, "The Seceders Sustained: Meeting at Memphis, Tennessee, Letter from Secretary Thompson, " June 2, 1860.

New York Times, May 4, 1865.

New York Times from *Washington Post,* "Interview with Jacob Thompson on Publication of Jeff Davis' Book Rise and Fall of the Confederate Government," June 10, 1881.

Oxford Constitution, Oxford, MS, March 22, 1851.

Pemberton John C., "Report of Lieut. Gen. Pemberton to Gen. S. Cooper, Adjt & Inspector General, Aug. 25, 1863 (Published by Order of Congress, 1864.)

"Proceedings of the Democratic National Convention, June 1-5, 1852 at Baltimore, Washington, DC, 1852."

"Proceedings of the National Railroad Convention at St. Louis, Missouri, November 23, 24, 1875."

Rainwater, P. L., "Letters to and from Jacob Thompson," *The Journal of Southern History, Vol. 6, #1, Feb. 1940.*

Robbins, Peggy, "The Greatest Scoundrel," *Civil War Times Illustrated, Vol. 31, #5* (Cowles Media Co., Harrisburg, PA, Nov/Dec 1992.)

Ross Carolyn, unfinished manuscript of Jacob Thompson (University of Mississippi Archives and Special Collections, University, MS.)

Thompson, Catherine, Letter to son Macon, October 21, 1865, Museum of the Confederacy, Eleanor S. Brockenbrough Library, Richmond, VA.

Thompson, Jacob, "Increase of the Army Speech in the House of Representatives, January 9, 1847" (Blair & Rives, Washington, DC, 1847.)

Thompson, Jacob, Letter to wife Kate, November 13, 1864, Toronto, Canada (unpublished, University of Mississippi Archives and Special Collections, Carolyn Ross Collection.

Thompson, Jacob, Letter to J. Black, July 6, 1865, Manuscript Division of Library of Congress D2.

Thompson, Jacob, Letter to Jeremiah Black, November 27, 1879, Dickinson College Archives and Special Collections, Carlisle, PA.

Thompson, Jacob, Letter to J. Black, October 9, 1865, mailed from Paris, France, Stanford University Libraries Special Collections, Stanford, CA, MISC 1815.

Thompson, Jacob, Property Ledger (1854-1856), Carolyn Ross Collections, University of Mississippi Archives and Special Collections, University, MS.

Wernick, Robert, "The Debts We Never Repaid," *American Heritage #1, 1964.*

Windham, Frank, editor, "The Letters of Kate Thompson to Mary Ann Cobb, 1858-1861," *Journal of Mississippi History 50/3,* (Jackson, MS, 1988.)

Internet Sources

Beauregard, P. G. T., "Report of General Beauregard C. S. Army, Commanding Army of the Mississippi at the Battle of Shiloh (Pittsburg Landing) www.civilwarhome.com/beau.html.

Caswell County Family Tree, Nicholas Thompson Genealogy and Will, www.rootsweb.ancestry.com/cgl-bin/igm.cgi?op=GET&db=caswellcounty&id=13917.

Chalmers, James, "Letter from General Chalmers to Jacob Thompson, December 15, 1863," www.civilwar-online.com/2013/12/december-15-1863-james-r-chalmers-to.html.

Isom, Joanna Thompson, The Federal Writers Project of the Works Progress Administration for the State of Mississippi, slave narratives, US Genweb African-American Griot Project, www.rootsweb.ancestry.com/~aagriots.

"Lake Thompson Recreation Area," www.gfp.sd.gov/state-parks-directory/lake-thompson.

Lively, Matthew W., "Yellow Fever Plot of 1864 Targeted Lincoln & U. S. Cities," www.civilwarprofiles.com/yellow-fever-plot-of-1864-targeted-lincoln-u-s-cities, July 13, 2014.

Luebke, P., "Kilpatrick-Dahlgren Raid," Encyclopedia Virginia, Virginia Foundation for the Humanities, encyclopediavirginia.org/Kilpatrick-Dahlgren_Raid.

Macon, Nathaniel Biography, www.ncpedia/biography/macon-nathaniel-0.

Mayfield, Jack, "The organization of Lafayette County—February 9, 1836," www.hottytoddy.com/2013/03/11.

Mayfield, Jack, "Oxford's Olden Days: The Gardener's Home—the Gatekeeper's Lodge," www.hottytoddy.com/2015/03/16.

"Secret Operations by the Confederacy," www.civilwarhome.com/canadaspies.htm.

Thompson, Jacob, "Letter to Governor of North Carolina," www.civilwarcauses.org/thompson.htm.

Thompson, Jacob, "Report of Colonel Jacob Thompson, C. S. Army, Aide de Camp to General Beauregard," www.civilwararchive.com/Research/1862/shilohcsa2.htm.

"Thompson House," www.tollisonlaw.com/about/thompson house.

Woodrick, Jim, "Jacob Thompson," www.andspeakingofwhich.blogspot.com, August 12, 2012.

ACKNOWLEDGEMENTS

Bill Rose, my former college roommate and long time friend, volunteered to edit this book. What a friend. Without his encouragement to proceed as well as utilizing his vast editing skills gleaned from a career doing just that, Accused would not have come to fruition.

Special thanks are also due the staff at the University of Mississippi Libraries, Archives and Special Collections for their kind and knowledgeable assistance.

Mary Ann, my wife, deserves a reward for tolerating me in this project, including repeated requests for computer help.

Finally, I am indebted to Neil White of Nautilus Publishing for making it happen.

Made in the USA
Columbia, SC
31 May 2019